KW-057-990

HIGHER EDUCATION IN
VIRTUAL WORLDS:
TEACHING AND LEARNING IN
SECOND LIFE

Related books

EVANS, HAUGHEY, & MURPHY	International Handbook of Distance Education
O'NEIL & PEREZ	Computer Games and Team and Individual Learning

WESTON COLLEGE

B70476

LibraryPlus

HIGHER EDUCATION IN VIRTUAL WORLDS: TEACHING AND LEARNING IN SECOND LIFE

EDITED BY

CHARLES WANKEL

St. John's University, New York, USA

JAN KINGSLEY

Association for Professional and Executive Learning, Barcelona, Spain

Emerald

United Kingdom • North America • Japan
India • Malaysia • China

Emerald Group Publishing Limited
Howard House, Wagon Lane, Bingley BD16 1WA, UK

First edition 2009

Copyright © 2009 Emerald Group Publishing Limited

Reprints and permission service
Contact: booksandseries@emeraldinsight.com

No part of this book may be reproduced, stored in a retrieval system, transmitted in any form or by any means electronic, mechanical, photocopying, recording or otherwise without either the prior written permission of the publisher or a licence permitting restricted copying issued in the UK by The Copyright Licensing Agency and in the USA by The Copyright Clearance Center. No responsibility is accepted for the accuracy of information contained in the text, illustrations or advertisements. The opinions expressed in these chapters are not necessarily those of the Editor or the publisher.

British Library Cataloguing in Publication Data
A catalogue record for this book is available from the British Library

ISBN: 978-1-84950-609-0

ISOQAR
QUALITY ASSURED
ISO 9001
✔
UKAS
QUALITY MANAGEMENT
026
Certificate number ....1985.........

Awarded in recognition of
Emerald's production
department's adherence to
quality systems and processes
when preparing scholarly
journals for print

INVESTOR IN PEOPLE

Contents

List of Contributors   vii

Acknowledgments   ix

Introduction   1

1. Overcoming the Entry Barriers to Second Life in Higher Education   11
   Gavin Dudeney and Howard Ramsay

2. Communication Challenges and Opportunities for Educators Using Second Life   29
   John C. Sherblom, Lesley A. Withers and Lynnette G. Leonard

3. Inclusion Benefits and Barriers of "Once-Removed" Participation   47
   Simon Ball and Rob Pearce

4. Opportunities and Challenges for Business Education in Second Life   65
   Edwin Love, Steven C. Ross and Wendy Wilhelm

5. Virtual Worlds and Business Schools – The Case of INSEAD   83
   Andreas M. Kaplan

6. Online Instructor Immediacy and Instructor-Student Relationships in Second Life   101
   Traci L. Anderson

7. Cross-World Branding – One World is Not Enough   115
   Nina Belei, Gwen Noteborn and Ko de Ruyter

8. Literary Analysis as Serious Play in Second Life   141
   Mary McAleer Balkun, Mary Zedeck and Heidi Trotta

9. Second Life – a Context for Design Learning   159
    Ning Gu, Leman Figen Gul, Anthony Williams and Walaiporn Nakapan

10. The Theatre of Performance Appraisal: Role-Play in Second Life   181
    Shona Morse, Fiona Littleton, Hamish Macleod and Rory Ewins

11. Using Second Life at the Open University: How the Virtual World Can
    Facilitate Learning for Staff and Students   203
    Steph Broadribb, Anna Peachey, Chris Carter and Francine Westrap

12. Aging, Lifelong Learning, and the Virtual World of Second Life   221
    Leslie Jarmon, Tomoko Watanabe Traphagan,
    John W. Traphagan and Lynn Jones Eaton

Author Index   243

Subject Index   249

List of Contributors

Traci L. Anderson	Saint Cloud State University, St Cloud, MN, USA
Mary McAleer Balkun	Seton Hall University, South Orange, NJ, USA
Simon Ball	JISC TechDis, York, UK
Nina Belei	Maastricht University, Maastricht, The Netherlands
Steph Broadribb	The Open University, Milton Keynes, UK
Chris Carter	The Open University, Milton Keynes, UK
Ko de Ruyter	Maastricht University, Maastricht, The Netherlands
Gavin Dudeney	The Consultants-e, Barcelona, Spain
Lynn Jones Eaton	University of Texas at Austin, Austin, TX, USA
Rory Ewins	The University of Edinburgh, Scotland, UK
Ning Gu	School of Architecture and Built Environment, University of Newcastle, NSW, Australia
Leman Figen Gul	Faculty of Engineering and Natural Sciences, International University of Sarajevo, Bosnia and Herzegovina
Leslie Jarmon	University of Texas at Austin, Austin, TX, USA
Andreas M. Kaplan	ESCP Europe, Paris, France
Lynnette G. Leonard	University of Nebraska at Omaha, Omaha, NE, USA
Fiona Littleton	The University of Edinburgh, Scotland, UK
Edwin Love	Western Washington University, Bellingham, WA, USA
Hamish Macleod	The University of Edinburgh, Scotland, UK
Shona Morse	The University of Edinburgh, Scotland, UK
Walaiporn Nakapan	Rangsit University, Patumthani, Thailand

Gwen Noteborn	Maastricht University, Maastricht, The Netherlands
Anna Peachey	The Open University, Milton Keynes, UK
Rob Pearce	Higher Education Academy Engineering Subject Centre, Loughborough University, Loughborough, UK
Howard Ramsay	University of Strathclyde, Glasgow, UK
Steven C. Ross	Western Washington University, Bellingham, WA, USA
John C. Sherblom	University of Maine, Orono, ME, USA
John W. Traphagan	University of Texas at Austin, Austin, TX, USA
Tomoko Watanabe Traphagan	Texas Education Agency, Austin, TX, USA
Heidi Trotta	Seton Hall University, South Orange, NJ, USA
Francine Westrap	Leighton Buzzard, Bedfordshire, UK
Wendy Wilhelm	Western Washington University, Bellingham, WA, USA
Anthony Williams	School of Architecture and Built Environment, University of Newcastle, NSW, Australia
Lesley A. Withers	Central Michigan University, Mount Pleasant, MI, USA
Mary Zedeck	Seton Hall University, South Orange, NJ, USA

Acknowledgments

The editors thank all of the following colleagues and authors for their contributions, suggestions and editorial comments:

Lavie-Dinur Amit, Traci Anderson, Mary Balkun, Simon Ball, Sandra Bassendowski, Nina Belei, Linda Berdayes, Zane Berge, Bret Bowers, Steph Broadribb, Chris Carter, Jason Caudill, Kenneth Day, Qingwen Dong, Friedman Doron, Uma Doraiswamy, Gavin Dudeney, Gerald Everett, Rory Ewins, Helen Farley, Nil Goksel, Ning Gu, Figen Gul, Lois Hamill, Robert Harbison, Yifeng Hu, Leslie Jarmon, Lynne Jeaton, Andreas Kaplan, Gülsün Kurubacak, Suellyn Lathrop, Christoph Lattemann, Lynette Leonard, Fiona Littleton, Edwin Love, Hamish Macleod, Nancy Marshall, Patricia McQuaid, Shona Morse, Timothy Mullin, Walaiporn Nakapan, Gwen Noteborn, Anna Peachey, Rob Pearce, Gay Perkins, Howard Ramsay, Ko de Ruyter, Steven Ross, John Sherblom, Michele Smith, Stefan Stieglitz, Helena Szrek, Elizabeth Thiry, John Traphagan, Tomoko Traphagan, Heidi Trotta, Francine Westrap, Wendy Wilhelm, Tony Williams, Lesley Withers, Haiwang Yuan, Karniel Yuval, Mary Zedeck and especially our Commissioning Editor Diane Heath.

We are appreciative of our research assistance provided by Kevin Heater and Shaun Malleck for their help with the project. We are also most grateful to Jill Harnington for the cover photographs.

The opinions expressed in this book are those of the chapter authors and not necessarily those of the editors — we have attempted to include a range of perspectives and case studies, and as is natural in these cases, there may be differing opinions expressed.

Introduction

Jan Kingsley and Charles Wankel

1. Why This Book?

Virtual Worlds (VWs) are no longer merely the domain of youthful "gamers" (Michael & Chen, 2006; Thomas & Brown, 2009) operating on the edges of the communications envelope. On the contrary, VWs and their associated avatars are taking a central place in the way that millions of people spend their time undertaking a wide variety of activities including socialising, commerce, business meetings, staff recruitment, testing and model-building, and yes, acting out their fantasies as well! (Beck & Wade, 2006; Percival, 2008; Aldrich, 2004; Gee, 2007; Terdiman, 2008; Gibson, Aldrich, & Prensky, 2007).

A range of training and development activities also take place in VWs, with academic institutions and companies exploring the benefits of an immersive environment in which participants can interact with each other as well as with their instructor, even if they are thousands of miles apart physically.

The term "exploring" is important: the use of VWs is still an emerging field, and although many experiments are in progress, it is still the case that only a tiny minority of people use VWs as an integral part of their professional lives. Indeed, as can be seen in the following chapters, none of the learners had had previous experience of Second Life. In June 2009, 69,000 people worldwide had a Positive Monthly Linden Flow (PMLF), that is, made more money than they spent in Second Life. There are possibly several thousand more who use Second Life for professional purposes with little or no financial impact (such as educators), but PMLF is a useful indicator of how many people are using Second Life "professionally" as a means of generating income.

In this book, we bring together a selection of chapters written by academics and practitioners who have been involved in developing learning activities using the Second Life platform. Our intention is to provide guidelines, suggestions and ideas as

Higher Education in Virtual Worlds
Copyright © 2009 by Emerald Group Publishing Limited
All rights of reproduction in any form reserved
ISBN: 978-1-84950-609-0

well as to highlight the potential issues and problems arising when thinking about the use of VWs for educational purposes.

As the world of learning becomes ever more complex, educators are faced with an almost bewildering choice of medium, and keeping up with developments can in itself prove a major challenge. Expectations on the part of learners are also broadening, placing an increased burden of responsibility on educators to develop a range of learning opportunities, including podcasts, wikis, social networking, VOIP support and VW activities.

The latter platforms started out in the early 2000s, and they are still undergoing development in a number of areas including the technological infrastructure, the social construct (e.g., the rules and regulations governing allowable activities in-world), the economic and financial models being applied, and the markets that they are addressing.

As Table 1 demonstrates, in June 2008, there were already over 200 million registered avatars in nine VWs, *excluding* fantasy world massively multiplayer online games (MMOGs) and other "closed" VWs.

Another interesting aspect arising from this table is that there are still relatively few people in the over 20 age range registered in VWs. Educators can be forgiven for thinking that their Higher Education students are not interested in these platforms and that perhaps investments, whether in terms of time or money, are not worthwhile.

However, the younger teen generation is growing up using VWs (such as *Penguin Club, Habbo, Gaia*) as an integral part of their social and online lives. Within five years, this generation will be seeking placements at universities and in companies, and it will be as natural for them to turn to VWs as it is for older people today to seek information on the Internet. This implies that Higher Education establishments have a window of five to seven years to develop their VW presence or risk losing market share. Those that invest now have the luxury of relatively cheap "research time." As the young teen generation comes of age, the investments required will increase dramatically with demand for qualified and experienced builders and script-writers outstripping supply (Heaton, 2007).

Table 1: Registered avatars in virtual worlds, June 2008.

	11–14 year olds	15–20 year olds	Over 20s	Web address
Whyville	3			www.whyville.net
Barbie Girls	13			www.barbiegirls.com
Club Penguin	19			www.clubpenguin.com
Habbo	100			www.habbo.com
Stardoll	21			www.stardoll.com
Gaia		13		www.gaiaonline.com
There		20		www.there.com
Second Life			15	www.secondlife.com
Activeworlds			1	www.activeworlds.com
Total (millions):	156	33	16	

It is not only the overall VW population that will increase. With the release of parts of its source code, Linden Labs has contributed to the development of the "OpenSim" project which in turn is spawning hundreds of new "worlds," many of which are being designed for specific groups or uses.

It is already possible to download VWs onto PDAs and iPhones, with 90% of South Koreans in their twenties and 25% of the country using *Cyworld* to communicate with each other on their mobile phones (Shin, 2009). The biggest technological leap will occur when avatars are able to move from one world to another seamlessly and visit 3D websites. Once that happens, everyone will be expected to have at least one avatar. Educators ignore this technological trend at the peril of their professional credibility.

With this book our aim is to provide suggestions as to how educators can use one of these VWs – Second Life – to provide immersive learning experiences for their students and programme participants.

2. Why Second Life?

We decided to focus on Second Life for a number of reasons:

- It is currently the most popular platform for educators: as of summer 2009, there were over 4000 people registered in the SL Educators List (SLED), and the number of academic institutions establishing islands in SL grows daily, already reaching several hundreds (Second Life and Education, 2009).
- It is not a "game" world such as *World of Warcraft* – there are no gaming rules, no "levels" to achieve, no pre-designated roles and no scores. On the contrary, Second Life was designed to be as "open" a society as possible, and it is only due to legal requirements in California that certain restrictions have been imposed (e.g., gambling is not allowed "in-world," and neither are there any banks).
- Unlike Forterra's *Olive* platform, anyone can enter Second Life for free, and it is only those that wish to do so who spend real money buying virtual clothes and other virtual goods – this makes Second Life a cost-effective starting point for using VWs and encouraging others to do so.
- Second Life has a real economy, using "Linden Dollars" that can be converted freely into US Dollars (Castronova, 2005). For certain educational uses, such as in Business Administration programmes, this holds out the promise of enabling students to set up a real business, take real-life decisions and witness the real-time impact of those decisions on a real society. All of this within a "safe" environment, where the financial stakes are (relatively-speaking) minuscule. Three of the chapters in this book are business-education-orientated, although it is not our intention to suggest how to use Second Life to make money!
- As an "open" society, Second Life provides an environment conducive to serendipitous encounters with other people who would otherwise never meet. Indeed, a good example of this is that the editors of this book met by chance in

Second Life! This factor can at times cause certain difficulties and stresses (not everyone in Second Life behaves "professionally"), and it is one aspect that might be cause for concern for educators. On the other hand, since it is a "virtual" world, the potential damage is limited, whereas the potential advantages can be leveraged by educators to provide their participants with a much wider range of learning opportunities.

- Second Life may not be as technically advanced as certain other VWs, and this can occasionally cause dissatisfaction, especially on the part of some "digital natives." However, there is a strong community of developers and programmers who are working to simplify the interface on the one hand while enabling a higher degree of integration with other platforms and programmes on the other. For "newbie" educators, this support network is of great assistance.

- Finally, although Second Life itself might not become the "killer app" it was originally heralded as, there can be no doubt that familiarity with its interface, opportunities and technical challenges will provide an excellent foundation upon which to build the competencies required to develop educational programmes in any other VW.

3.   Structure and Content of This Book

The book is broadly divided into two parts: the first part (Chapters 1–6 inclusive) is more theoretical in nature, with a number of general issues related to the use of Second Life being discussed, including linkage to other fields of academic study. The second part (Chapters 7–12 inclusive) describes specific case studies and presents examples of how Second Life has been used for particular groups ranging from undergraduates to retired professionals.

Faced with the plethora of potential projects and papers to include in such a book, the editors decided to take an inductive approach to accommodate the high-quality and important topics from among the many submissions received. An alternative approach would have been deductive, assigning pre-selected topics to certain writers. But the latter approach would have allowed bias to filter the tumultuous experimentation and innovation being researched in Second Life higher education. As we embark on the second decade of the 21st century, codetermination of key content is increasingly the norm and appears to suit both the topic and culture of VWs.

The resulting volume might therefore appear to some less than "neat" or "sufficiently academic" in nature. But we trust that readers will nonetheless find valuable insights and helpful suggestions for their own explorations into the virtual universe.

The book opens at what might be considered the "negative" end of the spectrum: in Chapter 1, Dudeney and Ramsay lay out in detail the challenges and hurdles facing educators when they first attempt to develop a Second Life project from a number of perspectives – institutional, technical, pedagogical and end-user. Almost mirroring the entry into Second Life itself (the "first-hour" syndrome), if these barriers can be overcome, then there are rewards to be obtained. Dudeney and Ramsey provide advice as to how to minimise these barriers so as to provide a rewarding experience for educators and participants.

In Chapter 2, Sherblom, Withers, and Leonard look at Second Life from the computer-mediated communications (CMC) perspective, concluding that despite the technological, instructional and interpersonal barriers arising, students find Second Life to be a versatile, useful communication medium through which to participate in group discussion, collaboration and brainstorming.

This chapter also highlights a recurring theme throughout the book: much of the feedback received from participants is not about the VW platform itself so much as the difficulties inherent in any online interaction, for example the difficulty in organising synchronous meetings, or the constraints of using text-chat, or the bandwidth requirements and occasional poor quality of voice chat (VOIP). As the technological infrastructure as a whole improves, so should these barriers tend to decline in importance.

Moving towards the positive end of the spectrum, in Chapter 3, Ball and Pearce suggest that the use of VWs for some learners is much more than a fad or gimmick – it is a way of interacting, developing skills and having experiences that simply could not occur in real life. VW platforms, while not a panacea to all pedagogic or access issues, are in the process of justifying their place as an addition to the suite of tools available to educators. This may be especially true in the case of learners who face accessibility issues, who are not as confident as others in real-world situations, or who have to practice entering stressful real-world scenarios.

Ball and Pearce provide a range of examples where Second Life has been used effectively to support learners facing such challenges, with the proviso that – as with all learning methodologies – educators need to ensure that they use the appropriate tool for the job at hand.

As previously mentioned, it comes as no surprise that academics are exploring Second Life's potential for business education. In Chapter 4, Love, Ross and Wilhelm present a survey into how business educators are using Second Life as a pedagogical tool, as well as the challenges they face before its full potential can be realised. They provide a sample lesson developed by a business professor, a discussion of students' responses to their Second Life experiences, and a note on the untapped potential of this VW for business education.

The benefits and challenges outlined in this chapter are by no means restricted to business education – on the contrary, there are insights and suggestions for educators for all subjects, including a list of SL tools that any Second Life educator will find helpful.

In Chapter 5, business education is again the focus, with Kaplan presenting the case study of how INSEAD Business School uses its presence in Second Life, along with suggestions as to how other educational institutions can best leverage their investment.

One of the issues he highlights is that to maximise its potential, Second Life should not be seen as merely an extension of a teaching situation into the VW – instead, institutions need to assess a range of investment options including promotion, student and staff recruitment, information provision and even in-world activities to attract casual passers-by. One of the greatest "turn-offs" to VW visitors is an empty island!

Moving from the institutional level to the individual level, and using a more formalised academic paper style, in Chapter 6 Anderson presents the results of her research into Instructor Immediacy and its impact on students in Second Life. Unsurprisingly perhaps, the research findings suggest that nonverbal immediacy is important for instructors who are currently teaching, or are planning to teach, in Second Life. What is interesting about this research is that immediacy behaviours are important at all – it relates not only to the fact that the instructor must be seen to be "present," but that his/her avatar should be seen to behave in a manner consistent with "good" teaching practice. For example, the instructor's avatar needs to face the student avatars, gesticulate appropriately, even smile and use other paralinguistic effects. This suggests that educators need to be keenly aware of the impact their avatars have on their students and be able to master a range of techniques within Second Life to enhance the feeling of proximity between instructor and student.

Chapter 7 opens the second part of the book where the focus shifts from more general concepts (albeit with examples) to specific case studies of how Second Life has been used within developmental programmes. Belei, Noteborn and de Ruyter describe how they provided an immersive experience for their Brand Management students, thus helping to bridge the gap between theory and practice. The project made use of Second Life's Linden Dollar economy to assess student creativity (in both SL and RL), commitment and understanding of marketing theory.

They conclude that:

> *(the use of virtual worlds) results not only in a competitive advantage in attracting good students, but ultimately provides a whole new dimension to the present teaching and learning environment.*

Balkun, Trotta and Zedeck present a case study in Chapter 8 which underscores the move from teacher as "communicator of knowledge" to student as "builder of knowledge." Over three different programmes, students of literature have built the House of 7 (after Hawthorne's novel, the House of Seven Gables) within Second Life, including highly detailed furnishings, interactive tasks for visitors and more general information about the literature of the period.

This case study provides an example of how Second Life projects can be presented to the "external" world: the build is open to the general public, thus providing a degree of motivation that can be missing from a "closed" class project. Knowing that their work will be scrutinised by passers-by, students clearly spent a great deal of time researching and scripting to achieve desired effects.

Additionally, the fact that the project has been incrementally improved by succeeding cohorts establishes a continuity that is perhaps lacking in other case studies. As the authors point out, the build provides a degree of permanence that is difficult to replicate in a normal educational setting. Most student assignments end up in instructors' filing cabinets, with some perhaps making it into a web repository.

In Second Life, the results of the students' energy and effort will remain for some time to come, a monument to their learning.

Although the focus of the previous chapter was on creativity rather than building, Chapter 9 is almost the reverse: Gu, Gul, Nakapan and Williams describe how they developed a programme for Design Learning across two university groups – one in Newcastle, Australia and the other in Thailand – that worked collaboratively on the design of virtual "homes." The freedom from gravity and other "worldly" constraints allowed the design students to build prototype virtual homes that stretched their creative and collaborative skills, allowing them to think "outside the box" and communicate synchronously in ways that would be extremely difficult to replicate using any other distance technology.

Both the following Chapters – 10 and 11 – deal with an area where VWs can also excel: their use for role play. In Chapter 10, Ewins, Littleton, Macleod and Morse provide an example of how Second Life can be used to enable students – in this case, following an MSc in E-Learning programme – to practice appraisal feedback skills in a manner that allows a degree of reflection and "separation" compared to role plays in "real life." Here, the authors conducted an experiment using volunteers from the programme and they report back on their findings, concluding that in the future, companies might use such an approach for appraisals in the "real world."

This links directly to Chapter 11, in which the Open University authors Broadribb, Peachey, Carter and Westrap have also experimented with using Second Life for performance appraisal training, in this case with staff members undergoing training provided by the HR department. This takes us beyond the envelope of "Higher Education" into the area of executive education, since the "students" are preparing to use performance appraisal skills not as part of a degree programme, but as part and parcel of their professional lives. Broadribb et al. underline the value of involving non-academic staff in VWs, as well as the challenges inherent in attempting to implement what some perceive as being a "frivolous game" into an organisation's development strategy.

In the final chapter of this book, Eaton, Jarmon, Traphagan and Traphagan again take us beyond Higher Education into the realm of Lifelong Learning, and specifically the potential benefits of Second Life (and other VWs) for the "silver" generation. Although only a few of the "students" on the programme actually made it into Second Life on their own, the possibilities of increased socialisation, improved communication with younger generations, the sheer fun of being able to visit virtual historical and cultural builds clearly had a positive impact on the target group. This chapter highlights the fact that VWs are not merely for the young, but rather for the young at heart, whatever their age and interests.

4. Some Initial Conclusions Arising

As with any emergent technology, there are a number of challenges to overcome in the use of VW platforms, not the least of which are the psychological and cultural barriers arising from the view that VWs are merely some kind of "game." Neither will VWs ever be able to supplant all the benefits of face-to-face interactions, especially as there are always likely to be technological glitches or time differences hindering smooth synchronous communication.

On the other hand, we can no longer avoid the fact that VWs, in one form or another, have become part of the technological infrastructure. There are millions of people, especially pre- and young teens, now using VWs as their networking platform of choice. The full impact of this has yet to be felt in Higher Education institutions, but some educational explorers are beginning to develop strategies and approaches that will stand them (and their institutions) in good stead when that moment arrives.

In this book, we have just begun to scrape the tip of a creative new world – there are hundreds of educational projects being developed in Second Life (de Lucia, Passero, Francese, & Tortora, 2009; Larvin, 2009) ranging from geographical through medical to archaeological. There will soon be thousands of such projects. We hope to have provided glimpses into the potential benefits and uses of virtuality without obscuring the issues involved.

We trust you enjoy your exploration of this "brave new world."
Jan Kingsley
Charles Wankel

References

Aldrich, C. (2004). *Simulations and the future of learning*. Wiley.

Beck, J., & Wade, M. (2006). *The kids are alright: How the gamer generation is changing the workplace*. Harvard Business School Press.

Castronova, E. (2005). *Synthetic worlds*. University of Chicago Press.

de Lucia, A., Passero, I., Francese, R., & Tortora, G. (2009). Development and evaluation of a virtual campus on Second Life: The case of second DMI. *Computers & Education, 52*(1), 220–233.

Gee, J. P. (2007). *What video games have to teach us about learning and literacy*. Palgrave Macmillan.

Gibson, D., Aldrich, C., & Prensky, M. (2007). *Games and simulations in online learning: Research and development frameworks*. Information Science Publishing.

Heaton, J. (2007). *Scripting recipes for Second Life*. Heaton Research Inc.

Larvin, M. (2009). E-learning in surgical education. *ANZ Journal of Surgery, 79*(3), 133–137.

Michael, D., & Chen, S. (2006). *Serious games: Games that educate, train, and inform*. Thompson Publishing.

Percival, S. (2008). *In world travel guide: Second Life*. Que Publishing.

Second Life and Education. (2009). Second life in education: Exploring the educations uses of second life. Accessed July 3, 2009, from http://sleducation.wikispaces.com

Shin, D. H. (2009). Virtual gratification of wireless internet: Is wireless portable internet reinforced by unrealized gratifications? *Telematics and Informatics, 26*(1), 44–56.

Terdiman, D. (2008). *The entrepreneur's guide to Second Life*. Wiley.

Thomas, D., & Brown, J. S. (2009). Why virtual worlds can matter. *Journal of Learning and Media, 1*(1), 37–49.

Author Biographies

Jan Kingsley is executive director of the Association for Professional and Executive Learning (ASPEL), and associate professor of Management at ESADE Barcelona and the Maastricht School of Hospitality Management. He has been involved with executive development for over 20 years with a wide range of clients from the corporate, government and NGO sectors throughout the world, specialising in leadership, organizational development, change management and large-scale project management. He has had an avatar – Berry Beattie – in Second Life for two years, developing his interest in using the platform for educational purposes. He has been invited to present at numerous workshops and conferences, including Online Educa 2008, and has audited E-Learning programmes for CEL – Technology-Enhanced Learning and delivery institutions for UNIQUe – European University Quality in eLearning.

Charles Wankel is Associate Professor of Management at St. John's University, New York. He received his doctorate from New York University. Charles has authored and edited many books including the best-selling *Management*, 3rd ed. (Prentice-Hall, 1986), *Rethinking Management Education for the 21st Century* (IAP, 2002), *Educating Managers with Tomorrow's Technologies* (IAP, 2003), *the Cutting-Edge of International Management Education* (IAP, 2004), *Educating Managers through Real World Projects* (IAP, 2005), *New Visions of Graduate Management Education* (IAP, 2006), *University and Corporate Innovations in Life-Long Learning* (IAP, 2007), *Innovative Approaches to Reducing Global Poverty* (IAP, 2008), *Alleviating Poverty through Business* Strategy (IAP, 2008), *Handbook of 21st Century Management* (SAGE, 2008), *Global Sustainability Initiatives: New Models and New Approaches* (IAP, 2008), *Innovative Approaches to Global Sustainability* (Palgrave, 2008), *Encyclopedia of Business in Today's World* (SAGE, 2009), and the forthcoming *Being and Becoming a Management Education Scholar* (IAP, 2008), *Emerging Ethical Issues of Life in Virtual Worlds* (IAP, 2009), and *Management through Collaboration: Teaming in a Networked World* (Routledge, 2010) an introductory management textbook with over 900 coauthors from 90 nations. He is the leading founder and director of scholarly virtual communities for management professors, currently directing eight of these with thousands of participants in more than 70 nations. Charles has taught in Lithuania at the Kaunas University of Technology (Fulbright Fellowship) and the University of Vilnius (United Nations Development Program and Soros Foundation funding).

Chapter 1

Overcoming the Entry Barriers to Second Life in Higher Education

Gavin Dudeney and Howard Ramsay

1.1. Introduction

At the peak of its uptake in early 2007, Second Life was perhaps the most discussed of the new rash of virtual worlds, with news stories appearing every day — most of them seemingly connected with controversy, divorce and human strife. At the same time, however, the education community in-world continued to grow at a startling pace, and that year saw the consolidation of many projects and initiatives, from the Second Life Best Practices in Education conference to the exponential growth of the Second Life Educators List (SLED).[1]

It is very much the case that certain facets of Second Life speak clearly to its usefulness in higher and further education, not least of which is the fact that it is perhaps currently the most economical way of experimenting with so-called web 3D technologies, thus giving educators their first experience of these environments and providing them with the necessary skill set to operate in virtual worlds and the criteria to enable them to evaluate other platforms for longer term implementation.

Couple this with the vibrant user community, easy availability of information and communication tools, and external support systems such as the SLED List mentioned above, and there are many good reasons to start any research into the possible uses of virtual worlds for educational purposes with Second Life.

While the administrative, research and teaching cultures of higher education institutions are as diverse as they are numerous, the issues that these institutions

---

1. The SLED List: https://lists.secondlife.com/cgi-bin/mailman/listinfo/educators.

Higher Education in Virtual Worlds
Copyright © 2009 by Emerald Group Publishing Limited
All rights of reproduction in any form reserved
ISBN: 978-1-84950-609-0

encounter when adopting new technologies in teaching and learning scenarios may be said to have rather more in common due to their analogous aims, needs and — in more practical terms — activities.

In this chapter, we break down the principal issues identified into four clear areas, examining each in turn before making general recommendations, which, it is hoped, will guide institutions as they plan any move into the adoption of Second Life in their research, teaching and learning activities.

Institutional barriers are those primarily pertaining to, or arising from, the inherent administrative and financial structures of college bodies and how technological innovation can be a barrier to end-users — researchers, teachers and students — and their fruitful use of the incoming technology. The institutional barriers related to Second Life are perhaps reinforced by the popular media's representation of the environment.

Pedagogical barriers are often barriers of perception: at one end of the scale, these might best be described as an inability to successfully transpose *real world* principles of teaching and learning to an online environment, whilst at the other end, we refer to the users' inability to sustain the required level of *suspension of disbelief* needed to fully engage in these kinds of environments.

Pedagogical barriers overlap with the ever-present issue of technical barriers in the sense that prosaic day-to-day technical issues can have negative effects on a teacher's or researcher's well-laid plans for pedagogical use or research.

High-end hardware requirements combined with network restrictions that often necessitate institutional IT service intervention, regular software upgrades and limitations on the opening of Second Life accounts all combine to make technology a potentially significant barrier for many institutions in purely practical implementation terms.

Finally, end-user barriers are examined. These span a wide variety of disparate areas, from Second Life client usability and instability to client configuration issues and accessibility. On the more practical implementation side, we also examine social issues of user training, e-safety, disruptive behaviour and undesirable content.

1.2. Institutional Barriers

The wide variety of purposes that multi-user virtual environments (MUVEs) are currently being put to include collaborative learning and design, seminars, workshops, tutorials, induction courses and tutorials.[2] It was noted that *internal institutional funding remains the predominant source of fiscal support.* However, the majority of these sources were projects internal to individual departments or units rather than centrally administered institutional resources. This suggests two possible scenarios: Either

---

2. The Autumn 2008 Snapshot of UK Higher and Further Education Developments in Second Life, Virtual World Watch, October 2008.

enthusiastic individuals or groups are receiving funding from lower down the institutional hierarchy with initiatives having yet to receive top-level acceptance. Alternatively, higher level management deems it more advantageous to let these projects grow in different directions and be allowed to independently succeed or fail depending on their uptake.

In addition, *a significant number of respondents were supported by external, often research-based funding.*[3] As such, in UK Higher Education at least, current developments are generally motivated by research and/or pedagogical aims. The report surveys institutional reactions to Second Life projects and reveals a complex range of reactions from *bizarrely hostile* to *extremely supportive*. Media coverage of occasional, but highly prominent salacious stories, appears to have informed the vocabulary of many of the negative comments quoted such as *only nutters use it*, *deeply disturbing* or *frivolous indulgence*. These issues have been unhelpful in communication with managers who have multiple constituencies to consider, from researchers whose *raison d'être* is to look beyond superficial representations to marketing departments that interface with tax payers who fund such *frivolous indulgences*.

It appears that superficial experience or knowledge of Second Life in an educational context can often result in Second Life being perceived as too different a tool, requiring too great a leap of faith from some institutions. Some practitioners report gaining funding by deliberately replacing terms such as Second Life *virtual island* in requests with the more palatable *Web Host server charge.*[4]

1.3.   The Hype Cycle

Much of the educational activity current in Second Life might be characterised by Thelander as the *Chaotic Sandpit* (Thelander, 2007). Zastrocky et al. coin terms for the management of expectations of the use of Second Life in Higher Education — the *Disciplined Engine Room* requires transition through the *Healthy Hothouse* stage (Zastrocky, Lowendahl, & Harris, 2007). With these terms, they illustrate four institutional scenarios to discuss technological transformation under Garner's widely discussed *Hype Cycle* (Fenn & Raskino, 2008). The Hype Cycle describes what Garner's researchers assert is a pattern in the adoption of technologies in Higher Education, cycling through triggers, inflated expectations, disillusionment, and growing enlightenment until a plateau of productivity is reached. Institutional barriers are present primarily in the first two stages. As yet, the use of MUVEs has not progressed to the level of central and stable funding to lead into the third stage of significant levels of disillusionment.

---

3. *Ibid.,*
4. This example from Sarah "Intellagirl Tully" Robbins was given in a panel discussion at the first Second Life Best Practices in Education conference in-world, May 25, 2007.

If a concept such as the Hype Cycle is to be accepted and applied to the adoption of MUVEs in Higher Education, the question becomes to what extent knowledge of the coming peaks and plateau can be usefully applied by both institutions and enthusiastic practitioners. Perhaps, after all, it is only in retrospect that the stages can accurately be identified. That said, the model does prepare managers and practitioners for short- and medium-term disappointment, which does not have to — and indeed should not — be taken as automatic long-term failure.

1.4. Recommendations Relating to Institutional Barriers

Institutional support should be sought by the use of analogy: a Second Life resource is an additional teaching or research tool and should not be placed in any special or new category for consideration, thus setting it apart from other tools and approaches and, as a consequence, building up unreasonable expectations. The potential for over-inflated expectations of educational or research results should be explored openly and, where possible, constrained to the realms of reality. Acknowledgement of the immaturity of the technology and the potential for negative attitudes towards it should also be acknowledged.

Similarly, institutional policies on accessing Internet resources judged to be of a potentially "adult" nature might also impede any implementation of public wide area networks such as Second Life. Early establishment of rules and permissions (for both academic staff and their students) with regard to conduct during in-world projects will be essential to their smooth running and, if well-formulated, should preclude the need for last-minute or *ad-hoc* solutions. The goal is to establish sustainable good practice.

Institutional participants (both educators and researchers) should seriously consider how to present themselves and their Second Life facility. Thought should be given to visual appearance, both of the virtual space and of the avatars operating within it, naming conventions for avatars, which can be easily linked to the physical institution, codes of conduct and, depending on buy-in from other potential stakeholders across the institution, branding and institutional design.

1.5. Pedagogical Barriers

Even for enthusiastic academic participants in a Second Life class or seminar, one of the first questions raised is, quite rightly, *How are we going to manage this?*, with the implication that a special protocol for behaviour is required of all participants in the event.

1.6. Protocols

This is a weak barrier since most aspects of such protocols have direct analogies in real-world classroom management. For example,

How will they ask questions? — in a real seminar room, a hand might be raised. In Second Life, a question could be typed if to speak it aloud would be considered an interruption. In larger events, a chairperson can be appointed much as would be the case in a real life event. The chairperson would select which questions to ask or invite people to speak just as they would in real life.

How do we stop people flying around? — Classroom or event management also carries over effectively from real life principles with participants generally responding to stated expectations of behaviour. Indeed, first-time attendees may find comfort in a crib sheet of dos and don'ts, but these are likely to be, in principle, very similar to those in any real life event.

A greater danger might be manifest in the potential presence of undesirable attendees. Having an educational space open to all comers is the least bureaucratic and time-intensive way of allowing people access (and of managing the space itself), but it does carry the danger — however small — of malicious individuals seeking to disrupt events held there. This is less of an issue where a long-term programme of events is designed for a closed or semi-closed group. In that case, entry rights to an area can be controlled by use of groups or land permissions. In the case of wholly open admission, it is prudent to have tutors and/or suitable administrators present with appropriate *eject* permissions to remove people if required. It should be noted that educational spaces in Second Life tend to suffer less from this process of "griefing" than other spaces; this may be due, in part, to anecdotal evidence that suggests that such spaces are inherently less interesting and therefore less of a challenge for the potential digital troublemaker.

1.7.   "But ... it's a Game ..."

The conceptual jump required by some to counteract negative connotations attributed to MUVEs as *games* is perhaps greater than towards other rising technologies in areas such as e-learning, distance education and online collaboration. Online video collaborations, whether through enhanced Voice Over Internet Protocol (VOIP) systems such as Skype or more sophisticated platforms such as Elluminate or Adobe Connect Professional, have had analogies in everyday culture for over a century in the form of the telephone and television to the use of video conferencing appearing in popular culture certainly as long ago as the 1960s (2001: A Space Odyssey). Without having used a MUVE, the closest analogy that a manager may fall back on is that of the video game. This is perhaps magnified by the requirement of a degree of what Coleridge describes as "that willing suspension of disbelief for the moment, which constitutes poetic faith" (Coleridge, 1817) in early experiences of Second Life. Originally, this referred to the reading of literature and how the reader must set aside their knowledge of the untruth of some or all of what they read. Similarly, participants in Second Life need to set aside the perception that participants are not collocated. The degree to which this "choice of perception" is successful establishes the initial attitude towards Second Life.

Seminars held by University of Strathclyde in Scotland in partnership with Dalhousie University in Canada in 2008[5] found a majority of participants present in Second Life for the first time. Several participants, both managers and academics, described after the event how the speaker and subject of the seminar had been much more important to them than the medium of delivery. *Suspension of disbelief* can be reinforced by a wide range of tangential strategies such as dressing avatars appropriate to their function, with badges making tutors immediately identifiable. The University of Strathclyde Business School Second Life project team, for example, dress as they would in real life — in business suits.

When an individual signs up for a Second Life avatar, they must choose a name. This allows free choice of forename and a choice from a list of around forty surnames, which change on a regular basis. Requests can be made to Linden Labs for the use of real names. However, the fees of $50 to allow an individual's real name to be used in Second Life are high in terms of the budgets available to many Higher Education pilot projects. This can result in staff using compromise or composite names such as JohnSmith (real-world forename and surname combined into first name) Magic (selected from the names offered on sign-up). One of the Strathclyde team managed, by pure chance, to assign his own real-world name to his avatar from the list of surnames on offer at the time of signing up. While this aided identification and reinforced the professional "corporate" image, the individual reported that this was an uneasy experience when surrounded by people who were all effectively using aliases. An alternative is to design a button or other accessory that displays the wearer's real name — this has the added advantage of being removable when not required.

The design and implementation of an educational space in Second Life is inextricably connected to its intended use, and thus it is essential that educators be involved in the design, layout, and construction of any such facilities. This requirement however, means that an existing level of experience in Second Life is necessary. While the visual simulation of aspects of a real-world facility (whether real or emulated) can ease the issues surrounding perception for both faculty and students (and indeed managers), additional factors might be considered. These can include factors such as the distance between event rooms to avoid audio spillover (thick walls usually sufficing in the real world), or the placing of "teleport" spots to enable participants to transfer themselves to a specific second location efficiently — a seminar break-out room, for example — the use of which might otherwise be quite complicated for new users. Factors such as these might not be immediately apparent and may not be crucial in isolation but ignoring them could, in combination, make an event fail.

These issues can be compounded by the troublesome *First Hour*. This is currently a widely-used term for what is acknowledged by Linden Lab to be one common result of an often complicated first experience of the Second Life software, controls

---

5. Strathclyde Business School Newsletter 2008: http://www.sbs.strath.ac.uk/newsletter/2008-11/index.html, accessed on 3 July 2009.

and environment:

> *Rosedale singled out search, the user interface and new user orientation as needing major improvements. "We need to collapse the orientation experience on learning the interface down to a 30-minute timeframe," he declared. "We're not there yet." Rosedale went on to describe the current interface as "overwhelming".*[6]

Tutors or event leaders must, therefore, streamline and simplify this first experience for new users as much as possible. New users to Second Life are led through a time-consuming induction, which, although a useful exercise for self-motivated students, is often ignored by a significant number of users motivated more by attendance at a seminar than by the novelty of the medium. Recent developments[7] have enabled first-time users to sign up for Second Life accounts and arrive immediately in, for example, their assigned classroom or seminar room, thus avoiding the orientation step, which is often arguably unnecessary if the student's use of Second Life is to be confined to the classroom spaces themselves. That said, practical participant instructions are invaluable even in this simple, controlled scenario. First-time attendees' instructions should be tailored towards the requirements of the event in hand. For example, if audio for communication is to be used, this should certainly be a training focus due to the array of potential challenges presented by individual technical setups. Indeed, pre-event in-world consultations to test attendees' hardware compatibility are useful for all participants and are definitely essential for key individuals (tutors, speakers or guests). This type of preparation combined with a simple protocol for engagement should serve as a sound basis for simple events or collaborations.

Arguing for a constructivist perspective, Whitton and Hollins note that of MUVEs *it is essential to have a clear educational purpose for their use, not simply because they are thought to be motivational* (Whitton & Hollins, 2008). On-going integral online socialisation of students and attendees at a MUVE seminar will probably be key to engagement and educational benefit (Nicol, Minty, & Sinclair, 2003). This suggests that courses seeking to take advantage of the socialisation potential of Second Life must develop a longer term strategy for the participants to benefit from the platform.

1.8. Technology Barriers

Another area that presents significant challenges to the implementation of Second Life is that of technology and the demands made on physical installations, support staff and end-users to ensure a reliable and sustainable teaching experience.

---

6. http://www.thestandard.com/news/2009/01/30/exclusive-linden-lab-executives-plot-second-life-growth-interface-concerns-persist. Accessed on August 2009.
7. http://join.secondlife.com. Accessed on August 2009.

The general hardware and connection requirements of the platform[8] have experienced a steady increase in the six years of its development and now represent an appreciable demand on institutions.

One of the biggest obstacles is Second Life's inability to function with most standard graphics adaptors, as it is almost entirely restricted to the nVidia GeForce, ATI Radeon and Intel 945 chipset cards. It provides very poor support for other cards, especially the onboard sets found in many budget or bulk-purchase systems. In the second half of 2008, when major developments were finally incorporated into both the server and the client, many institutions that had successfully been using Second Life in their teaching found their computers suddenly unable to run the client and were either forced to abandon their use of the platform or engage in a lengthy and expensive upgrade process. This can be particularly problematic in areas where finance for regular upgrades is not readily available. Bob Boufford,[9] Lead of E-learning Support and Technical Development at the University of Alberta, Canada, reported in an email interview:

> All of our labs are pretty good for standard web browsing, viewing media and using MS Office. However, the graphics are embedded Intel chips, so Second Life runs poorly and will give a poor experience, thus becoming a barrier to end-users (...) the current state of the economy will result in very slow upgrades of the labs.

Coupled with these hardware issues are frequent updates of the Second Life client or viewer, which can test the patience of most institutional support services.

It is often the case with the client that the first install is sanctioned by IT support, but further updates become the responsibility of the person implementing it with their students, often necessitating cumbersome workarounds with pen or networked drives, and this has led to tension between academic staff wishing to use Second Life and the technical support services responsible for the equipment.

Even when the previously mentioned hardware and software issues have been resolved, there often remain significant challenges, which are discussed below.

1.8.1.   Access

One of the biggest issues for institutions is the requirement to open a set of ports for Second Life to be able to connect and operate properly (443/TCP, 12035/UDP, 12036/UDP and 13000-13050/UDP). Support services often take issue with this request, citing security reasons. This obstacle is akin to ones presented by VOIP services (see below), messaging clients and many Web 2.0 collaborative environments such as *Facebook*, *Flickr*, *YouTube* and others. Academics attempting to

---

8. http://secondlife.com/support/sysreqs.php. Accessed on August 2009.
9. http://www.spoke.com/info/p6JkYAk/BobBoufford

communicate a difference between Second Life and these online services have reportedly often been met with a general lack of comprehension. While some institutions might open these ports on a per-machine or per Internet Protocol (IP) address, many institutions use dynamic, that is, constantly changing IP addresses (or simply wireless connections), which may necessitate IT services opening the appropriate ports for virtually all IP addresses (and, as a consequence, all machines) that might potentially connect to Second Life. While in theory connecting to Second Life over Third Generation High Speed Packet Access (HSPA) cellular phone networks should provide sufficient bandwidth for a stable user experience, tests by the University of Strathclyde in 2008 showed that the variation in signal over time and location made this no more than a last resort contingency method.

1.8.2. Account Creation

Account creation has proven to be a major stumbling block for many institutions, especially when done as part of an introductory session before the start of an actual course within Second Life, largely due to Linden Lab restrictions on multiple-account creation from the same IP address. This has also been the subject of many discussions on the SLED List, with suggested solutions including the use of proxy servers and the possibility of having institutional IP addresses "white listed" or added to an approved list by Linden Lab. Whilst some people have successfully been white listed for this purpose, the effects have proven to be less than long-lasting and a number of educators have found themselves facing the same situation in subsequent iterations of courses or modules. Peter Miller,[10] lecturer in Biological Sciences at the University of Liverpool, UK, reported:

> *Experienced significant problems white listing adequate number of PCs via LL (Linden Labs) tech support; should probably have gone via concierge service; even now, only 30% of our PCs are (somewhat arbitrarily) white listed. LL should really sort out the first-contact issues.*

To date, the only reliable method of avoiding this issue appears to be to have students create their accounts outside the institution's network. In this case, it also means outside of any halls or other university accommodation where institutional IP addresses are often also shared.

1.8.3. Voice

The inclusion of synchronous VOIP services in 2007 (through a partnership with Vivox) has also occasioned a set of problems that will be familiar to users of other

---

10. Peter Miller's experiences on teaching in Second Life can be found on his blog at http://tidalblog.blogspot.com/

similar services such as Skype. These include the need for good-quality audio equipment on each computer, with USB headsets being the preference, setup problems within the client itself and patchy service on many occasions in-world. Further to this, VOIP services are often prohibited in certain parts of the world, and this has occasioned feelings of isolation for some users. Users with hearing or speech difficulties have also reported such feelings.

1.8.4. Bandwidth Requirements

For the end-user experience to be enjoyable and to a standard suitable for instruction, Second Life makes significant demands on available bandwidth. The SimTeach wiki (http://www.simteach.com) describes the bandwidth requirements thus:

> *Each computer running Second Life will need an average of 80 kbps downstream, spiking at about 400 kbps on initial connect and during teleports. Upstream is much lower, requiring 30 kbps on average.*

However, these are basic requirements and do not take into consideration large quantities of avatars in a single space, nor complex and multi-textured builds nor indeed streaming media, all of which can push average usage on a single computer well into double-digit gigabyte downloads per month.

1.9. Recommendations Relating to Technology Barriers

- Good communications with technical support groups in each institution are paramount to the successful implementation of Second Life, in terms of both the provision of suitable hardware (from graphics cards through to good-quality headsets for voice communication) and in ensuring that access through the opening and monitoring of the required ports is unhindered.
- Sign-up to Second Life is a one-off requirement, and this need not be done by teachers or researchers if an administrator or educational technologist can do it, thus facilitating the acquisition of usernames and passwords as well as ready-made avatars. Student induction into Second Life can be facilitated with the provision of a registration API-enabled institutional website and ensuring that the institution allows for large-scale avatar registration through the white listing process detailed above.

1.10. End-User Barriers

Related to these are specific barriers for the end-user, not least of which is the user interface of the client itself, which has often been criticised for being clumsy and unintuitive.

Featuring eight button options along the lower part of the screen, as well as three media controls and a text communication panel, coupled with seven text-based menus at the top (combining over 100 options), the interface bears little more than a passing resemblance to the more familiar features of most software or web-based interfaces.

This visual density is further complicated by sub-menus of many of these options (the "Build" button being an obvious candidate, where users are often quite able to place a simple primitive shape in-world but are then equally often incapable of working with that object due to the complexity of options that may be applied to it) and on-screen overlaid informational panels and heads-up displays (HUDs are controls for add-on visual displays and helper applications that the user may choose to incorporate in their client). All this can lead to a high degree of confusion in first-time users and a sense of being overwhelmed by the available options.

Coupled with a lack of immediately noticeable goals or courses of action, this complexity has led to a high degree of shallow, one-time engagement with the environment. Linden Labs have made various attempts at mitigating against this early confusion, most noticeably with "orientation spaces", which attempt to orientate new users and guide them through the basic operations of movement, object interaction and communication with other users, but these have proven unpopular, with many users viewing them as yet another obstacle to get past before entering Second Life itself.

These orientation spaces have been adapted to several languages and for specific purposes, including education, but are still severely underused by most new users. Several contributions towards mitigating against the complexity of the interface have been made (as well as adding to it, in certain cases) with a plethora of community-developed viewers. A full list of current viewers can be found on the Second Life wiki at http://wiki.secondlife.com/wiki/Alternate_viewers#Third-party_Viewers.

Other less immediately noticeable issues with the interface include less than satisfactory building tools, poor physics and lighting, and an unreliable search feature (somewhat improved in late 2007 when Linden Lab incorporated Google Search Appliances in the indexing and results display). Users falling into Prensky's[11] category of the "digital native" are also often disappointed by the quality of graphics within Second Life, and this can lead to some degree of scepticism on the part of younger users.

The interface is also unwieldy for users with visual or aural difficulties with its reliance on on-screen text or voice for communications and no set standards in terms of font sizes or colour schemes, and its over-reliance on textures for displaying important information, thus rendering it illegible by standard screen readers.

Hearing-impaired users benefited indirectly from a variety of plug-ins to synthesise text chat to voice developed in 2006 and early 2007, but development on these was largely discontinued once voice was finally implemented. The work of

---

11.   http://www.marcprensky.com/writing/Prensky%20-%20Digital%20Natives,%20Digital%20Immigrants%20-%20Part1.pdf. Accessed on August 2009.

White, Fitzpatrick, and McAllister (2008) at the University of Sussex, UK, on access for blind and visually impaired users is worth noting, and there were various fruitful discussions on the SLED List during 2008.

Once issues of access and interface usability have been solved, the next significant barrier encompasses the need for user-training in both general and tools or task-specific areas of client use, made especially complicated at a distance due to the instructor's inability to see what is happening on the students' screens.

This training is particularly important at the initial stage. John Miller,[12] nursing instructor at Tacoma Community College, USA, focused on this in an email interview:

> *Another important hurdle to overcome is the complexity of the user interface of Second Life. I am currently struggling with that issue in my orienting students in a face to face situation, which requires much time and can affect a budget in education. This is a most essential activity for learner so that they become moderately capable in using learning objects, use of cameras, moving and communicating. Extensive one-on-one training is needed especially for many adult learners, students and teachers alike (…)*

In more general terms, there are several ongoing issues connected with daily use. These are discussed below.

1.10.1.   Client Crashes

Whilst platform stability improved greatly in 2008, dropping from 1.2% of total client logins per month in September 2007 to 0.2% in the same period in 2008, statistics on viewer crashes for September 2008 were still running at around 20% of total user sessions,[13] and this represents a significant challenge to running programmed courses and to class schedule completion when extrapolated over a whole course or module. It is not unusual, in the authors' experience, to spend up to 20% of class time waiting for students to log in after a viewer crash or to solve other related problems such as temporary loss of voice service (see below) or the inability to teleport.

1.10.2.   Audio

The main barrier to the use of voice lies in the configuration options. Again, in the authors' experience, a fair degree of class time can often be lost due to issues with all

---

12. http://www.educause.edu/Community/MemDir/Profiles/JohnMiller/65303. Accessed on August 2009.
13. http://secondlifegrid.net/technology-programs/service-metrics#outages. Accessed on August 2009.

students being able to hear at the same time. Controls for switching speech on and off while using Second Life, as one example, are an obstacle to first-time users who are often confused as to when they are broadcasting, when they are not and when they should "push to talk", that is, hold down an interface button to speak. These problems, it must be noted, are not necessarily specific to Second Life but can occur in any VOIP platform where end-user configuration plays a significant role in the overall experience.

1.10.3. Griefing

Griefing describes the action of disturbing other users of Second Life with verbal, visual or physical activity designed to limit the user's ability to carry out his/her intended aims in-world. This often involves the use of "weapons", which physically effect movement, or visual displays resulting in reduced visibility and thus impacting on the user's ability to interact with their environment. There have also been reports of griefers using voice and/or text chat to inhibit effective communications. Education projects in Second Life suffer less from this problem as they tend to be based on private island spaces where considerably superior access controls are in place, but educators who choose to leave their spaces as open access — precisely because of the interaction possibilities inherent in open spaces — occasionally have to deal with occurrences of griefing during class time.

1.10.4. E-safety

Coupled with the issue of griefing is the possibility of end-users coming into contact with inappropriate or disturbing content. Second Life mirrors real life in terms of users and spaces, and there is a bewildering array of builds devoted to various potentially problematic areas, not least of which is the large sex industry in-world.

Linden Lab have taken steps to clean up Second Life, prohibiting in-world banks and gambling and pursuing potentially offensive sexual, political and social materials, but there is still some way to go and there exists a high probability that students using the platform who leave the safety of their institutional setting will come into contact with some of this.

In the report of their presentation given at ReLIVE08 Liz Thackray, Good, and Howland (2008) reveal

> *Students needed to be introduced to SL and made aware of some of the risks inherent within the virtual environment. (...) Although it could be argued that, as a rule, we are unaware of what students do in their lives outside the real life classroom, it is also true that we do not ask them to do any particular activities in their lives beyond the classroom which would lead them into personally risky situations. (...) The written material introducing students to the course included information about*

> *how to register an avatar and alerted students to the risks in SL, providing strategies for avoiding, or if necessary escaping from, situations where they felt vulnerable or at risk. Although some risks might have been mitigated by purchasing our own island, we felt it was important for students to explore the affordances of SL for themselves.*

Much has been made of this potential problem on the SLED List in recent months and opinion is divided as to how much responsibility educators have outside class hours or outside institutional builds in-world.

1.11. Recommendations Relating to End-User Barriers

- Teachers should receive training in appropriate uses of Second Life as an educational platform: first-hour orientation should depend on the extent to which the user will be engaged in Second Life, whilst one-off users should be provided with a limited set of tools and instructions that will enable them to carry out the activities they will need to implement. Most importantly, they should be able to avoid the standard first-hour orientation and connect directly to the institution's Second Life facility as soon as possible after first sign-in to the virtual world. For longer running projects, training should include coaching to competency in the basic functions in Second Life — physical orientation and basic environment manipulation.
- A comprehensive support package for students should also be developed. This should include basic items such as default avatar designs, clothing and useful study tools, orientation exercises and advice, support for dealing with issues of potential disruption or distress such as griefing, contact with "alternative lifestyle" residents and other elements that are not normally encountered in more traditional learning environments.

It should be noted that at the time of writing, Linden Lab had announced a consultancy period into the implementation of a new division of the Adult Grid allowing for both PG and Adult content in separate "continents" with relevant search and access restrictions. Whilst this will not affect private island estates (which comprise the large majority of educational spaces in Second Life), it may make the current "mainland" safer and more acceptable for education and pave the way for more interesting and international projects. Commentators on the Linden Lab blog also note that this appears to be paving the way for the eventual merging of the Teen and Adult Grids into one world.

1.12. Conclusions

As we have seen in the course of this chapter, Second Life — along with the vast majority of other economically viable MUVEs currently available to educators —

has not yet reached a level of maturity or professionalism that easily allows for successful implementation in Higher Education contexts without considerable compromise and accommodation on the part of the institution.

However, it is evident when discussing Second Life with early adopters in the education field that it is precisely the "amateur" nature of the platform that is considered one of its most attractive facets. Equally evident in these conversations is the need for more skilled and experienced educator-users to take the next steps beyond Gartner's *slope of enlightenment*, where research is now beginning to clearly demonstrate some of the advantages of using virtual worlds in certain educational scenarios,[14] to Gartner's *plateau of productivity* where it can be applied with less effort — both administrative and technical. For this to happen, it would seem vital that educators be given the support and training to break down all the barriers explored in this chapter and allow them to leverage these spaces effectively and productively in their teaching.

Equally clear in this putative adoption and development cycle is the urgent need for "hybrid" instructors who combine a set of skills, which are often not required in everyday teaching — skills ranging from the more prosaic ability to be able to understand and work with the complex user interface, to more advanced skills such as an understanding of the Second Life building interface and scripting language. Any implementation of Second Life at this level will require significant investment from institutions, and it is perhaps the demonstrable lack of this level of buy-in which is proving more of a barrier than any other.

The barriers to the adoption and use of technologies such as Second Life can be considered in many ways analogous to those present in the adoption of any other novel or disruptive approach, requiring similar amounts of investment in the change management process within institutions.

Despite a large-scale increase in the use of — and research into — virtual worlds in education, it is still too early to make a convincing argument for Second Life's value or to dismiss its potential. The calculation for many institutions may be one of whether the costs of dismantling the current barriers are worthwhile or whether it is more prudent to adopt a "wait and see" approach towards the efforts of other institutions and early adopters.

1.13. Recommendations

In this final section, we bring together the major recommendations of this chapter in list format for quick reference purposes.

- Institutional support should be sought by use of analogy: a Second Life resource is an additional teaching or research tool and should not be placed in any special or

---

14. http://www.virtualworldsnews.com/2008/09/quick-stat-seco.html. Accessed on August 2009.

new category for consideration, thus setting it apart from other tools and approaches and, as a consequence, building up unreasonable expectations. The potential for over-inflated expectations of educational or research results should be explored openly and, where possible, constrained to the realms of reality. Acknowledgement of the immaturity of the technology and the potential for negative attitudes towards it should also be acknowledged.

- An appropriate level of institutional technical support should be gained at the commencement of any Second Life project. As one example, it is conceivable that an institution's particularly inflexible provision of technical support may preclude the use of Second Life from, behind restrictive firewalls.

- Similarly, institutional policies on accessing Internet resources judged to be of a potentially "adult" nature might also impede any implementation of public wide area networks such as Second Life. Early establishment of rules and permissions (for both academic staff and their students) with regard to conduct during in-world projects will be essential to their smooth running and, if well-formulated, should preclude the need for last-minute or *ad-hoc* solutions that may not lead to sustainable good practices.

- Institutional participants (both educators and researchers) should consider seriously how to present themselves and their Second Life facility. Thought should be given to visual appearance — both of the virtual space and of avatars operating within it — naming conventions for avatars, which can be easily linked to the physical institution, codes of conduct (where necessary), and — depending on buy-in from other potential stakeholders across the institution — branding and institutional design.

- Sign-up to Second Life is a one-off requirement, and this need not be done by teachers or researchers if an administrator or educational technologist can do it, thus facilitating the acquisition of usernames and passwords as well as "ready-made" avatars where feasible. Care should be taken to facilitate student induction into Second Life with the provision of a registration API-enabled institutional website, and care should be taken to ensure that the institution allows for large-scale avatar registration through the white listing process detailed above.

- Teachers should receive training in appropriate uses of Second Life as an educational platform: first-hour orientation should depend on the extent to which the user will be engaged in Second Life, whilst one-off users should be provided with a limited set of tools and instructions that will enable them to carry out the activities they will need to implement. Most importantly, they should be able to avoid the "normal" first-hour orientation and connect directly to the institution's Second Life facility as soon as possible after first sign-in to the virtual world. For longer running projects, training should include coaching to competency in basic functions in Second Life — physical orientation and basic environment manipulation.

- A comprehensive support package for students should also be developed. This should include basic items such as default avatar designs, clothing and useful study tools, as well as orientation exercises and — where desirable — advice and support for dealing with issues of potential disruption or distress such as griefing, contact with "alternative lifestyle" residents and elements that are not normally encountered in more traditional learning environments, specifically pornography and other examples of the less educational aspects of Second Life.

- When using Second Life for teaching rather than research or development work, care should be taken to involve the students at design and implementation stages and to leave space on the institutions land for student creativity and experimentation. Having a stake in the overall project should ensure that overall uptake of any Second Life project will have a higher chance of success across all constituencies.

References

Coleridge, S. (1817). Biographia Literaria.

Fenn, J., & Raskino, M. (2008). *Mastering the hype cycle: How to choose the right innovation at the right time*. Boston, MA: Harvard Business School Press.

Nicol, D. J., Minty, I., & Sinclair, C. (2003). The social dimensions of online learning. *Innovations in Education and Teaching International, 40*(3), 270–280.

Thackray, L., Good, J., & Howland, K. (2008). Difficult, dangerous, impossible…: Crossing the boundaries into immersive virtual worlds. Paper presented at Relive 08 and available on request from Thackray-E.J.Thackray@open.ac.uk. Available at http://www.open.ac.uk/relive08/

Thelander, N. (2007). A university's digital migration, Educause 2007, Paper No 29.00.

White, G. R., Fitzpatrick, G., & McAllister, G. (2008). Toward accessible 3D virtual environments for the blind and visually impaired. In: Proceedings of the 3rd international conference on digital interactive media in entertainment and arts Athens, Greece, September 10–12, 2008. DIMEA '08, vol. 349. ACM, New York, NY (pp. 134–141). Available at http://doi.acm.org/10.1145/1413634.1413663. See also White's blog at http://www.blindsecondlife.blogspot.com

Whitton, N., & Hollins, P. (2008). Collaborative virtual gaming worlds in higher education. *ALT-K, 16*(3), 221–229.

Zastrocky, M., Lowendahl, J.-M., & Harris, M. (2007). *Technology adoption in higher education: Know your businesses*. Stamford, CT: Gartner.

Author Biographies

Gavin Dudeney is project manager for The Consultants-E, an online training and development consultancy, which has won various awards for its professional publications and online course design. The Consultants-E have been working in education in Second Life for more than two years and manage and run three full island sims. They have designed and built Second Life presence for Higher Education colleges in Switzerland, The United States, Finland and the United Kingdom and run the annual SLanguages Conference in-world. Gavin Dudeney is also a member of the international advisory board, *International Journal of Virtual and Personal Learning Environments*.

Howard Ramsay is an educational technologist at the University of Strathclyde Business School in Scotland. He has been using Second Life since 2004 and now runs the Strathclyde Business School Second Life island, initially providing online seminars for international postgraduate and doctoral distance students. He has published articles on the use of technology in teaching and learning natural language and is pursuing doctoral studies in online and distance collaboration and engagement.

Chapter 2

Communication Challenges and Opportunities for Educators Using Second Life [☆]

John C. Sherblom, Lesley A. Withers and Lynnette G. Leonard

2.1. Introduction

A number of scholars (Allen, 2006; Patterson & Gojdycz, 2000; Witmer, 1998; Wood & Fassett, 2003) identify the communication challenges and opportunities that educators face in using computer-mediated communication (CMC) in their courses. These challenges include helping students develop competence with the technology, learn strategies to communicate effectively through the medium, manage the interpersonal communication, and communicate effectively in groups. The opportunities are identified as providing students with the potential to engage in more critical thinking, collaborative learning, interactivity, and team-based problem-solving activities (Gaimster, 2007; Schrire, 2004, 2006; Vess, 2005; Wood & Fassett, 2003).

Few scholars, however, have looked specifically at the communication challenges and opportunities of using Second Life in the classroom (Sherblom, Withers, & Leonard, 2009). This chapter examines these communication challenges and opportunities by first reviewing the CMC literature and identifying the issues relevant to communication in Second Life. Then the chapter presents data from a thematic analysis of student responses. These responses are obtained through a focus group reflection on the communication occurring during a collaborative project undertaken as part of an undergraduate course offered in Second Life. The description and analysis of these responses delineate the communication challenges

[☆]This research was sponsored in part by a grant from the Center for Collaboration Science at the University of Nebraska at Omaha.

Higher Education in Virtual Worlds
Copyright © 2009 by Emerald Group Publishing Limited
All rights of reproduction in any form reserved
ISBN: 978-1-84950-609-0

and opportunities that student groups and educators face when using Second Life in the university classroom.

2.2. The Technology

More than half (55%) of U.S. employees who use computers in the workplace report experiencing computer anxiety and feeling unprepared to competently use the available communication technologies (Scott & Timmerman, 2005). A lack of skill and training with a specific CMC task increases participant anxiety and reduces communication competence in using the technology (Wrench & Punyanunt-Carter, 2007). Unskilled and ineffective use of text-based CMC increases an individual's computer anxiety, writing apprehension, and apprehension with CMC and negatively affects their communication effectiveness (Cornelius & Boos, 2003; Wrench & Punyanunt-Carter, 2007). Furthermore, Benoit, Benoit, Milyo, and Hansen (2006) report that students who have difficulty with the technology early in a course become frustrated and express decreased satisfaction with the course in general.

2.3. Interpersonal and Group Communication in CMC Contexts

In addition to computer anxiety, CMC poses a challenge for the communication processes used to establish interpersonal social presence, express personal identity, manage impressions, reduce interpersonal uncertainty, and develop ongoing relationships (Sherblom, 2009). Short, Williams, and Christie (1976) argue that this lack of social presence inhibits the expression of social-emotional communication and limits interpersonal relationship development. Daft and Lengel (1986), Trevino, Daft, and Lengel (1990), and McGrath and Hollingshead (1994) suggest that the lack of multiple simultaneous verbal and nonverbal cues, synchronous feedback, and vocal inflections to convey emotion, lead to interpersonal impressions that are less sociable, relational, and effective for developing relationships (Hancock & Dunham, 2001; Walther, Loh, & Granka, 2005).

However, Walther et al. (2005) assert that communicators can adapt to this paucity of nonverbal vocal and physical cues in CMC by adjusting their social information processing expectations and their communication strategies. They indicate that participants use verbal, rather than nonverbal, messages to express themselves and focus on contextual stylistic cues to obtain the necessary information about other participant's characteristics, attitudes, and emotions. Using these different communication strategies, communicators, with time, can learn to both express and acquire the social-emotional and relational information needed to develop interpersonal relationships in a CMC medium (Walther, 1996).

Postmes, Spears, and Lea (1998), however, caution that the visual anonymity of CMC obscures personal features, reducing the individuality of participants. This visual anonymity can result in a depersonalizing of the individual as it shifts a participant's attention to word choice, paralinguistic decisions, and typographic information more indicative of gender, social class, race, ethnicity, and group identities than personal characteristics (Hancock & Dunham, 2001). Thus, a stereotyped, de-individuated social identity may be communicated in which a person is more associated with social group membership and less defined by individual, personal characteristics (Hancock & Dunham, 2001; Lee, 2004). Walther (1996) recognizes this impoverished social presence and constrained relational development, and accepts that de-individuated, stereotypic impressions of communicators are often made. However, he suggests that available back-channel responses, language selection, and message construction cues are useful in reducing interpersonal uncertainty and developing personal relationships.

Collectively, these scholars suggest that CMC provides a medium in which communicators must: (a) cope with reduced social cues; (b) use alternative cues to create, and take time to process, social information; (c) be concerned about making stereotyped impressions; and (d) selectively attend to verbal style, word choice, and paralinguistic cues to reduce interpersonal uncertainty and develop personal relationships.

In sum, users of a CMC medium must manage both the technology and the communication aspects of the medium. Learning the necessary computer skills, overcoming techno-anxiety, and developing effective strategies for managing specific characteristics of the technology are important for increasing communication competence in any CMC medium. In addition to these skills, however, participants must develop communication strategies to effectively interpret the interpersonal meanings of others, manage their own personal expressions, and develop working relationships with others through a medium having reduced social cues available. Overcoming these challenges takes communication, awareness, and practice.

2.4. Interpersonal Uncertainty Reduction and Relationship Development

Some interpersonal communication processes become more difficult when communicating through CMC. At the same time, CMC eases the way for other aspects of interpersonal communication. Interpersonal uncertainty reduction, for example, is made more of a challenge by the lack of nonverbal cues available through the CMC medium. To build interpersonal relationships and understandings, CMC participants must develop and use different uncertainty reduction strategies than they do in face-to-face conversation (Walther et al., 2005). Email communicators have been shown to use more frequent and intimate personal questions and self-disclosures to reduce their interpersonal uncertainty than communicators in face-to-face contexts (Tidwell & Walther, 2002). Some research, however, indicates that other interpersonal communication challenges may be eased through CMC. Participants with high communication apprehension often find it easier to make a good impression through CMC, and as a written medium, CMC may be useful for highly apprehensive communicators who sometimes are avoidant in face-to-face situations (Patterson & Gojdycz, 2000;

Scott & Timmerman, 2005). In addition, participants with high communication apprehension often feel free to communicate more openly in their CMC sessions (Campbell & Neer, 2001). However, some participants who have high communication apprehension express concern about receiving more critical feedback through CMC and report no greater satisfaction with CMC than with face-to-face communication (Campbell & Neer, 2001). The results of this research suggest that Second Life's potential for facilitating the interpersonal communication processes of uncertainty reduction and relationship development should be considered.

2.5. Interpersonal Expression and Identity

Differences between the medium of face-to-face and CMC communication also elicit differences in interpersonal expression and group participation. Face-to-face communication relies heavily on vocal and other nonverbal social cues, maintains a higher level of social presence, provides a salience to personal characteristics, and is more likely to use observable social status characteristics in establishing group leadership. Text-based CMC depends on the primarily verbal cues of written communication, facilitates greater anonymity, and often its users are more likely to view members of out-groups as possessing stereotypically extreme views and traits (Ho & McLeod, 2008).

The absence of nonverbal cues expressed through CMC can make an individual's statements appear more anonymous and less individuated to other discussion participants. By reducing observable status differences, perceived anonymity can promote more egalitarian participation, create a more comfortable environment in which to contribute, and stimulate greater idea generation among students (Ho & McLeod, 2008). Sassenberg and Boos (2003) argue that when anonymity is coupled with fewer social contextual cues, lower self-awareness, and reduced self-regulation, participants experience a state of de-individuation that can result in more extreme opinions and behavior. When personal identity is salient and some degree of self-awareness is maintained or increased, individuals and groups tend toward less extreme opinions and behavior.

2.6. Group Communication and Participation

The social interaction and communication patterns of CMC participants are affected by normative group pressure (Lee & Nass, 2002). A CMC culture can be nurtured that develops politeness and inclusiveness in the electronic classroom. CMC users often adapt their messages to fit into a positive, affective, relational communication culture; and the use of the CMC medium itself has been shown to be an important influence on the verbal politeness and communication style of participants (Bunz & Campbell, 2004; Byron & Baldridge, 2007).

In a positive, supportive communication culture, CMC participants engage in collaborative processes more frequently. These processes facilitate learning and higher levels of cognitive performance and critical thinking (Schrire, 2004, 2006). Students exhibit greater interactivity and cognitive effort, engage in more collaborative learning, and participate in vigorous debate during their CMC collaborations (Vess, 2005). CMC also supports a positive team-building environment that promotes engagement, dynamic learning, and collaborative problem solving (Gaimster, 2007). In addition, students become more familiar with the educational material, feel better prepared, and are more willing to discuss their ideas in the face-to-face classroom once they have expressed their thoughts online (Vess, 2005). Wood and Fassett (2003) argue that CMC stimulates student learning; empowers students to take more responsibility for their participation in the classroom; and allows them to renegotiate their classroom social positions, their perception of the teacher's role, and the educational process itself. The networked conferencing style of CMC de-emphasizes the instructor as an authority figure, facilitates active participation and collaborative learning, and increases student participation in the learning process. However, greater technical skills are demanded of the individual and the group; and the potential for groups meeting through CMC without adequate prior training may reduce meeting coherence and group consensus (Cornelius & Boos, 2003). Speaker turn-taking and listening roles may be ignored by group participants and messages may be addressed to the group and receive little response. When this occurs group decisions are often less clear and groups become less task oriented, experience reduced group cohesion, and achieves less satisfaction (Cornelius & Boos, 2003).

Cornelius and Boos (2003) suggest training CMC groups to create more conversational coherence around topics and to collaboratively develop them by actively adapting communication behavior to the requirements of the medium. They further recommend teaching CMC group participants to make explicit references to a topic, to directly repeat key words, and to respond to a person's comment by addressing the person by name. These techniques enhance conversational coherence. In addition, they suggest asking direct questions and giving specific answers to help facilitate the conversational flow.

In sum, the effect of the communication medium on interpersonal and group communication processes must be considered. The characteristics of interpersonal uncertainty reduction, communication apprehension, interpersonal expression, and group conversational participation are influenced by the medium. Much of this influence can be perceived as positive as the medium facilitates a degree of anonymity, reduces some types of apprehension, and increases the possibilities for collaborative learning and participation. However, the communication medium can present a challenge for group communication and task achievement that is likely to influence group communication in Second Life.

2.7. Interpersonal and Group Communication in Second Life

Many of these findings of the CMC research literature are likely to be applicable to the interpersonal and group communication of Second Life where the communication most often occurs in a relatively anonymous, text-based medium. Even when voice communication is available and when communicators share some "real life" recognition of each other, participants frequently use text rather than voice and retain some sense of anonymity in their communication with each other. In this way, communicating through Second Life shares many of the challenges of other text-based CMC contexts such as email and instant messaging, in the need for developing technological competence, communicating effectively, managing interpersonal relation-ships, and working effectively in groups. However, through the visual representation of the user as an avatar participating in a three-dimensional space, Second Life also provides additional opportunities for developing a sense of social presence, expressing personal identity, managing impressions, reducing interpersonal uncertainty, and developing relationships that are not readily available in other text-based forms of CMC. For example, researchers have shown that Second Life offers a fuller range of interpersonal uncertainty reduction strategies to communicators than do other forms of text-based CMC. To reduce their interpersonal uncertainty in Second Life, communicators can use unobtrusive observation, draw comparisons with others, watch a person's less inhibited communication, listen for self-disclosed information, engage in deception detection, and use verbal questioning (Sherblom et al., 2009). Little research has been conducted on other interpersonal and group communication processes as they occur in Second Life, and even less research has investigated Second Life communication in the classroom and in the educational experiences of students.

Nesson and Nesson (2008) argue that Second Life, in its presentation of a virtual space that is similar to physical space, can offer advantages for developing interpersonal and group communication norms and behaviors that enhance the classroom and educational experience. Even for a student and instructor who never meet face to face in a physical classroom, the shared norms about classroom spatial configurations and behavioral norms learned through years of schooling help to organize the Second Life educational experience with rules for when to speak, where to sit, and when it is appropriate to enter and leave the classroom space. The look and feel of the virtual classroom space signals that classroom norms are in effect. Second Life can trigger social norms, build expectations about appropriate classroom behavior, incorporate communication expectations, and invoke implicit meaning structures for an educational environment (Nesson & Nesson, 2008). Second Life also provides an environment in which an instructor can take advantage of other shared real-world social norms for interaction, ritualized manners, and conversational rules. Through these implicit communication expectations and structures, Second Life can overcome many of the educational concerns for CMC in:

(a) building a classroom community,
(b) enhancing a student's communication with the instructor and other students,
(c) developing a peer group and the opportunity to learn from others,
(d) judiciously using peer pressure and competition in a positive way, and
(e) instilling a personal sense of responsibility for learning among students (Nesson & Nesson, 2008).

In addition, as a CMC medium, Second Life may facilitate certain types of communication that are not part of a traditional classroom context, but that may enhance the learning experience.

To investigate the challenges and opportunities of interpersonal and group communication in Second Life, the present study undertakes an analysis of student responses to participating in a collaborative group project. The study uses a focus-group methodology to investigate these communication challenges and opportunities of the Second Life classroom. The focus group was conducted near the end of the Second Life portion of a college course and inquires about the effect of the technology and communication medium on the students' interpersonal and group communication while participating in the collaborative group project.

2.8. Method

2.8.1. The Project

The instructors of classes at three different, geographically distanced U.S. universities initiated the collaborative project. Over the period of several weeks of the semester, students were trained to use the Second Life platform and instructed in how to complete a number of individual and dyadic tasks designed to reinforce the lessons. Then students were assigned to groups for the collaborative project. This project required students at two different mid-sized Midwestern universities separated by approximately a thousand miles, who were enrolled in classes (with class sizes of 29 students and 14 students, respectively) that had never met face to face, to work together and communicate using Second Life text chat. Students from each university were assigned to one of eight collaborative groups consisting of five or six students each. Each group was given the task of developing a proposal for helping an existing non-profit organization meet one of its organizational objectives through the use of Second Life. Students were required to research several charitable organizations as a group and select one organization for their project. The groups used Second Life for their group decision-making discussions about the organization and their proposed project. To accomplish the goals of this project, each group had to engage in a coordinated research effort to examine the non-profit organization, brainstorm ideas together, and develop a workable proposal with a timeline, events, and budget. Each group created a proposal indicating how the non-profit organization might use Second Life to meet an organizational need such as publicity, fund raising, or organizational outreach.

The 20 students enrolled in a third class held at a mid-sized northeastern university were trained separately and assigned to a review team charged with critiquing the proposal groups' projects. These review teams had to independently research the same non-profit organizations, develop a set of criteria for evaluating the effectiveness of the group proposals, and provide evaluative feedback on the proposals based on that set of criteria. Review team members met in Second Life throughout the course of the project, and also interacted in Second Life with the proposal groups to articulate the criteria and provide two rounds of evaluative feedback on the proposals. Upon the completion of the project, the proposal groups and representatives of the review teams met in the Second Life classroom for a focus group discussion of the Second Life group communication processes in which they had just engaged. Second Life provides an option to record and store synchronous communication text on a participant's computer hard drive. This option was used to produce a transcript of the focus group local text chat.

2.8.2.   The Focus Group

Approximately 40 students actively participated in the 40-minute focus group chat. One of the course instructors moderated the discussion by posing questions to which any student could respond. The focus group began with the facilitator saying: "*So, let's start with any comments you have about the collaboration project. What did you like about collaborating in* Second Life?", "*What were the challenges?*" Student responses to topics were encouraged through reflective, supportive responses to their comments such as "*ah, good,*" or with paraphrasing statements such as "*so Second Life is an efficient way to collaborate?*" and "*interesting, Do others also think you were better able to get to know one another through Second Life?*"

2.9.   Results

To learn about the students' experiences of communicating in these groups, we analyzed the resulting transcript of this focus group session using a constant comparative method of analysis (Glaser & Strauss, 1967; Strauss & Corbin, 1998a, 1998b). Student responses were iteratively coded, categorized, and continuously refined into a set of core categories and themes. This process of conceptual immersion into the focus group responses works to identify a pattern of interactions and relationships among the communication technology, medium, interpersonal, and group experiences. The themes identified in Table 2.1 and supported by the thematized respondent statements presented in Table 2.2 emerged from this analytic process.

The focus group discussion asked students to respond to the opportunities and challenges of Second Life communication in four general areas of interest to the researchers: the use of the technology, the human communication aspects of the computer-mediated medium, the influences on the interpersonal communication, and the effects on group communication.

Students describe Second Life as a new, useful, and versatile tool for group communication. One commented: "*As a tool, Second Life is sweet!*" They especially like the ability to multi-task, the immediate feedback, and the ability to transmit ideas and brainstorm as a group. However, the Second Life technology poses challenges, as well. Access to Second Life outside of class time was difficult for some students whose personal computers would not run the client software and for whom accessing the campus computer labs to use the Second Life platform was less

Table 2.1: Opportunities and challenges of Second Life as a communication medium.

Second Life as a communication medium	Opportunities	Challenges
The technology	New, versatile, useful Ability to multi-task Better than email	Access Distractions Computer lag
Computer-mediated communication	Efficient and Useful	Frustrating Chat obsessive Communication difficulties
Interpersonal communication	Get to know people Separate task and personal	Missing nonverbal cues Deception detection Anonymity Criticism
Group communication	Professional orientation Participation Collaboration Brainstorming	Group meeting challenges Connecting, pleasing

convenient. The Internet and Second Life itself also provide numerous opportunities for distraction, and computer slowness at times creates an annoying lag in the conversation.

Overall, students' comments suggest that Second Life provides an efficient and useful human-CMC medium, although it can be frustrating, chat obsessive, and challenging. Comments include: *"It can be useful to get assignments done,"* but it is also frustrating when *"I just wanted someone to talk to, instead of typing."* *"It's like writing a novel when you chat with someone."* *"It seems that I'm constantly staring at the local chat,"* and *"It really challenges everyone's communication skills and patience."*

Second Life does allow users to *"get to know others better"* as they work together, and through their posted profile statements. Also, as a medium, Second Life is efficient in separating group task discussion from personal comments. However, many *"nonverbal cues are missed in Second Life,"* making it *"difficult trying to figure out if group members are frustrated,"* and it is sometimes *"a strain to say the right thing because of not seeing reactions face-to-face."*

Deception, anonymity, and criticism are all issues discussed in multiple ways by students. Deception is hard to detect, but considered less likely the longer group members work together. Anonymity may mean that *"it is harder to get to know someone in Second Life, because people can be anything,"* *"but [also] we made choices based on something in real life."* When *"we lose the anonymity we have to start checking ourselves."* A lack of anonymity inhibits an *"ability to get to know class members on a different level than real life."* Criticism maybe *"a little easier,"* with *"less emotion,"* but often *"it does sound mean,"* may *"sound harsher,"* and *"coming across nice can be*

Table 2.2: Focus group themes of opportunities and challenges of Second Life.

The technology
  Opportunities
    New, versatile, useful
      As a tool, Second Life is sweet!
      It offered a new perspective into group processes
      There are so many versatile aspects of what you can do in Second Life
      The potential is there to transmit ideas and projects of any sort through
          Second Life
      I find it very useful for some of the real life things I am involved in
    Ability to multi-task
      Being able to multi-task and that being okay is a plus too
      Yeah, I love being able to multi-task
    Better than email
      Better than email; it made email seem so limited once I experienced Second Life
      Immediate feedback is important, more like face-to-face than email
      Second Life was much better than email for brainstorming
  Challenges
    Access
      Many group members could not use Second Life outside of class time which made
          it hard to communicate as much as we liked before using email in addition to
          Second Life
    Distractions
      There were a lot of distractions
      I think the Internet is very distracting
      I get distracted by the avatars
      It's so much easier in Second Life to get off topic
      It was hard keeping the group on the same page. There would be distractions in
          Second Life as well as on the Internet
    Computer tag
      Lag was the worst part
      Private chat didn't work that often either
      Lag and set-up time were downfalls
      Definitely, the lag time has been a problem
      I was seriously lagging. It would really slow down the process
      I think the medium itself was a disadvantage for me. The group chat lagged so
          much I was almost 5 minutes behind the rest of the group

Computer-mediated communication medium
  Opportunities
    Efficient, useful
      It can be efficient
      It can be useful to get assignments done
  Challenges
    Frustrating
      Not being able to see someone when I am talking to them is difficult
      I would get frustrated at times because all I can see is text. I am more of a
          nonverbal person, I like to see facial expressions and hear all the nonverbal
          sounds people make.
      Sometimes I just wanted someone to talk to me, instead of typing

Table 2.2: *(Continued)*

Chat obsessive

You essentially have to obsessively love chatting

Requires an extensive attention span

I don't like to convey information through a chat; It's slow and messages become lost or mistranslated

It's like writing a novel when you chat with someone

I am a very visual person and when there is nothing but chat and dancing avatars I have a hard time taking the conversation seriously

It seems that I'm constantly staring at the local chat

I am having trouble keeping up. It [the chat log] goes by really fast

I think a lot of conversations took place in private IM boxes

Communication difficulties

It really challenges everyone's communication skills and patience

I wanted to pull my hair out a couple of times

You had to work harder to get your point across

I think face-to-face is the best way, depending on what the desired outcome is

I seemed hard to get little things done unless someone was adamant

Sometimes it was hard to get your point across and not sound mean at the same time

At times to get your point across you had to say it more than once because someone may have skipped over reading it, or was too busy typing and they missed it

Another disadvantage was working through any disagreements. It's easier to reach consensus face-to-face because there may be more pressure, or you may see someone's idea more accurately face-to-face. Second Life was chaotic at the start

Too much going on in one little window and nothing going on around me in real life

Interpersonal communication

Opportunities

Get to know people

You get to know the others better

Somewhat better, but sometimes it was still hard

I think some character qualities showed through the more we worked together

You can to look at a profile someone has taken the time to fill out with useful information about them, but also their clothing serves as a nonverbal artifact about the person

Separate task and personal

Good when you need to meet with a lot of people and have less time

You can keep the discussion official in the local chat and keep the chit-chat to the personal IM window. That makes a big difference, especially when you have deadlines to meet

Challenges

Missing nonverbal cues

Non verbal cues are missed in Second Life

I wish I could see the nonverbal communication between group members in Second Life

It's hard to interpret how people are feeling in Second Life

The fact is there is someone on the other side with a different view

Table 2.2: (*Continued*)

I miss the chance that I don't really know who I am talking to

It is difficult trying to figure out if group members are frustrated

It is also harder to connect with others

Even when we use emoticons they can get misinterpreted. A smile can mean someone is being nice, or that someone is making fun of you or being sarcastic

I found it a strain to say the right thing because of not seeing reactions face-to-face

It's hard to express something; inflections don't exist in text, only conversation

Deception

I can't detect deception on Second Life

I can make my avatar look like I am a real party girl or a focused professional, and it is hard to tell which I am

So we can only base our judgment on what was said and the contribution that was made

I think Second Life does open the door of opportunity for deception

We had the opportunity to be deceptive, but when we were working how many of us continued to be deceptive. We revert to our own personalities. You learn a lot through the way one writes

I think it is harder to get to know someone in Second Life, because people can be anything and they may appear to be someone that they are not

Anonymity

We all represent ourselves in a particular fashion on here, and could be completely different in real life, but we made choices based on something in real life whether it was a dream, or the actual person

I didn't know anyone from my group because they were all from another college, so I was able to keep myself fairly professional

I really didn't like finding out who my real life classmates are. When we lost the anonymity we have to start checking ourselves

I didn't realize who my real life classmate in my group was until halfway through the project so I maintained the same relationship with them as I did with the other students

We knew from day one who was in our group in real life because the class was small. That inhibited my ability to get to know class members on a different level than real life

Criticism

I think that it makes criticism a little easier. There is less emotion and more fact behind it

It is never pure fact. It is your interpretation of what is happening

It is hard to type criticism because it does sound mean

When people would offer criticism it would sound harsher than it would have face-to-face

Being honest, but coming across nice can be difficult

I think that since we have a project to do and limited time: honesty is important. Being nice can take a second

Also, there are no repercussions in Second Life about what is said

You don't want to make people mad but don't want others to take over or not do their part, so being honest is necessary.

Table 2.2: *(Continued)*

Group communication
  Opportunities
    Professional orientation
      Second Life forms a sort of work ethic that would help residents communicate better
      We are able to accomplish a lot in a short period of time because of the lack of socio-emotional chatter
      It is easier in Second Life to say, ok, are we done here, cool, and leave; in real life there would have been times you wouldn't want to be that person to say: "Can we disperse?"
      I like Second Life for business, but it would be hard to develop strong personal relationships, unless you have a similar frame of reference
    Participation, collaboration, and brainstorming
      We had a lot of group participation in our group
      I think an advantage to using Second Life would be to have a lot of people collaborate on ideas together that otherwise wouldn't be able to meet in person
      I enjoy brainstorming ideas outside of the universities' classrooms
  Challenges
    Group meeting challenges
      It was hard to get a group to meet somewhere the first time
      It was easier for she and I to work together than the whole group. It's the medium's fault
    Connecting and pleasing everyone
      I feel more connected with the students in my real life classroom
      I think it was kind of tough to please everyone in Second Life
      It's hard to please everyone in a group in face-to-face, too

difficult." Still, "*being nice can take a second*," "*there are no repercussions in Second Life about what is said*," and "*you don't want to make people mad but don't want others to take over or not do their part, so being honest is necessary.*"

Finally, group communication takes on a professional orientation that invites participation, collaboration, and brainstorming. "Second Life forms a sort of work ethic," so participants "*are able to accomplish a lot in a short period of time.*" Second Life facilitates "*a lot of group participation,*" allowing "*a lot of people [to] collaborate on ideas together*" and "*enjoy brainstorming ideas.*" However, group meetings can challenge group members to find a place to meet, to feel connected with one another, and to please everyone in the group.

2.10.   Discussion and Implications

Clearly, students find Second Life to be a versatile, useful communication medium through which to participate in group discussion, collaboration, and brainstorming.

They experience numerous challenges in gaining access, managing Internet and Second Life distractions, and coping with computer lag and its detrimental effects on the continuity of their group conversations. The written nature of the chat can be challenging and frustrating, and the interpersonal communication made more difficult by the absence of many nonverbal cues. There are interpersonal communication issues surrounding deception, anonymity, and criticism, and group meetings require more effort, attention, and patience. However, Second Life is perceived as efficient and useful in facilitating the process of getting to know people, in separating personal from task communication, and in fostering a professional orientation to group participation, collaboration, and brainstorming. Overall, Second Life communication is rated more favorably by the students than email communication, although not quite as favorably as face-to-face communication, for accomplishing their group work. Despite all of the challenges articulated in its use, *"Second Life is sweet"* as a medium *"to transmit ideas and projects of any sort."*

Of additional interest in interpreting this thematic analysis is that students do not mention some of the concerns that have been raised in the previous literature on other CMC text-based contexts. Students do not mention computer anxiety in using Second Life, although they are forthright in their frustration with the lag. The students' ability to establish a sense of social presence in their working groups, to engage in social-emotional communication, and to develop interpersonal working relationships all appear assumed as they focus on the communication issues surrounding and following from the development of that social presence, communication, and relationship development. For example, students are articulate in their discussion of communication being more challenging with the lack of many nonverbal cues, the potential for deception, the pros and cons of personal anonymity, and the sensitivity to the need for and difficulty in giving criticism. This articulated sensitivity itself suggests a degree of social presence, interpersonal communication, and relationship development among communicators who are consciously working through and adapting to the communication medium to achieve their goals.

Of equal importance are the communication challenges identified by students in achieving those goals. Communication takes more effort and is harder in Second Life than face-to-face. Typing all of one's comments and reading quickly enough to keep up with the group chat both appear to be challenges. Beyond that, getting a discussion point across to the group, being recognized, and being heard by the group, can challenge everyone's communication skills and patience. These aspects of group communication pose the biggest challenges for group collaboration in Second Life. Participants do not express concerns with interpersonal uncertainty reduction, communication apprehension, or relationship development. The interpersonal expression and identity issues surrounding deception, anonymity, and criticism are raised, taken into account, and discussed in sophisticated ways that suggest that they are not problems for the group's development, communication, and task accomplishment. The real challenges appear at the group meeting level, and in feeling connected to and pleasing everyone within the group. Even these challenges, however, are offset by the group communication opportunities afforded by Second

Life, that is, a professional orientation for developing group participation, collaboration, and brainstorming.

In addition, there are some concerns raised by participants in the present study for speaker turn taking and listening roles such as those previously identified by Cornelius and Boos (2003) in other CMC contexts. Turn taking becomes an issue, especially within the discussion of lag. Listening arises as an issue in the discussion of getting a point across and being acknowledged. However, much more of the interactivity, collaborative learning, team building, and group problem-solving processes documented by Gaimster (2007), Schrire (2004, 2006), Vess (2005), and Wood and Fassett (2003) in other CMC environments are evident here in the students' discussion of their participation in the Second Life group communication. The opportunity to engage in these interactive processes raises the potential for teaching courses in Second Life that compare favorably to courses taught in a face-to-face classroom. So (2009) argues that time and physical constraints often limit opportunities to initiate, participate in, and sustain discussions in traditional face-to-face classrooms so that, unfortunately, despite efforts toward a learner-centered pedagogy, the traditional instructor initiation-student response-instructor evaluation model still dominates most face-to-face undergraduate classrooms today. Yildiz (2009) argues that learning occurs best within a social interaction in which learners socially negotiate meaning through a mutual process of reflection-collaboration-articulation. The role of the teacher becomes that of facilitator and knowledge is socially, rather than individually, constructed through group participation, collaboration, and brainstorming. Learning is facilitated through social interaction. The present set of student responses suggest that this type of learning occurred in the collaborative group project participation in Second Life. Some limitations to participation and collaboration are noted, such as the challenge for some students of gaining access to Second Life outside of the classroom. However, even with these limitations, student-centered learning appears to have occurred. Other limitations, such as computer access and lag, will lessen as the technology improves over time. The opportunities for truly synchronous group participation and collaboration will continue to grow and develop. With these two technological trends, Second Life will overcome many of the challenges and will continue to offer exciting new opportunities as a communication medium for educators and for the classroom of the 21st century.

References

Allen, T. H. (2006). *Is the rush to provide on-line instruction setting our students up for failure? Communication Education, 55*, 122–126.

Benoit, P. J., Benoit, W. L., Milyo, J., & Hansen, G. J. (2006). *The effects of traditional vs. web-assisted instruction on student learning and satisfaction.* Columbia, MO: The Graduate School, University of Missouri.

Bunz, U., & Campbell, S. W. (2004). Politeness accommodation in electronic mail. *Communication Research Reports, 21*(1), 11–25.

Byron, K., & Baldridge, D. C. (2007). E-mail recipients' impressions of senders' likability. *Journal of Business Communication, 44*, 37–160.

Campbell, S. W., & Neer, M. R. (2001). The relationship of communication apprehension and interaction involvement to perceptions of computer-mediated communication. *Communication Research Reports, 18*, 391–398.

Cornelius, C., & Boos, M. (2003). Enhancing mutual understanding in synchronous computer-mediated communication by training. *Communication Research, 30*, 47–177.

Daft, R., & Lengel, R. (1986). Organizational information requirements, media richness, and structural design. *Management Science, 32*, 554–571.

Gaimster, J. (2007). Reflections on Interactions in virtual worlds and their implication for learning art and design. *Art, Design & Communication in Higher Education, 6*(3), 187–199.

Glaser, B. G., & Strauss, A. L. (1967). *The discovery of grounded theory: Strategies for qualitative research*. New York: Aldine de Gruyter.

Hancock, J. T., & Dunham, P. J. (2001). Impression formation in computer-mediated communication revisited. *Communication Research, 28*, 325–347.

Ho, S. S., & McLeod, D. M. (2008). Social-psychological influences on opinion expression in face-to-face and computer-mediated communication. *Communication Research, 35*, 190–207.

Lee, E. (2004). Effects of visual representation on social influence in computer-mediated communication. *Human Communication Research, 30*, 234–259.

Lee, E., & Nass, C. (2002). Experimental tests of normative group influence and representation effects in computer-mediated communication. *Human Communication Research, 28*, 349–381.

McGrath, J. E., & Hollingshead, A. B. (1994). *Groups interacting with technology*. Thousand Oaks, CA: Sage.

Nesson, R., & Nesson, C. (2008). The case for education in virtual worlds. *Space and Culture, 11*(3), 273–284.

Patterson, B. R., & Gojdycz, T. K. (2000). The relationship between computer-mediated communication and communication related anxieties. *Communication Research Reports, 17*, 278–287.

Postmes, T., Spears, R., & Lea, M. (1998). Breaching or building social boundaries: SIDE effects of computer-mediated communication. *Communication Research, 25*(6), 689–715.

Sassenberg, K., & Boos, M. (2003). Attitude change in computer-mediated communication: Effects of anonymity and category norms. *Group Processes & Intergroup Relations, 6*(4), 405–422.

Schrire, S. (2004). Interaction and cognition in asynchronous computer conferencing. *Instructional Science, 32*, 475–502.

Schrire, S. (2006). Knowledge building in asynchronous discussion groups: Going beyond quantitative analysis. *Computers & Education, 46*(1), 49–70.

Scott, C. R., & Timmerman, C. E. (2005). Relating computer, communication, and computer-mediated communication apprehensions to new communication technology use in the workplace. *Communication Research, 32*, 683–725.

Sherblom, J. C. (2009, April). The promise and challenge of CMC for the classroom. Paper presented at the Eastern Communication Association conference, Philadelphia, PA.

Sherblom, J. C., Withers, L. A., & Leonard, L. G. (2009, February). Interpersonal uncertainty reduction in *Second Life*. Paper presented at the Western States Communication Association Conference, Phoenix, AZ.

Short, J., Williams, E., & Christie, B. (1976). *The social psychology of telecommunications*. London: Wiley.

So, H. J. (2009). When groups decide to use asynchronous online discussions: Collaborative learning and social presence under a voluntary participation structure. *Journal of Computer Assisted Learning, 25*, 43–160.

Strauss, A., & Corbin, J. (1998a). *Basics of qualitative research: Techniques and procedures for developing grounded theory*. Thousand Oaks, CA: Sage.

Strauss, A., & Corbin, J. (1998b). Grounded theory methodology: An overview. In N. K. Denzin & Y. S. Lincoln (Eds), *Strategies of qualitative inquiry* (pp. 158–183). Thousand Oaks, CA: Sage.

Tidwell, L. C., & Walther, J. B. (2002). Computer-mediated communication effects on disclosure, impressions, and interpersonal evaluations: Getting to know one another a bit at a time. *Human Communication Research, 28*, 317–348.

Trevino, L. K., Daft, R. L., & Lengel, R. H. (1990). Understanding manager's media choices: A symbolic interactionist perspective. In: J. Fulk & C. Steinfield (Eds), *Organizations and communication technology* (pp. 71–94). Newbury Park, CA: Sage.

Vess, D. (2005). Asynchronous discussion and communication patterns in online and hybrid history courses. *Communication Education, 54*(4), 355–364.

Walther, J. B. (1996). Computer-mediated communication: Impersonal, interpersonal, and hyperpersonal interaction. *Communication Research, 23*, 3–43.

Walther, J., Loh, T., & Granka, L. (2005). Let me count the ways: The interchange of verbal and nonverbal cues in computer-mediated and face-to-face affinity. *Journal of Language & Social Psychology, 24*(1), 36–65.

Witmer, D. F. (1998). Introduction to computer-mediated communication: A master syllabus for teaching communication. *Communication Education, 47*(2), 162–174.

Wood, A. F., & Fassett, D. L. (2003). Remote control: Identity, power, and technology in the communication classroom. *Communication Education, 52*(3/4), 286–296.

Wrench, J. S., & Punyanunt-Carter, N. M. (2007). The relationship between computer-mediated-communication competence, apprehension, self-efficacy, perceived confidence, and social presence. *Southern Communication Journal, 72*(4), 355–378.

Yildiz, S. (2009). Social presence in the Web-based classroom: Implications for intercultural communication. *Journal of Studies in International Education, 13*(1), 46–65.

Author Biographies

John C. Sherblom teaches graduate and undergraduate courses in communication and technology, research methods, and organizational communication at the University of Maine. He has published more than 30 research articles and given numerous conference presentations. Much of his research has focused on the development of computer-mediated communication. He is the author of a textbook on Small Group and Team Communication that is in its fourth edition. He is currently teaching a course in Second Life. His research interests focus on issues of individual identity, presentation of self, and participation in group decision making in Second Life.

Lesley A. Withers is an interpersonal scholar who has published research on computer-mediated social support, and presented at academic conferences on teaching and communication in Second Life. She teaches graduate and undergraduate courses in the area of interpersonal communication, nonverbal communication, and research methods at Central Michigan University (CMU). Over the past year, she has taught courses in Second Life during two semesters and engaged in research on the effects of student experiences of communication apprehension, competence, and social presence on their class participation in Second Life. She serves as chair of the Second Life learning community at CMU.

Lynnette G. Leonard's research and teaching interests include communication and new technology. She has been active in Second Life since 2006 and has integrated Second Life into her communication classes since Spring 2007. She has been integral in the development of the University of Nebraska at Omaha (UNO) School of Communication's Second Life campus. She has presented on Second Life and education to the faculty at UNO, the Omaha Public School District, and the Lincoln Public School district. Along with Lesley Withers, she conducted a training workshop entitled, "unCONVENTIONal teaching: The pedagogical potential of Second Life." at the National Communication Association meeting in November 2008.

Chapter 3

Inclusion Benefits and Barriers of "Once-Removed" Participation

Simon Ball and Rob Pearce

> *As with any other technology applied in the support of education we need to be careful to make use of the opportunities that virtual worlds afford in ways that align with our, and our students', learning objectives, rather than deploying the technologies for their own sakes. But along with the inevitable mistakes there would seem to be considerable potential.* (Macleod, 2007)

3.1. Introduction

Computer-generated virtual worlds in various forms have existed since the mid-1970s with the first educational applications appearing in the late 1980s (Slator, Beckwith, & Chaput, 2006). The phenomenally successful computer games industry and the development of the Internet into the world's first practical and powerful world-wide public computer network have brought about yet more opportunities for educational applications. This socio-technical revolution has created a new generation of three dimensional (3D) savvy students who arrive at university with an easy familiarity, refined skills and a permanent change in expectations. This has not gone completely unnoticed within the academic community and pioneering work has begun.

A great example and a popular choice for academics is Second Life, which is, for now, the most common choice for development (Kirriemuir, 2008). Second Life requires users to adopt an alter ego, an avatar whose appearance and characteristics can be modified by the user at will, which enables users to indulge in "once-removed" participation – that is, participation through an alter ego whose real-life controller remains anonymous if desired. The relationship between an avatar and its real-life controller has been discussed very effectively by Warburton (2008). Embodiment in

Higher Education in Virtual Worlds
Copyright © 2009 by Emerald Group Publishing Limited
All rights of reproduction in any form reserved
ISBN: 978-1-84950-609-0

this sense is described by Biocca (1997) as "users' mental model of themselves inside the virtual world". This is made possible within virtual environments by giving the participants the aforementioned digital representation of themselves, their avatar. It is through the use of avatars that "users do not simply roam through the space as 'mind', but find themselves grounded in the practice of the body, and thus in the world" (Taylor, 2002).

There are difficulties with "once-removed" participation or embodiment for some users, however. Childs and Kuksa (2009) surveyed students about their experiences of learning in virtual worlds, discovering that a sense of "presence" is vital for students to feel the learning experience is effective and engaging.

> *The apparent inability of some students to experience embodiment therefore raises a new form of accessibility concern in using virtual worlds in education.* (Mark Childs, personal communication)

The contrasting reception given to virtual world learning activities is highlighted in the Childs and Kuksa study, where some students reported the experience of observing theatres in Second Life as "you just feel like you're just watching a game" and "you don't have the feeling of it," whereas others reported the exercise of walking around as almost a physical experience.

Since its release in 2003 the number of UK academics who are developing or operating teaching and learning resources in Second Life has grown rapidly, particularly in the past 2 years.

> *While an accurate figure is difficult to determine (partially due to the non-public nature of some developments), as a rough estimate some three-quarters of UK universities are actively developing or using Second Life, at the institutional, departmental and/or individual academic level. Of these, many institutions support several ongoing Second Life developments, often involving groups of people rather than individuals.* (Kirriemuir, 2008)

Despite some obvious access requirements (a powerful computer, institutional access permission and a certain degree of visual acuity, for instance), there are emerging a range of potential benefits associated with adding this tool to the teacher's palette. Naturally, issues regarding inclusion of visually impaired users should be explored when considering the implementation of virtual world learning and teaching elements. Those issues have been, and continue to be, very effectively discussed in a number of fora (Abrahams, 2007; Hanson, 2008; Kelly, 2008) and effective solutions to aspects of those issues are regularly proposed (Adams-Spink, 2007; Jaime, 2007; Milena, Alissa, & Ron, 2007; White, 2007). There are even prototype working interfaces that give blind users the ability to participate in many virtual world activities (Carr, Sapre, Yuan, & Folmer, 2008, Carter & Corona, 2008a, 2008b).

Perhaps less obvious to the casual user of virtual worlds are the pedagogical possibilities that virtual worlds raise with regard to problem-based and experiential learning, simulation and social and peer learning.

> *As an experiential environment, Second Life enriches students' learning experiences in ways that are not possible with traditional texts or standard course management systems that depend on text-based assignments.* (McKinney, Horspool, Willers, Safie, & Richlin, 2008)

Directly supporting the use of virtual worlds for teaching, learning and assessment are the possibilities, many of them benefits rather than barriers, to the continuum of learner needs pertaining to social interaction, ranging from shyness and reluctance to engage in face-to-face discussion through to autistic spectrum characteristics, together with the potential for virtual worlds to enable individuals to engage with scenarios they would not be able to experience in real life.

> *Second Life [has the] potential for fostering cooperative and individual learning activities, which is one of the Multi-User Virtual Environment's greatest merits.* (Childress & Braswell, 2006)

Conversely, the stripping away of many of the established methods, protocols and habits of communication and learning is not always a positive experience for learners. Some potentially valuable projects are currently underway that will substantially add to the canon of knowledge in this field (for example, transferring problem-based learning techniques and technologies into virtual worlds, PREVIEW-Psych, 2009); generating solutions to the challenges of teaching, learning and collaboration in Multi-User Virtual Environments (Open Habitat, 2009); and modelling the processes needed to enable groups of students from Higher Education environments to establish their socialisation and engagement for more productive information and knowledge exchange and learning through the medium of online 3D Multi-User Virtual Environments (MOOSE, 2009). In this chapter, we highlight the pedagogical advantages of using virtual worlds in higher education for learners with various needs alongside the potential pitfalls.

3.2. Building Social Confidence Virtually with Students on and off the Autistic Spectrum

Although it might seem an unusual approach to group together autism and Asperger's syndrome with shyness and social interaction issues, for the purposes of this discussion, the effects are quite similar. When designing learning activities that involve discussion, oral contribution or social interaction of any kind, from small group work through to delivering presentations and speaking in front of a wider cohort, there will always be a group of learners for whom the experience does not provide the best means of displaying their learning or understanding. Whatever the cause, be it an impairment, condition, learning style, preference, personality trait or simply a particular preference at a particular moment in time, there are potentially many learners for whom interaction via a virtual world can provide experiences that would be difficult, traumatic, less pleasant, and sometimes impossible experienced in a face-to-face scenario.

At the simplest level, those for whom social interaction itself is a difficult act to perform can practice interaction when in a virtual world, never needing to know (or care) who the people that they are interacting with really are. They can practice making small talk, or discussing specific topics and delivering into the discussion their own personal opinions, from not only their "own computer, own room, own space" (David Savill, quoted in Saidi, 2008) but also without even having to reveal their identity or their impairment. There is even evidence that using and interacting with others within virtual worlds improves real-life social skills (ScienceDaily, 2008). Imagine a classroom-based discussion on an ethically sensitive topic such as abortion – there will undoubtedly be a proportion of the learners who do not feel sufficiently confident or able to voice their opinion on such a controversial subject in a public forum. However, put each learner behind an anonymous alter ego, effectively "once-removed" participation, and they may feel more able to contribute openly, leading to a much richer experience for the entire cohort.

It is possible to provide not only learning experiences in virtual worlds that enable a fuller and wider contribution from all learners but also specific activities targeting those students for whom the experience offers the greatest benefit over traditional classroom scenarios – for instance, those learners with more severe social isolation or awkwardness, eccentric behaviour or obsessions, or inability to "read" body language or facial expression. These are all traits experienced by many people with Asperger's syndrome or autistic spectrum conditions, and there is a particular location within Second Life that has been set up to allow them to experience their new mode of interaction with others who understand their position before moving out into the "wider world" – Brigadoon (Blanc, 2009) is a private island constructed by John Lester, one of the Directors of Linden Lab.

> *The group wanted to socialise and meet people but found it frightening and communicating difficult. [Brigadoon] built up everyone's confidence. After a while they felt comfortable enough in their social abilities to leave the island and explore the rest of Second Life.* (Deeley, 2007)

Tartaro and Cassell (2007) describe a series of experiments in using virtual peer technology with children with autism, enabling children to take "buddies" to develop social skills, and there is no reason why this principle should not extend to adults with similar difficulties (Biever, 2007). Following these "confidence building" activities, learners with particular social difficulties may well be able to perform much better in a range of learning experiences, both those utilising virtual worlds as well as more traditional classroom-based activities. Research undertaken with young people with autism suggests benefits with theory-of-mind impairments (Moore, Cheng, McGrath, & Powell, 2005).

Traditional learning activities may also cause particular difficulties for learners with mental health issues, introducing anxieties that prevent them from delivering their best performance. Users with mental health issues or autistic spectrum disorders that cause any introduction to new situations to become extremely stressful can potentially be given a "taster" of the new situation in a virtual world, from within their "comfort zone" of home or another familiar environment. Simon Bignell of the University of Derby (Milton Broome in Second Life) comments on his Linden-approved research in Second Life:

> *[my interest] stems from being particularly interested in the use of Second Life to reach out to groups of people who show communication and social impairments. The unique virtual world of Second Life could provide an environment where interventions and experiments that may be considered unethical or impossible in real life can be easily conducted whilst assuring the safety of the participants.* (Bignell, 2008)

So even if the traditional learning experience is maintained rather than delivering it through a virtual world, learners are better facilitated to perform to the best of their ability if they can experience an "acclimatisation" or "familiarisation" activity in a virtual environment.

3.3.   The Pedagogical Implications of "Once-Removed" vs. True Representation

The real power of virtual worlds to act as both an accessibility and a pedagogical benefit in teaching and learning is inherent in the very nature of once-removed participation. Everyone who enters a virtual world does so by creating a character, or avatar, that can look and act like whoever their creator chooses. This acts as a "leveller" meaning all learners potentially get to "start again" and interact without the characteristics or "baggage" of their everyday lives. This can be of particular benefit to those who, rightly or wrongly, face issues relating to the way they look or behave in real life (people with self-confidence issues, people who use wheelchairs, people with facial disfigurements, people of different racial groups etc. may all experience prejudices and assumptions about themselves in real life), should they choose it to be so, can eliminate those issues in a virtual world. The ability, to an extent, for any user to "stand in another's shoes" in this way is an insight hard to create in the real world. Indeed, many users of Second Life operate several avatars, though the reasons for this (albeit clearly related to identity) and the statistics to measure this trend are nearly impossible to accurately establish.

The benefits to teaching and learning of removing "baggage" in this way are potentially great. Classroom discussions are almost always, despite the best efforts of the facilitator, biased towards a small number of individuals who have the knowledge, social confidence or desire for self-promotion to engage and dominate. The remainder of the cohort will contribute to a lesser degree than their knowledge or understanding would suggest, due to the relative dominance of this vocal minority. As time proceeds on a course, these behaviour patterns will become established within the cohort and thus self-sustaining. A discussion where everyone has an equal chance to add comment would be hugely beneficial in this kind of scenario, not only enriching the discussion but of course developing further the analytical and reasoning skills of the learners who would not have contributed in the face to face discussion. An anonymised "once-removed" discussion also has the potential to move in deeper and more sensitive directions due to the removal of social constraints – an example being the design classes of Ian Truelove (SL: Cubist Scarborough) where peer critiquing is made easier by being avatar-to-avatar (White & Truelove, 2009).

The reconstructing of traditional educational frameworks by using virtual worlds will bring benefits to different groups of learners in very different ways.

> *The visual nature of Second Life provides students who are challenged by the mechanics of writing with an alternative mode for demonstrating mastery of course material.* (McKinney et al., 2008)

Moreover,

> *Second Life's environment lends itself to student interaction and collaboration; as a result, it can facilitate peer teaching.* (Carr & Braunger, 1998)

In addition to the potential for improved interaction and learning, the use of virtual worlds may provide unusual life skills development opportunities for learners. There exists a recognised effect of the use of avatars in virtual worlds on the displayed personality traits of the participants, the "Proteus effect" (Yee & Bailenson, 2007). The Proteus effect suggests that participants develop or emphasise certain characteristics dependent on the appearance of their avatar (tall avatars behave more confidently in negotiation than smaller avatars, for example, regardless of the physical characteristics of the user controlling the avatar). This effect could potentially help to develop skills that may be difficult for individuals to otherwise acquire – for instance, could a wheelchair user, always used to participating in real life debates from a seated perspective, use some of the skills acquired from operating a tall, standing avatar, to enhance their seated participation in future real life debates?

Certainly in terms of disability, virtual worlds such as Second Life offer the opportunity to not only contribute on an equal basis with everyone else, but to have experiences, albeit vicariously through the avatar, that would not be possible in real life (Crichton, 2007). A *Youtube* video highlighted by the Royal National Institute of Blind People (RNIB, 2007) shows a person with cerebral palsy operating an avatar in Second Life using a head wand and extolling the virtues of being able to use or discard a wheelchair at will and being able to fly. However, the realities of the comparison are brought home through an incident in an online nightclub where she was dancing, chatting and generally being included in the social discourse when appearing without her wheelchair. Upon returning with the chair she was ignored. This anecdotal evidence must be balanced with the observation that in an environment where disability is "optional" along with the inherent anonymity buffer between virtual and real identity, this use of the wheelchair could have been misinterpreted by her fellow clubbers as an affectation merely for effect. Henry Swan of Opera Software argues that

> *[online worlds offer] a sense of connectedness and community to those that may otherwise struggle to leave the house or who have limited opportunities to interact with others beyond carers and immediate family.* (Carr, 2009)

Peter Abrahams makes the point of Second Life being a great leveller.

> *Second Life is a place where everyone is as able as each other. This may well be one of its major shortfalls as it removes some of the diversity of Real Life that makes it such an interesting place. On the other hand it does give people the opportunity to experience, even somewhat vicariously, being one of a bigger crowd.* (Abrahams, 2006)

On the contrary, Simon Stevens, the creator of Wheelies Club in Second Life,[1] refuses to appear online without his wheelchair, for the very reason that people should be accepting of impairments and learn to deal with whatever disabilities a given situation produces, and to "deny" one's disability online just makes it easier for people to ignore that responsibility. Not that he denies other people's right to choose a non-disabled persona if they so wish:

> *The avatar is a powerful device in ensuring an inner self-identity…So for some disabled people, Second Life is an opportunity to escape from their impairment…There is, however, a group of disabled people, including myself, who wish to appear disabled within Second Life…Within an environment which is perceived to be barrier free, it challenges the very nature of impairment and disability when someone chooses to appear disabled.* (Stevens, 2007)

It may even be deeply insulting to those who feel they are partly or wholly defined by aspects of their physical appearance or disability to suggest that they might wish to appear without those characteristics online. There is a distinct community of deaf people who view Deafness as their culture as well as being a disability in a largely hearing society (a lack of hearing is rarely a disability when interacting with other

---

1. http://slurl.com/secondlife/Taupo/168/86/23.

Deaf people) (Baker & Padden, 1978); and of course there are those whose religious beliefs extend to the way they dress – both groups may wish to represent those defining characteristics in an online persona.

The once-removed persona not only provides the potential for a more personal and deeper engagement with academic discourse as described earlier but may also directly enable a deeper understanding in those students who, for various reasons, are unable to engage with learning in a traditional manner. The Literature Alive! programme has recreated Dante's Inferno in Second Life as an interactive learning experience.[2] Note cards for learners and tutors are dotted throughout the various circles of hell, which one can traverse through gondola tours or self-directed, providing the opportunity to chat to Virgil and Dante, partake in learning activities, and understand the notions behind the medieval Divine Comedy works. The penetrability of this "once-removed" representation of the original concept is greatly enhanced for a wide range of learners for whom penetrating the bare text would be difficult. Modern day allegories such as the allocation of politicians and stars from the entertainment industry to the various circles of hell enable the learner to frame a classic work of literature in modern conceptual terms, greatly enhancing its accessibility.

3.4. Harmless Deception or Deceptions that Harm?

The usage of avatars in teaching and learning, while providing the opportunities for liberation and levelling of interactions described earlier, may also potentially produce third party confusion. It was described earlier how individuals with Asperger's syndrome or autistic spectrum disorders may experience difficulty in interpreting body language or facial expression. The use of Virtual Worlds allows them freedom from having to face this complication, but adds another in its place. If students are used to interacting together as a cohort, and then move into a virtual world, only to witness some members undergo a significant change in mannerisms, language and opinions, drastically different from what is "known" about that person, what issues does that raise in terms of group dynamics?

Students are advised to respect each other's beliefs and opinions, but this becomes increasingly difficult when one is able to make statements at odds with one's true beliefs, when in the guise of the avatar. Virtual Worlds provide huge socialisation benefits to distance learning cohorts, yet the lack of first hand experience of fellow students can further increase the opportunities for subterfuge. There is anecdotal evidence from distance learning tutors utilising this technology, for the most part very effectively, of the portrayal of "falsehoods" within the cohort, where such deceptions threaten to multiply and potentially wreck the group's sense of community. Of course, this brings enormous opportunities for sociological, ethical and anthropological subject areas, but the potential for psychological harm also

---

2. Pasteur, 2008, http://world.secondlife.com/region/21408c6c-ebd7-48d8-9fdc-40fe9cc79735.

needs to be considered. Further discussion in this area perhaps needs to be reserved for a separate paper, but it needs to be borne in mind by teachers venturing into virtual worlds for teaching and learning.

One widely used exemplar of the exploitation of this potential for third party image confusion is that of Wilde Cunningham (New World Notes, 2004) an orange-skinned avatar created and operated simultaneously by a team of severely disabled individuals from a residential care centre in the United States. The members of the team individually would have difficulty creating and controlling an avatar, but together they have the skills necessary. This is a wonderfully empowering example of the possibilities of technology, but it also raises the issue of confusion – the avatar is controlled by smaller subgroups of different team members on different days (rarely are all nine participants available and willing to join in on every occasion), and therefore, it will display different characteristics on different occasions. If the avatar then participates in any group activities, the other group members will experience a different "personality" coming through each time they meet. In terms of teaching and learning, this raises issues of identity – students may have several avatars or may even operate each other's avatars at times, and learning activities therefore need to be designed to minimise the impact of this behaviour.

The once-removed manner of participation in virtual worlds also allows learners a range of freedoms they may not otherwise have. Although it is possible to set up access-controlled rooms and buildings in virtual worlds like Second Life, much of the benefit of using these media is that students can move around the worlds and learn from their experiences. This is potentially hugely beneficial for all students, and especially those whose real world situation means they are unlikely to encounter certain particularly valuable scenarios (for example, for various reasons certain students may find it difficult to travel to the country whose language or culture they are learning about, but could interact with students from, or virtual locations based on, that country readily via a virtual world). But it should also be borne in mind that this also raises the possibility of highly unusual experiences occurring that would not be likely in real life, and so may be beyond the capability of some students to deal with. For example, it is highly unlikely – although not unheard of – that a person would undress themselves in a real lecture, but quite possible to achieve instantaneously in a Second Life classroom – see Ellis (2007) for a frightening example of what vulnerable students may encounter.

"Griefers," trouble-makers in Second Life, who can orchestrate anything from harmless pranks to sustained assaults, are numerous. Deliberate acts aside, there is also much discussion in academic circles of the importance of dress (and anatomy?) codes for students attending learning activities in virtual worlds. What might the effect be upon students who find themselves in an unpleasant situation? How do we create support systems that deal with this? The solution of course lies in the efficacy of the support systems, rather than in avoiding the technology altogether for fear of what might happen. Oliver (2007) states that:

> *recognising that there are negative as well as positive aspects to this process [of engaging in community activities in Second Life] may help in*

> *establishing realistic expectations about what engaging with communities*
> *[in real life] will be like. For teachers, it emphasises that risks will arise*
> *if learners are expected to engage in existing communities.*

The once-removed manner of participation in virtual worlds may also lend itself to the support of students with particular difficulties. It may be much easier, for example, for a student to make virtual rather than face-to-face enquiries regarding matters relating to sexual health or mental health (for example, one assumes it would be much easier for an anonymous avatar to walk into a virtual world clinic and ask "what should someone do if they got drunk last night and slept with someone without protection?" than for the student concerned to seek advice in real life). Indeed areas in Second Life such as the University of Plymouth's Sexual Health SIM (Bouloth & Toth-Cohen, 2008)[3] enjoy success as an information outreach centre.

The final issue to be addressed regarding once-removed participation is the role of the tutor. What might be the issues associated with discovering that the purple biker gorilla lurking in the corner is, in fact, your teacher? This would be perfectly acceptable to many learners, who may appreciate the removal of traditional roles in the learning process, but learners from cultures with more formal teacher–learner roles and relationships may find it particularly difficult to deal with, introducing a barrier or complication to their learning that would otherwise not exist.

3.5.   Failing without Consequences – the Academic Benefits

In addition to the accessibility benefits and barriers of using virtual worlds to enable those with particular impairments to interact with others and the world around them in a different way, virtual worlds can provide students with opportunities that simply would not be achievable in real life. For example, the testing of trauma nurses' decision-making processes cannot be effectively simulated in the real world other than by text-based "role-play scenarios" (Dev, Youngblood, Heinrichs, & Kusumoto, 2007). In virtual worlds, students can begin to learn "on" and "in" a safe environment, so that they can practice scenarios and examine their behaviour during their intervention, in addition to reflecting on their practice after the event.

The E-Doctoring virtual world constructed by the Universities of Newcastle (UK), Davis (California, US), Los Angeles (California, US) and Seattle (Washington, US) allows medical students to examine patients, make clinical decisions (if necessary within a given time frame), perform surgical procedures and so on, all within the safety of a virtual world, although certain skills such as catheterisation will always need to be refined on a physical 3D patient model before their use in practice. If, in a virtual world scenario, a message flashes up during a complex procedure that they just killed their patient, it is perhaps preferable that this is a virtual world scenario, where they can rewind and have another go. E-Doctoring (2008) provides 10 scenarios that cover the

---

3. http://world.secondlife.com/place/d26dc21f-612f-710b-490d-eccc2492fa79.

full range of ethical and social issues relating to genetics, including aspects of law, communication and culture as well as the medical side. There can be no doubt that these scenarios provide a case-study style of education but with an added element of "reality" that can only assist the students in translating their learned knowledge and skills into practical scenarios. Kingston University uses virtual worlds to teach learners how to use radiography appropriately in the treatment of cancers (Elliott, 2008). The Ann Myers Medical Center (2008)[4] provides a host of in-world scenarios for nursing and medical students that greatly increases the number of different case experiences they can have during their course (Mesko, 2007). Similarly the Synthetic Environments for Emergency Response Simulation project (SEERS) is funded by the US Department of Homeland Security to provide cost effective mission rehearsal tools for emergency response personnel (SEERS, 2008).

This kind of virtual world scenario has even made its way into game format, with the Nintendo Wii now supporting "Trauma-center-second-opinion" which works in a similar manner to E-Doctoring but is aimed not at medical students but at the general game-playing generation, like an updated version of the family board game "Operation" (Nintendo, 2008).

And then there are more complex representations and simulations – students can gain real-life experience of nuclear fission (a nuclear reactor is currently under construction (Guess, 2007)), an ocean trench, controlling a chemical plant or investigating a delicate archaeological dig.

In Canada at the Loyalist College in Ontario, Customs and Immigration students participated in a Canadian border simulation to learn and practice interview skills. The results of the project were dramatic, with student learning and skills retention better than previous students who did not have the benefit of the simulation (Hudson & Hubble, 2008).

A recent development at the University of Derby in the UK is a huge virtual quarry for quarrying students developed in conjunction with the Institute of Quarrying. It is still work in progress and is intended to replicate real quarrying situations (some of which are hazardous) such as dangerous overhangs, explosions and hazardous working vehicles and enables students to move around the quarry identifying those hazards (EduServ, 2009).

How in real life could students be given an insight into what life is like with various mental or psychological conditions? The Virtual Hallucinations tour[5] offers users a small insight into what life is like with auditory hallucinations. Of course there are well-trodden arguments about the value of simulations and that they can never provide users with an experience that approaches equity with "the real thing" but they certainly can offer some valuable insight, and this is an excellent example of that. "Using traditional educational methods, instructors have difficulty teaching about the internal phenomena of mental illnesses, such as hallucinations," (Peter

---

4. http://world.secondlife.com/place/b2f0f3c4-c6b7-2267-9cc1-e83776c01c39.
5. secondlife://sedig/26/45/.

Yellowlees, quoted in UCDavis Health System, 2007). Yellowlees and his team created the virtual environment to replicate the experiences and world of a schizophrenia patient (Yellowlees & Burrage, 2005) to provide medical students with a better understanding of this mental illness. When comparing virtual world technology with other possibilities for achieving this aim, Yellowlees explained "Compared with custom software development, using an existing software system cut development time for our psychosis environment by a factor of 10." In addition to the replication of conditions virtual worlds can be used directly in the support of trauma – the army is using scenarios constructed in virtual worlds to assist personnel with managing post-traumatic stress (Rizzo, 2006).

Virtual environments also enable tutors to monitor students' readiness to go on practice placements. Virtual worlds can be used as measures to prepare students for real life practice by making them aware of their strengths and areas that they need to develop before working with, or on, real people. Virtual worlds can also be used to help repeatedly assess students' learning and fitness to move forward – particularly students who need more reinforcement of their learning in order to proceed successfully. For example,

> a properly structured Second Life environment could allow biology students who are learning about DNA replication to receive continuous, immediate assessment and feedback via in-world exercises. This feedback would allow students to gauge knowledge acquisition and determine if they need additional support in order to master the concepts. Moreover, this feedback and assessment could take place beyond the temporal constraints imposed by the scheduled class period. (McKinney et al., 2008)

which would benefit students with dyslexia, for example, to an even greater extent than their peers.

Virtual worlds can enable opportunities for tutors to provide interdisciplinary learning opportunities in a way that "real world" limitations cannot. For example, you may be able to synchronously provide learning opportunities through virtual scenarios for large numbers of students who you could not cater for in a physical setting such as a lecture theatre. This way the students can engage with and learn about each others' professions. This may potentially have useful implications for the increasingly intertwined health and social care fields.

3.6. Conclusions

It is evident that the use of virtual worlds in general creates a range of pedagogic possibilities that potentially can benefit all learners but that often have much greater potential to provide an equal experience for learners with particular needs or preferences. There are potentially disproportionate benefits for various different types of users in addition to creating barriers for those who cannot access the interfaces used. Universal Design for Learning principles (Burgstahler, 2008) highlight the need for learning activities to be designed so that they are simple, intuitive and flexible in their use (not necessarily in their subject matter, under UK law it is imperative that accessible design is implemented to support, not diminish academic standards). These principles "dictate that curricula enable all individuals to gain knowledge, skills and enthusiasm for learning" (Rose & Blomeyer, 2007).

It is even more imperative that ways and means are found of enabling those who are currently excluded from engaging in these activities, as more benefits of their use become evident. Applying the principle of once-removed participation to virtual workspaces and learning scenarios may elicit a whole series of resultant effects, many of which will be positive. Concomitantly some of the effects may be negative, for which tutors should not only be prepared, but should welcome as an opportunity to further improve the learning process. We hope to have established in this chapter that the use of virtual worlds for some learners is much more than a fad or gimmick, it is a way of interacting, developing skills and having experiences that simply could not occur in real life. They are not a panacea to all pedagogic or access issues, but undoubtedly they are in the process of justifying their place as an addition to the suite of tools available to educators.

Finally, Virtual Worlds are not necessarily games; they exist often for other purposes because they are immersive, persuasive and hugely flexible. It is a measure of their strength that they capture the popular imagination. Academe can be assured that such a solid endorsement will place this technology alongside others pressed successfully into service as pedagogical support tools such as television, radio and the Internet. It is our responsibility as educators to ensure that we exploit all the potential benefits for our students.

References

Abrahams, P. (2006). *Second life class action.* Accessed July 3, 2009, from www. it-analysis.com/blogs/Abrahams_Accessibility/2006/11/second_life_class_action.html

Abrahams, P. (2007). *Second Life is now too important not to be accessible.* Accessed July 3, 2009, from www.it-analysis.com/blogs/Abrahams_Accessibility/2007/12/second_life_is_now_too_important_n_.html

Adams-Spink, G. (2007). *Virtual worlds open up to blind.* Accessed July 3, 2009, from http://news.bbc.co.uk/1/hi/technology/6993739.stm

Ann Myers Medical Centre. (2008). *The future of medical education.* Accessed July 3, 2009, from http://ammc.wordpress.com/

Baker, C., & Padden, C. (1978). *American sign language: A look at its story structure and community.* Silver Spring: Linstok Press.

Biever, C. (2007). Web removes social barriers for those with autism. *New Scientist* 2610.

Bignell, S. (2008). *Milton Broome's virtual psychology.* Accessed July 3, 2009, from www.miltonbroome.com

Biocca, F. (1997). The cyborg's dilemma: Progressive embodiment in virtual environments. *Journal of Computer-Mediated Communication, 3*(2), Retrieved July 3, 2009, from http://jcmc.indiana.edu/vol3/issue2/biocca2.html

Blanc, A. (2009). *Brigadoon: An innovative online community for people dealing with Asperger's Syndrome and Autism.* Accessed July 3, 2009, from http://braintalk.blogs.com/brigadoon/

Bouloth, M.N.K., & Toth-Cohen, S. (2008). *A sexual health sim in second life*. Accessed July 3, 2009, from http://sl-sexualhealth.org.uk/?cat = 4

Burgstahler, S. (2008). *Universal design of instruction: Definition, principles and examples*. University of Washington. Accessed July 3, 2009, from http://www.washington.edu/doit/Brochures/Academics/instruction.html

Carr, D. (2009). "Virtually accessible." Access: the inclusive design journal, Spring 2009. RNIB.

Carr, M. S., & Braunger, J. (1998). *The curriculum inquiry cycle: improving learning and teaching – an overview* (In: McKinney et al. (2008)). Portland, OR: North West Regional Educational Laboratory.

Carr, D., Sapre, M., Yuan, B., & Folmer, E. (2008). *Text Second life: A second life client for visually impaired and blind users*. Accessed July 3, 2009, from http://textsl.org/

Carter, B., & Corona, G. (2008a). *Visual worlds user interface for the blind*. Accessed July 3, 2009, from http://services.alphaworks.ibm.com/virtualworlds/

Carter, W.S., & Corona, G.D. (2008b). Exploring methods of accessing virtual worlds. *Access World, 9*(2). Retrieved July 3, 2009, from www.afb.org/afbpress/pub.asp?DocID = aw090207

Childress, M. D., & Braswell, R. (2006). Using massively multiplayer online role-playing games for online learning. *Distance Education, 27*(2), 187–196.

Childs, M., & Kuksa, I. (2009). "Why are we in the floor?" Learning about Theatre Design in Second Life™. EDULEARN09 International Conference on Education and New Learning Technologies, Barcelona (Spain), July 6–8, 2009.

Crichton, P. (2007). *Second hand look at second life*. Accessed July 3, 2009, from www.bbc.co.uk/blogs/access20/2007/04/second_hand_look_at_second_lif.shtml

Deeley, L. (2007). *Is this a real life, is this just fantasy?* Accessed July 3, 2009, from http://women.timesonline.co.uk/tol/life_and_style/women/body_and_soul/article1557980.ece

Dev, P., Youngblood, P., Heinrichs, W., & Kusumoto, L. (2007). Virtual worlds and team training. *Anesthesiology Clinics, 25*(2), 321–336.

EDoctoring. (2008) *Edoctoring*. Accessed July 3, 2009, from http://edoctoring.ncl.ac.uk

Eduserv. (2009). *Virtual quarry in second life*. Accessed July 3, 2009, from http://virtualworldwatch.net/2009/01/19/survey-response-pete-radcliff-university-of-derby/comment-page-1/

Elliott, J. (2008). *"Treating cancer" in a virtual world*. Accessed July 3, 2009, from http://news.bbc.co.uk/1/hi/health/7648170.stm

Ellis, W. (2007). *Second life sketches: Please stop doing that to the cat*. Accessed July 3, 2009, from http://secondlife.reuters.com/stories/2007/02/23/second-life-sketches-please-stop-doing-that-to-the-cat/

Guess, A. (2007). *In second life, there's no fallout*. Accessed July 3, 2009, from www.insidehighered.com/news/2007/08/20/secondlife

Hanson, S. (2008). *Virtual worlds: Synopsis of user interfaces and accessibility initiatives*. Accessed July 3, 2009, from http://ausweb.scu.edu.au/aw08/papers/refereed/hansen2/paper.html

Hudson, K., & Hubble, K. (2008). *Applied training in second life: Canadian border simulation at loyalist college*. Accessed July 3, 2009, from http://www.loyalistcollege.com/news/loyalist-college-at-forefront-of-virtual-world-edu

Jaime, S. (2007). A model to design interactive learning environments for children with visual disabilities. *Education and Information Technologies, 12*(3), 149–163 (cited in Hanson, 2008).

Kelly, B. (2008). *Is second life accessible?* Accessed July 3, 2009, from http://ukwebfocus.wordpress.com/2008/01/14/is-second-life-accessible/

Kirriemuir, J. (2008). *A Spring 2008 "snapshot" of UK higher and further education developments in second life*. Accessed July 3, 2009, from www.eduserv.org.uk/upload/foundation/sl/uksnapshot052008/final.pdf

Macleod, H. (2007) Holyrood park: A virtual campus for Edinburgh. Virtual worlds, real learning? Eduserv Foundation Symposium 2007, Thursday, May 10, 2007, Congress Centre, London.

McKinney, S., Horspool, A., Willers, R., Safie, O., & Richlin, L. (2008). Using second life with learning-disabled students in higher education. *Innovate: Journal of Online Education, 5*(2).

Mesko, B. (2007). *Virtual medical center: The future of medical education*. Accessed July 3, 2009, from http://scienceroll.com/2007/04/24/virtual-medical-center-the-future-of-medical-education/

Milena, D., Alissa, A., & Ron, W. (2007). Exploring ambient sound techniques in the design of responsive environments for children. Paper presented at First International Conference in Tangible and Embedded Interaction (cited in Hanson, 2008).

Moore, D., Cheng, Y., McGrath, P., & Powell, N. J. (2005). Collaborative virtual environment technology for people with autism. *Focus on Autism and Other Developmental Disabilities, 20*(4), 231–243.

MOOSE. (2009). *Investigating the scaffolding and processes needed to enable groups of students from HE environments to establish their socialisation and engagement for more productive information and knowledge exchange and learning through the medium of online 3-D Multi User Virtual Environments using Second Life – a collaboration between the University of Leicester, London South Bank University and the Beyond Distance Research Alliance.* Accessed July 3, 2009, from http://www.le.ac.uk/beyonddistance/moose

New World Notes. (2004). *The nine souls of Wilde Cunningham, part I*. Accessed July 3, 2009, from http://secondlife.blogs.com/nwn/2004/12/the_nine_souls_.html

Nintendo. (2008). *Trauma center second opinion*. Accessed July 3, 2009, from www.nintendo.co.uk/NOE/en_GB/games/wii/trauma_center_second_opinion.html

Oliver, M. (2007). *Exclusion as an aspect of communities in Second Life*. Accessed July 3, 2009, from http://learningfromsocialworlds.wordpress.com/exclusion-community-in-second-life

Open Habitat. (2009). *Taking an innovative approach to encouraging creative online collaboration in Multi-User Virtual Environments (MUVEs) – a collaboration between the University of Oxford, Leeds Metropolitan University, King's College London, the University of Essex and Dave Cormier, based at the University of Prince Edward Island.* Accessed July 3, 2009, from http://www.openhabitat.org

Pasteur, E. (2008). *Cat in hell's chance. Blog of Eloise Pasteur, member of Dante's Inferno build team.* Accessed July 3, 2009, from http://eloisepasteur.net/blog/index.php?/archives/136-Cat-in-Hells-chance.html

PREVIEW-Psych. (2009). *Problem-Based Learning in Virtual Interactive Educational Worlds for Psychology – a collaboration between the University of Derby, Aston University, Coventry University and the Higher Education Academy Psychology Network.* Accessed July 3, 2009, from http://previewpsych.org

Rizzo, A. (2006). A virtual reality exposure therapy application for Iraq war military personnel with post traumatic stress disorder: From training to toy to treatment. In: M. Roy (Ed.), *NATO advanced research workshop on novel approaches to the diagnosis and treatment of posttraumatic stress disorder* (pp. 235–250). Washington, D.C.: IOS Press.

RNIB. (2007). *Wheelies in second life*. Accessed July 3, 2009, from www.rnib.org.uk/wacblog/category/virtual-worlds

Rose, R.M. & Blomeyer, R.L. (2007). *Research committees issues brief: Access and equity in online classes and virtual schools.* Vienna, VA, North American Council for online learning. Accessed July 3, 2009, from http://www.inacol.org/resources/docs/NACOL_EquityAccess. pdf

Saidi, N. (2008). *"Naughty auties" battle autism with virtual interaction.* Accessed July 3, 2009, from http://autisticsavant.blogspot.com/2008/05/ireport-naughty-auties-battle-autism.html

ScienceDaily. (2008). *Second life improves real-life social skills.* Accessed July 3, 2009, from www.sciencedaily.com/releases/2008/07/080717210838.htm

SEERS. (2008). *Synthetic environments for emergency response simulation.* Accessed July 3, 2009, from http://www.ists.dartmouth.edu/library/118.pdf

Slator, B. M., Beckwith, R. T., & Chaput, H. (2006). *Electric worlds in the classroom: Teaching and learning with role-based computer games* (ISBN 0807746754, 9780807746752, pp. 105–108). New York: Teachers College Press.

Stevens, S. (2007). *Wheeliecatholic blog.* Accessed July 3, 2009, from http://www.simonstevens. com

Tartaro, A., & Cassell, J. (2007). Using virtual peer technology as an intervention for children with autism. In: J. Lazar (Ed.), *Universal usability: Designing user interfaces for diverse user populations* (pp. 231–262). Hoboken, NJ: Teachers College Press.

Taylor, T. L. (2002). Living digitally: Embodiment in virtual worlds. In: R. Schroeder (Ed.), *The social life of avatars* (pp. 40–62). London: Springer-Verlag.

UCDavis Health System. (2007). *Virtual psychosis environment helps understanding of schizophrenic hallucinations.* Accessed July 3, 2009, from http://www.ucdmc.ucdavis.edu/ newsroom/releases/archives/psychiatry/2007/virtual_hallucination3-2007.html

Warburton, S. (2008). *Loving your avatar: Identity, immersion and empathy.* Accessed July 3, 2009, from http://warburton.typepad.com/liquidlearning/2008/01/loving-your-ava.html

White, G.R. (2007). *Second life for the visually impaired-accessibility analysis and review.* Accessed July 3, 2009, from http://blindsecondlife.blogspot.com/2007/11/accessibility-analysis.html

White, D., & Truelove, I. (2009). OpenHabitat, using multi-user virtual environments in higher education, Orange Island Education Days Conference, Tuesday, April 28, 2009.

Yee, N., & Bailenson, J. N. (2007). The proteus effect: The effect of transformed self-representation on behaviour. *Human Communication Research, 33,* 271–290.

Yellowlees, P., & Burrage, K. (2005). *Virtual hallucinations.* Accessed July 3, 2009, from http:// www.ucdmc.ucdavis.edu/ais/virtualhallucinations/

Author Biographies

Dr Simon Ball is Senior Advisor for Higher Education with JISC TechDis, the UK advisory service for inclusive use of technology. Simon specialises in the accessibility issues involved in E-Assessment; the inclusive use of technologies to support teaching and learning, in particular virtual worlds such as Second Life; and the use of organisational policy to embed an inclusive approach to technology right across the operations of higher education institutions.

Rob Pearce, Information Systems and E-learning Manager, Higher Education Academy Engineering (Loughborough University) and Materials (Liverpool

University) Subject Centres. Rob has responsibility for the development and application of web technology, online resource dissemination and e-learning initiatives. He has over 20 years experience working as an engineer and with information technology, with 11 years spent in academic organisations. Rob's role includes communicating the impact and potential opportunities provided by cutting-edge Internet technologies to the higher education community in the UK. He is a Chartered IT Practitioner. Current work includes managing two UK wide projects to investigate the widespread release of Open Educational Resources and the establishment of a unified interoperable calendaring standard.

Chapter 4

Opportunities and Challenges for Business Education in Second Life

Edwin Love, Steven C. Ross and Wendy Wilhelm

4.1. Introduction

Second Life has become a vast seeding ground of entrepreneurship. Thanks in part to the intellectual property ownership policies of Linden Lab and the existence of a meaningful currency of Linden Dollars, business people, artisans, speculators, and artists from around the world have developed start-ups selling virtual goods and services inside this virtual world. Many see this as an extension of their real-world businesses, whereas others view their businesses as a means to support their virtual lifestyle. Linden Lab reports that in the month of February 2009, more than 400,000 customers made roughly 25 million transactions in Second Life. Although the dollar value of each transaction is nearly always miniscule in real world business terms, the aggregate effect of these transactions is to create a vibrant business commercial ecology. Since minimal business start-up costs help to keep barriers to entry low, this is an environment that is ripe for experimentation and exploration.

This broad and accessible ecology of micro-commerce makes Second Life highly attractive to business educators. It makes possible field studies, role plays, simulations, and many other activities that are particularly relevant in fields such as management, marketing, and entrepreneurship. Instruction in "numbers-based" fields such as accounting can be enriched and made relevant through activities such as student bookkeeping of virtual enterprises. Perhaps more importantly, Second Life has become the venue of choice for IBM, Colgate-Palmolive, Kraft, Cisco, and many other firms for work in virtual teams or convening meetings with employees in multiple locations. Business graduates are made more valuable by preparing them as students to work together in a virtual world (Love, Wilhem, Chapman, summerfelt, & Kedzior, 2008).

Higher Education in Virtual Worlds
Copyright © 2009 by Emerald Group Publishing Limited
All rights of reproduction in any form reserved
ISBN: 978-1-84950-609-0

Although there appears to be considerable interest among our colleagues in using Second Life as a pedagogical tool, and several case studies of how business educators use it in specific courses have been published (e.g., Mennecke, Hassall, & Triplett, 2008), we know of no empirical research that has examined, across disciplines, how business faculty are using Second Life in their courses. This chapter describes our findings from an exploratory study of business educators in both the United States and abroad who appear to be actively engaged with Second Life as a pedagogical tool. Specifically, we wished to obtain answers to the following research questions:

- Do educators perceive unique pedagogical advantages of Second Life over traditional B-school learning environments?
- What are some current examples of how business schools are using Second Life to enhance student learning? to experiment with new pedagogical approaches? and
- As early adopters of Second Life, what are the challenges that business faculty are facing?

4.2. Research Methodology

An online survey was developed to address each of these research questions. The survey questions were open-ended to encourage respondents to answer each question in depth. The survey was pre-tested with a number of colleagues familiar with Second Life, resulting in several changes in question wording to improve respondent comprehension.[1]

A list of business faculty who are currently using the Second Life environment for pedagogical purposes was generated from in-world[2] and real world sources such as higher education listservs and wikis. This search generated 35 business faculty from a cross-section of universities and disciplines, both in the United States and abroad. The request for participation and a link to the survey were sent through email to all respondents. Each participant who provided an avatar name was given a payment in Second Life (worth approximately US$4.00) for participation, and one was randomly selected to receive free use of a plot of land on the Second Life mainland area for six months (a US$150.00 value).

Data collection took place over a four-week period in January 2009. The survey was sent to 35 faculty and 19 faculty responded, a 54% response rate. The sample represents a diverse group in terms of business discipline, business school size, and geographical location.

---

1. "Survey." .Qualtrics. Accessed July 3, 2009, from http://wwucbe.qualtrics.com/SE/?SID = SV_5q1d6TPcBr0BH92&SVID = Prod.
2. "In-world" is an adjectival term used for activity conducted while logged in to Second Life.

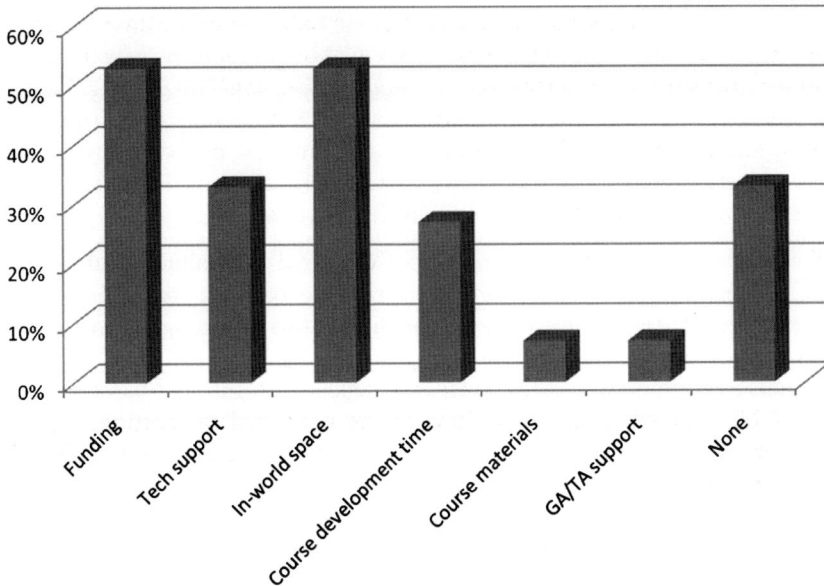

Figure 4.1: Sources of faculty support for Second Life campuses/activities

4.3. Findings

70% of respondents indicated that they do receive some support from their universities to develop and maintain their in-world campuses or activities (Figure 4.1). The support includes funding, technical support, and assistance in developing coursework, among others.

4.4. Unique Pedagogical Advantages of Second Life

The business faculty we surveyed identified several pedagogical advantages associated with Second Life over traditional business school learning environments.

High engagement: Several respondents identified an "engagement factor" or "deeper memory creation through the rich-media experience" that is not easily duplicated in a typical classroom or distance learning environment. Students see other persons in realistic settings and interact with them through either text messages or voice chat. Although the medium does not allow for the physical, non-verbal cues of an actual face-to-face meeting, it does allow for richer interaction over distance and provides settings (i.e., a retail store or a factory floor) that cannot be duplicated on most campuses.

Stimulation of creativity: Business students are often exhorted to be "creative" in their approaches to problem solving, but it is difficult to teach students how to think "outside the box" in a traditional face-to-face or online learning environment. The development of an alter-ego in the form of an avatar can *"loosen them up a bit"* and *"help to shake at least a few of them out of plodding along and into dancing,"* according to one respondent. The ability to engage in 3D modeling of various objects (products, fashion, structures), and to create machinimas, mixed-reality events and in-world advertising and branding materials were also mentioned as creative exercises that are typically unavailable in a classroom setting.

Social presence and real-time interaction: Compared to online/distance learning courses, Second Life offers students a much richer experience that engages more of the senses. Many of the faculty surveyed mentioned this advantage, using terms such as "networking" and "collaboration" and "real-time interaction with students or practitioners elsewhere" to describe their experiences with Internet-based classes held in Second Life. Of particular interest were the perceived motivational aspects of Second Life immersion. Several educators noted that students were more inspired or motivated to cooperate and collaborate with each other in Second Life and that team performance was superior vis-à-vis traditional online or classroom environments. One university's conceptualization of a virtual business classroom may be found in Picture 4.1.

Ability to undertake immersive simulations and experiments: Many of the business faculty surveyed see Second Life as a microcosm of the "real world" in which to test new business concepts or run experiments. As one respondent stated, *"Students can actually run a business in Second Life and experience many of the same pitfalls as in a*

Picture 4.1: A virtual classroom in Second Life

real-world situation." With many firms moving to virtual meetings, and with team members in disparate locations, Second Life offers business educators an environment in which to teach students the virtual teaming skills they may one day need to be effective managers.

4.5.   Educational Uses of Second Life

Respondents represent a broad spectrum of disciplines, but the types of educational uses exhibit some commonalities (Figure 4.2). All faculty, regardless of discipline, mention the use of Second Life for 3D distance learning, including group meetings, classroom discussions, mixed reality events bringing guest speakers and students together, and learning events with students from different countries or regions. Business simulations and role plays that attempt to replicate real world business situations are other frequently mentioned uses of Second Life. These activities include mock interviewing, test marketing of new products, experimenting with branding/advertising information, design and testing of retail/factory layouts, and event planning and implementation. Setting up and conducting interviews and panel discussions in Second Life are also commonly mentioned (e.g., having students locate and interview Second Life entrepreneurs about their business models). Others have gone further, assigning actual projects such as developing business plans for in-world entrepreneurs, conducting surveys or focus groups with Second Life consumers as part of a marketing research course, or designing training to be delivered through Second Life for a collaborative decision support project.

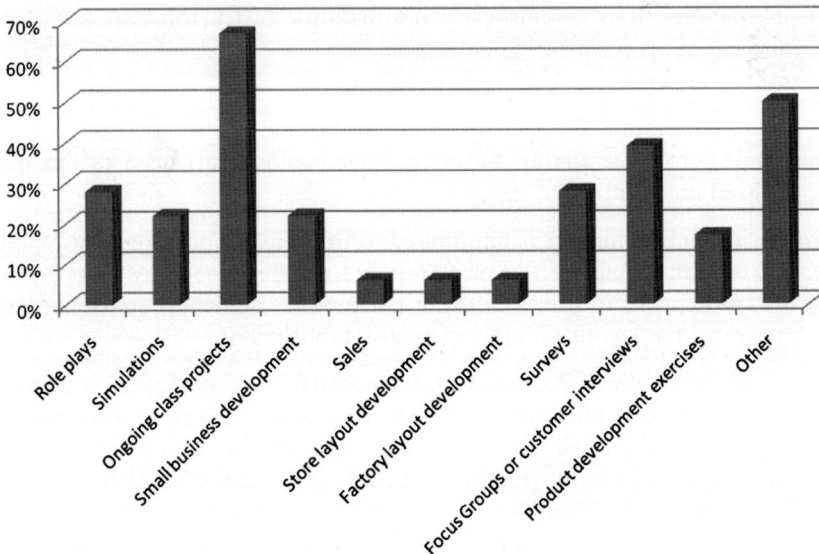

Figure 4.2: Common uses of Second Life for business education

4.6.   Tools Used by Business Educators

Our respondents mentioned a number of tools and features that are useful in their educational endeavors. First we present those that are a part of the Second Life client software, then an assortment of other tools available from third parties.

4.7.   Features Contained in the Second Life Client

Text chat and chat logging: The fundamental means of communication in Second Life is text chat entered through a keyboard. The software can be configured to write the transcript of the conversation to a text file on the client computer, enabling later analysis of a conversation, which can be helpful in the critique of a business negotiation exercise. Normal chat is "heard by" (displayed on the screen of) every avatar within 20 meters of the speaker.

Instant messaging and IM logging: Instant messaging can occur among avatars anywhere in the Second Life grid. As with text chat, it is entered through the keyboard and can be logged. Instant messages can be between two or more avatars. IMs are private, so the technique is sometimes used when conversing with an adjacent avatar to maintain confidentiality – which instructors might find very useful in coaching role players.

Notecards: These are text documents that are used to pass information and instructions. The notecards themselves are plain text, but can contain links to other documents, pictures, and landmarks to destinations. Instructors can give students instructions and assignments using notecards; students can record conversations and send them to their instructors using this medium.

Voice: Voice chat (local) and calls (distant) are also available. In-world recording does not appear to be available, but a recorder could be attached to the speaker output of the client computer.

Camera: Vision in Second Life is not limited to the avatar's position. The "camera" can be used to look at one's self or moved quite some distance away from the avatar to view distant items or to gain a different perspective. Students can use the camera to quickly survey the layout of a commercial establishment.

Creating/modifying objects: As noted on its website, "Second Life is a free online virtual world imagined and created by its Residents." Most of the creation is accomplished using the build menu to create objects from primitive shapes (cube, sphere, cylinder, etc.) and covering those shapes with textures. Creations vary from the small and simple, for example, a gold bracelet, to the grand and complex, for example, a replica of the Eiffel Tower. Some find building to be a straightforward process of combining precisely positioned pieces; others find it a hopelessly complex task. A requirement that all students build complex objects would be risky, but enabling students to use simple objects and texture application allows for the development of realistic retail or manufacturing facilities.

Snapshots: The client includes a screen capture/picture-taking utility. This can be used to document situations and scenes, and to supplement instructions.

4.8. Available from Third Parties

Note: Although specific products are listed here, there are alternatives to most of these. The References section contains links for each item mentioned.

Freeview TV: This and similar products allow the viewing of media streamed from a web address (which could include, of course, a university source). The most current version of QuickTime must be installed on the client computer for the video to be seen.

Presentation whiteboard: This will hold a series of textures (e.g., saved PowerPoint slides) and allow their display in order.

Message whiteboard: This allows avatars to write and display notes in the virtual world, just as if they were using flipcharts to record ideas in a real life group meeting.

4.9. Potential for Discipline Specific Usage

Our findings suggest that, thus far, the pedagogical uses of Second Life are quite limited, although opportunities to augment course content within each traditional business school discipline are plentiful. To understand the potential business uses of Second Life, it is first necessary to understand the different kinds of assets: memberships, Linden dollars, objects, and land.

Membership is the account by which an avatar is created and the person is able to log in to Second Life. There are two types: Basic membership is free – basic members can own L$ and objects, but cannot own land. Premium membership costs US$9.95 per month (less if paid on a quarterly or annual basis) – premium members can own land as well as L$ and objects.

Linden dollars (L$) are the in-world medium of exchange. They can be bought and sold (using real-life [RL] currencies) and transferred to other residents (avatars). L$ have a fairly steady value vis-à-vis RL currencies and there are a number of exchanges, including one operated by Linden Lab. At the time of this writing, the exchange rate was approximately L$275 = US$1.00. Each resident has his or her own L$ and US$ account balance; individual transactions for the past 30 (L$) or 45 (US$) days can be viewed on line and saved to spreadsheets.

Objects can be created; held in one's own inventory; transferred to/from others (with proper permissions); copied (with proper permissions); and modified (with proper permissions). All inventory items are programmed objects, and thus are intellectual property. The metric of inventory items is "primitive shapes," known as "prims." The simplest prims are shapes such as a cube, cylinder, or sphere varying in size from 0.010 meters to 10.000 meters in length, width, and height. Complex objects such as a castle are composed of hundreds or even thousands of prims. There is no charge for holding objects in inventory, but to create an object or leave it permanently in the world one must have access to land on which building is permitted.

Land is an address in a virtual spatially defined grid. Holding land allows one to place (build or "rez") objects in the virtual world; the more land, the more objects. Objects are defined in terms of the number of prims from which they are composed. The largest single unit of land is a simulated region, known as a "sim," which is 65,536 square meters (sm), 256 meters on a side. A sim is divisible into 16 sm pieces, and parcels in second life are often in multiples of 1024 sm. Most sims hold a maximum of 15,000 prims, evenly allocated across the area, so a 1024 sm parcel is allocated (1024*15,000/65,536 =) 234 prims. Linden Lab receives most of its revenue from the land, requiring those who own an entire sim (65,536 sm) to pay US$195 per month (called "tier" payments because the charges are a step function). Persons who hold less land pay lower fees (e.g., US$40/month for 8,192 sm), but at a higher rate per square meter. Once acquired from Linden Lab, land areas can be divided or combined and sold to other residents.

The functional areas of business can use the L$ currency, objects, and land to supplement their curriculum. Goods may be constructed and marketed to either a select group (e.g., classmates) or to the entire populace of Second Life.

Accounting: Accounting in Second Life is primarily on a cash basis, individually assessed. Groups do not hold cash; any proceeds or charges are normally passed on to individuals within 24 hours. Some managerial planning can be done around cash flow (e.g., timing to ensure the ability to pay monthly land costs).

Business policy and strategy: One can certainly create and operate a business in Second Life. There is quite a learning curve, however, and it would be difficult for students to conceive, create, and operate a substantial business enterprise in the time frame of a typical class.

Economics: Long-term historical records of L$ and land transactions are closely held, if available at all, therefore macro-economic studies might be difficult to complete. On the contrary, Second Life has a viable currency and thriving market place, so students could certainly establish an enterprise and test various concepts.

Finance: There are some issues that are in the realm of managerial accounting or cash-flow management. Many of the typical topics of finance, such as investment strategy, stocks, and bonds, however, are not supported within the framework of Second Life. In fact, banking-like organizations were removed from Second Life due to regulatory (and fraud) concerns.

Human resources management and organizational behavior: Businesses in Second Life can operate 24/7/365, which leads to some interesting staffing challenges. On the contrary, many operations can be automated (such as processing of purchases and invitations to groups). We see several possibilities for HR-related role playing in Second Life, especially if voice is used (e.g., learning and practicing job interviewing techniques).

International business: Second Life is very international in scope, with large populations from all the English-speaking countries, most Western European countries, Russia, Japan, and Korea. Currency is not an issue per se, although there are some border opportunities since EU residents have to pay VAT if they deal with Linden Lab but not if they deal with other residents.

Management information systems: Second Life is an interesting programming environment, with a specialized scripting language and the ability to create programmable objects. There are some possible applications of MIS tools (such as spreadsheets and databases) to manage enterprises in Second Life, but data transfer is rarely easy.

Marketing: Marketing may find the most interesting analogs in Second Life. Products (and services) can be created and sold, pricing decisions are very important, promotion is critical. Placement is less of an issue due to the ability to deliver electronically and instantaneously. Customer relations are critical, since switching costs are virtually nil – even for moving one's building from one location to another.

Operations management: The virtual nature of most resources makes some operations management topics less relevant. Products can be delivered any time anywhere in the Second Life world and raw materials are virtually infinite. One can use the building capabilities in Second Life to model and demonstrate topics such as facility layout.

4.10. Challenges Faced by Business Faculty as Early Adopters of Second Life

In general, the educators that we surveyed were very positive about their experience with Second Life. Those who had not yet added a virtual world experience to their courses either had concrete plans to do so or were actively investigating the environment. This is not to say that the experience of these early users has been entirely positive. They identified clear challenges they face in adapting their classes to the Second Life environment.

Funding: Funding and other support from universities was often missing. Although eight of our respondents indicated that they received some degree of technical support or other assistance in the development of in-world real estate, many others responded that they received no support whatsoever. This funding problem was compounded by the fact that several respondents identified cost of land and technical support as a major barrier to adoption of the platform.

Educators who wish to have a permanent presence in Second Life must somehow acquire land. One option is to buy an entire "island" – a sim of 65,536 sm which costs a US$700 initial setup fee and US$147.50 per month "tier" fee (educational rates are about 75% of normal). A second option would be to rent or buy a smaller parcel of land on the main grid of Second Life, and pay the going rate – probably at least US$25 per month for a piece of land large enough to support a simulated office or small retail complex.

Second Life initiatives will continue to be a challenge for instructors. Given the current economic climate, instructors will need to provide an especially compelling case for the allocation of resources to the further development of virtual projects. Although a compelling case may be made for expanding online course offerings given their low cost relative to traditional campus offerings, the effectiveness of Second Life as a pedagogical tool has not yet been made sufficiently clear to justify a shift in funding for most universities. Smaller institutions, however, may find that Second Life provides them with a cost-effective means of enhancing their courses and attracting students who are interested in the technology and the virtual environment.

Learning the platform: Several respondents stated that they had either experienced a steep learning curve or had found that their students had to spend too much time developing their avatars and learning the interface. This time spent learning to operate in Second Life erodes the course time left for valuable in-world educational experiences. This is clearly a case in which the early adopters are at a disadvantage relative to later users. Should the platform be adopted across multiple courses, then later courses need not devote time to "learning the world." Alternatively, instructors may seek ways to facilitate this process through pre-built avatars or other means. It should be noted that recently Linden Lab simplified the process of setting up an account and getting started in Second Life. Assuming no technical problems, a new user may now be exploring in less than 10 minutes.

Technical barriers: Instructors intimated that they encountered multiple technical problems that either diminished the quality of the experience or prevented them from implementing their projects at all. These barriers included the lack of access to computer systems with adequate specifications (e.g., they had insufficient RAM) or networks with adequate bandwidth to support a class full of students logged in simultaneously. Where sufficient bandwidth exists, IT departments at some universities have restricted access to Second Life by blocking the site on their network servers. Even individual users of Second Life struggle with the bandwidth issue, which is exacerbated by frequent upgrades to the system. Many users also complain of unplanned downtimes, which are an obvious risk to the execution of a scheduled in-world group experience.

Respondents expressed frustration with software barriers as well. Tools and applications such as PowerPoint and Excel are commonly used in business courses, and business students are expected to become proficient in these applications through in-class experience and assignments. The architecture of Second Life makes it difficult for instructors to use these applications. Although it is possible to provide links to spreadsheets and presentations outside of Second Life, this approach can erode the rich experience of interacting in the virtual world.

Social factors: One respondent commented that it felt *"disingenuous"* to interact through avatars when you are also interacting in a real world classroom. Although it may be easier to learn how to use Second Life in a computer lab or similar environment, physical proximity may take away from the realism of the in-world environment.

Educators also expressed concern about the sexual nature of many areas of Second Life. There is a need to be able to keep instructional areas sealed off from sex and pornography; the search system is only somewhat effective in identifying inappropriate areas. Furthermore, many people who are familiar with Second Life associate it with sexual activity, making it difficult to make the case that it is a suitable educational platform. The physical attractiveness of most Second Life avatars tends to validate this concern among new users.

One respondent suggested a strategy for dealing with this problem. Before starting a project in Second Life, it may be helpful to hold a class session on computer ethics and to set specific rules and protocols about networking with others in Second Life. It may also help to implement a dress code.

Finally, some students have difficulty seeing value in learning how to use, work, and interact in Second Life. Some have expressed the belief that Second Life is now *"old news"* and do not see how learning to use it will improve their attractiveness to future employers. They worry that Second Life is not distinguishable from a game and that the time they spend in Second Life will cause others to perceive them as "slackers."

Limits to business simulation: Computer code determines what is possible and what is not possible in this virtual world. For example, in a world where physics will not allow, say, a cell phone to operate, such devices will have no value (Ostrander, 2008). Lawnmowers are worthless when grass grows only as instructed. Marketers expect products to do well only insofar as they satisfy consumer needs, so any application of consumer need based on market research conducted in Second Life to the real world environment must be met with considerable skepticism. Even products such as hair and skins that have direct analogs in the real world like cosmetics will be valued differently between the virtual world and the real world. And ultimately, it is for the real world that we must prepare students.

Also, much has been made of the "post-scarcity" world created by web 2.0, one in which information can be easily shared between individuals instantly and at no cost. In that the world of Second Life consists only of information, one may argue that the only scarcity in Second Life is that which is imposed by the creators of objects. As has been observed in the ongoing difficulties with knock-off virtual products (fashion designers have been particularly hard hit), even creators have difficulty imposing scarcity once a product has been created.

This lack of scarcity creates even greater limitations on the extensibility of in-world findings to the real world. Where, say, an automobile has so little value that it is commonly given away, or a motorcycle may be a gift with purchase, we must expect market research to be seriously skewed.

4.11. Conclusions

Findings from this exploratory study suggest that Second Life has the potential for enhancing student learning and teaching effectiveness for those business faculty who are willing to invest the time and effort necessary to become comfortable with the platform. Respondents consistently noted that, for students, the immersive environment is more engaging, stimulates greater creativity and offers a distinct advantage – the 3D environment – over traditional B-school and distance learning courses. To experience the environment for ourselves, we developed a sample lesson and also asked two of our students to explore Second Life campuses.

4.12. Business Education in Second Life: A Sample Lesson

To test the feasibility of conducting a learning exercise in Second Life, one of the authors created a lesson about "Assets in Second Life." The lesson is designed to familiarize students with the four types of assets mentioned earlier in this chapter. It includes a slide show viewed in-world, a handout available from a web site, and tasks to be accomplished both in-world and on the Second Life web site. Following are the thoughts of the lesson's author, followed by thoughts and observations of others on the lesson and the process.

4.13. Reflections on Lesson Creation

Lessons created in Second Life must be constructed with great detail and an understanding of the student's current level of competency with the software. As with most lessons, the greatest challenge was thinking through the points to be learned and how to craft the lesson activities. This lesson consists of a handout, a slide show, and specific tasks the student must accomplish. The handout, with very precise steps, was not too difficult to compose for one who teaches in the field of information systems, but other instructors might find it more difficult to write at that level of detail. The author of such materials must be able to "think like a naïve user." Creating the slides in PowerPoint, saving them as BMP files, and then uploading into Second Life presented no challenges. The resources used in the "classroom" included commercial products for the slide show, product vendor, and real estate vendor. These are reasonably straightforward to set up.

4.14. Practical Task

Following some detailed guidance on how to operate in Second Life, students are assigned the following task.[3]

---

3. The full lesson plan handout is also available at http://www.cbe.wwu.edu/ross/ProfMeredith/Assets_in_Second_Life.pdf

At the conclusion of this assignment you should be able to develop a business plan incorporating requirements for primitive objects, land area, cost of the land and projected revenue.

You would like to create a mall in which people can sell their items. You've decided to use the building in which this lesson was conducted (the builder has agreed to let you have a copy) and the type of product vendor you saw on the wall.

1. *Determine total prim requirements for the building and twelve (12) vendors.*
2. *Determine how much land (in square meters) you would need to hold the building and vendors.*
3. *You will want extra prims for landscaping and other amenities, so round your land requirements up to the next multiple of 1024 sm.*
4. *Visit the land vendor and look for parcels of land that are appropriately sized. This vendor displays land that is currently for rent and is subject to change on a regular basis. As in real life, you might not find a parcel that is the exact size you seek. Choose one you like, note the name of the parcel, its location, the exact number of prims, and the price per week.*
5. *You expect your mall to have an 80% occupancy rate.*
6. *Given the rental price of the land, the maximum occupancy, and the expected occupancy rate, what weekly rent would you have to charge your tenants so your expected revenue would exceed your weekly land cost?*

4.15. Reflections on the Lesson Plan

This exercise provides an excellent means for students to familiarize themselves with Second Life, and a good basis from which to develop future lessons. Although the exercise is certainly feasible as is, there exist certain factors that will create challenges for instructors and students who are new to the environment. For example, the fact that a whiteboard can only be moved and not copied creates limits on the number of locations used within a single exercise. Furthermore, the need to upload each slide as a bitmap becomes cumbersome as slides require updating.

The need to jump between the web and SL in this lesson detracts somewhat from the sense of immersion. It would be preferable to have a section of wall that could function as a browser, making it feel as if it were the avatar and not the student who was browsing the web. The frequent need to download new versions of the software also detracts from immersion and could limit student ability to use Second Life in computer labs with restrictions on software. If the computer in the lab does not allow the software to update, then the student may not be able to complete the activity.

Another limitation to this exercise is that it requires students to operate their avatars in a confined virtual space. This limits the number of students who can engage in the exercise at a single time. Such a limitation may lead to frustration among students, especially where the exercise is used with a large class size. Expanding the space in Second Life may not resolve this issue, since participants need to "see" the whiteboard and other course elements.

A broader issue for these exercises in general is that the use of Second Life may further detach students from their instructors. Using the whiteboard exercise as an instruction tool to teach concepts such as the types of assets available in Second Life, for example, limits student/teacher interaction and discussion. The sharing of ideas is an important part of business education.

All this being said, in-world exercises such as this will be a useful complement to other classroom activities.

4.16. Business Education in Second Life: Two Students' Perspectives

At the request of the authors, two undergraduate business students, Max and David, took a tour of virtual campuses in Second Life. During their visits, they interviewed students at several universities and provided a report of their findings as well as their personal reflections.

Second Life learning is unique: After several hours of firsthand experience, both Max and David were enthusiastic about the potential of Second Life as a teaching and learning tool. "*I was intrigued by the notion that the whole way we learn could change in the coming years*," said Max, "*An in-world college campus is very different from the real world counterpart.*" He later noted that "*Second Life learning is unique enough from traditional learning that it has the ability to turn into a major teaching tool.*" "*Second life is primarily being used as a functional playground for experimental, cutting-edge professors, or as a tool for new information delivery for more mundane teachers,*" added David.

Modes of learning in Second Life differed from those in a traditional campus. Max noted, "*Most of the learning is done through interaction and viewing the virtual world around you.*" This interaction was present not only in field work, but also in the classroom. Max went on to elaborate: "*Plain text is also used in which a student can click on an object to view pertinent information the professor has distributed for the class that day,*" although he did note the presence of more traditional tools as well. "*PowerPoint slides are utilized mostly in lecture sessions.*"

Improvements are necessary: Education in Second Life clearly holds great promise for the students, although they felt that the platform was a long way from its full potential. Max: "*I found that video, audio, and other graphics are used less due to lack of technology in Second Life and other virtual worlds. This obviously differs from traditional real world education in which most of our understanding comes from listening to your professor and taking notes in class.*"

"*Upgrading the current feature set on Second Life like better video and audio capabilities would be very helpful in creating a better classroom environment,*" echoed David.

"*I also think that the learning curve for using Second Life is something that needs to be kept in mind when think about the potential for using SL for higher education class,*" added Max. "*I was able to figure out the basics of Second Life but there is so much to learn that a professor wanting to utilize it for his class might risk cutting some of his or her course material due to time constraints. While it is possible to conduct a class or start a business in a virtual world I don't feel that a student can get the same amount of education with a day's worth of time using Second Life compared to a real world classroom until improvements are made.*"

David agreed that education in Second Life held great promise, although not every student avatar he interviewed agreed. "*Primarily, respondents to my survey fell into one of two categories: those who believed there was a future for second life as an education application, and those who thought its use was a trend, limited by current technology.*"

The benefits of experiential learning are apparent: The greatest, or perhaps most apparent, educational benefit realized through the environment was clearly access to field experience. "*Unique to Second Life education is the emphasis on communication and practicing skills taught in the classroom inside a virtual world,*" noted Max, "*This is something traditional education can't easily offer students and is a real advantage to help a student fully take in what he or she has learned. Most students on Second Life I talked to want more than just listening to a lecture, reading a textbook, and jotting down notes. A student can take their knowledge in the field of sales and marketing to start a business in Second Life. This provides the educators the ability to see if what they are teaching their students is truly sinking in and provides students an opportunity to test what they have learned before they go out into the real world where mistakes can be more costly.*"

David gave the example of one student who started his own business in Second Life as a way of covering his in-world expenses. He added that "*several of the students that I talked to were using second life for scalable business applica-tions. By experimenting in-game with owning their own stores, they were gaining practical experience into management of their own funds and management of retail sites.*"

David noted that "*one could use the Second Life engine to run anything from group simulations for Management classes to test-marketing of products within a simulated environment.*"

Second Life is Web 2.0: David in particular emphasized the importance of the social aspect of the environment. "*The first person I interviewed was a male student in his first quarter of class online…He was in his sophomore year, so he had some experience with college education. He really enjoyed meeting online, and had great things to say about it. He mentioned how Second Life allowed him to be more "real" and speak up* more in class. He explained how he really enjoyed the potential in Second Life to meet new people."

To David, Second Life clearly falls in the domain of Web 2.0. He went on to say, "*This was not the first time I ran into the concept of social networking in SL. The next person I talked to had quite a few interesting things to say about in-world networking. He was also a non business student, and he explained how he was using Second Life for networking. His social circle all had Second Life accounts, and they were using it as a replacement Facebook.*"

4.17. The Untapped Potential of Second Life

Second Life offers a rich, interactive, highly configurable environment for simulating various business and organizational settings. We expect many educators will find uses for Second Life as a stage to enact various short-term situations – much like a role-play in class – but where the players could be anywhere in the world. We wonder, however, whether Second Life could also be a platform to support a real business exercise (not a simulation). Students could be given the modest amount of money and other support (e.g., land) necessary to establish a presence in-world. They would then be expected to create and operate a business where the market is other players spending "real" money – whether a defined group of residents (e.g., other classmates) or the entire population of Second Life.

References

Love, E., Wilhem, W., Chapman, C., Summerfelt, H., & Kedzior, R. (2008). Emerging opportunities for teaching and research in virtual worlds. Special Session, Academy of Marketing Science 2008 Annual Conference, Vancouver, Canada.

Mennecke, B., Hassall, L., & Triplett, J. (2008). The mean business of Second Life: Teaching entrepreneurship, technology and e-commerce in immersive environments. *Journal of Online Learning and Teaching*, 4(3).

Ostrander, M. (2008). Talking, looking, flying, searching: information seeking behaviour in Second Life. *Library Hi Tech*, 26(4).

LINKS TO THE PRODUCTS MENTIONED IN THE CHAPTER. THESE CONNECT TO XSTREETSECOND LIFE, THE ON-LINE SHOPPING WEBSITE MAINTAINED BY LINDEN LABS.

Freeview TV. Accessed August 21, 2009, from https://www.xstreetsl.com/modules.php?name = Marketplace&file = item&ItemID = 419124

Presentation Whiteboard. Accessed August 21, 2009, fromhttps://www.xstreetsl.com/modules. php?name = Marketplace&file = item&ItemID = 309204
Message Whiteboard. Accessed August 21, 2009, fromhttps://www.xstreetsl.com/modules. php?name = Marketplace&file = item&ItemID = 346426

Author Biographies

Edwin Love is Assistant Professor of Marketing at Western Washington University. His research interests include innovation, marketing strategy, new product marketing, behavioral decision theory, choice modeling, and preference formation. His research on knowledge flow has recently appeared in *The Journal of Knowledge Management*. With Wendy Wilhelm, he co-chaired a special session on emerging opportunities in teaching and research in virtual worlds at the conference of the Academy of Marketing Science (2008). He has more than 10 years of professional experience as an entrepreneur, management consultant, project manager, and financial analyst. He received his PhD in Marketing from the University of Washington in 2008, his MBA from University of Arizona in 2001, and his BA from The Evergreen State College in 1990.

Steven C. Ross received a BS in History from Oregon State University (1969) and MS and PhD in Business Administration from The University of Utah (1976, 1980). He has been on the faculties of Marquette University (1980–1988), Montana State University (1988–1989), and Western Washington University (1989–present). He is currently Professor of MIS and Chair of the Department of Decision Sciences at WWU. His field of study is management information systems, including pedagogy and instructional applications, and most recently focusing on database and Internet applications. He is the author or coauthor of 27 journal articles, 35 books, and numerous conference presentations and other research papers. His publications have appeared in *Journal of Informatics Education Research, Communications of the Association for Information Systems, Journal of Cases on Information Technology, Journal of Consumer Affairs,* and *Journal of Professional Nursing,* among others. Dr. Ross has been an avid user of Second Life since October 2007 and is a partner in a thriving real estate rental business in SL.

Wendy Wilhelm received her BA in Psychology and French from Tufts University, her MBA from Cornell, and after several years working in brand management, returned to the University of Washington for her PhD in Marketing (1987). Dr. Wilhelm has been on the Marketing faculty in the College of Business and Economics at Western Washington University since 1986. Her teaching and research interests include marketing research, "new media," and curricular innovations in marketing, with a particular interest in incorporating sustainability into marketing coursework. Her most recent work appeared in the *Journal of Consumer Affairs* and the *Journal of Marketing Education,* and she serves on the Board of Directors and

Editorial Review Board for JME. Fascination with Second Life and its possibilities for business education led to two conference papers on this subject presented at the *2008 Academy of Marketing Science* (w/Ed Love and Chris Chapman) and *2008 Marketing Educators' Association* conferences. Dr. Wilhelm is currently exploring opportunities for using *SL* in her *Marketing Research* and *Sustainable Marketing* courses.

Chapter 5

Virtual Worlds and Business Schools – The Case of INSEAD

Andreas M. Kaplan

5.1. Introduction: Business Schools Using Virtual Worlds?

Over recent months, several multinational enterprises such as Adidas, Dell, and Wells Fargo have entered (and left) Second Life (SL) to test its potential as a new marketing channel or simply to get press attention in Real Life (RL) print media. Yet what may be surprising to most of us is that major universities such as Harvard, Princeton, and Stanford are also represented in this virtual world. At SimTeach[1] – a community where faculty and others can get information and share experiences of designing, teaching, and administering classes in immersive environments – one can find around 200 universities and colleges that are present in SL.

Business schools have also started to show an interest in SL, publishing an increasing amount of articles about virtual worlds and related topics (e.g., Hemp, 2006; Holzwarth, Janiszewski, & Neumann, 2006; Schlosser, 2003, 2006). However, the first major business school that entered the online economy, rather than merely studying it, was INSEAD, an international graduate business school and research institution founded in 1957 with campuses in France and Singapore. INSEAD's main differentiation factor lies in its global perspective and cultural diversity, making it a veritable "Business School for the World." INSEAD makes ample use of SL by holding in-world lectures, maintaining virtual research laboratories, and inviting prospective students or potential employers to get in touch with the institution.

---

1. http://www.simteach.com/wiki/index.php?title = Institutions_and_Organizations_in_SL

Higher Education in Virtual Worlds
Copyright © 2009 by Emerald Group Publishing Limited
All rights of reproduction in any form reserved
ISBN: 978-1-84950-609-0

SL's possibilities for expansion on cultural diversity and outreach make the virtual jump particularly interesting for INSEAD.

The objectives of the chapter are: a) to introduce the reader to the opportunities of SL for business schools, using several examples from different countries, b) describe in detail the case of INSEAD to provide an in-depth analysis of the potential benefits and challenges of this new medium, and c) discuss the key insights as well as future developments of virtual social worlds within a business school context.

5.2. How Business Schools Make Use of Second Life

Having analyzed the different uses business schools make of SL, one can see four different approaches: communication and public relations; virtual education; the management of internal processes and student recruitment; and finally for research purposes. Each of these applications, which are all very similar to corporate activities in *SL* (Kaplan & Haenlein, 2009d), will be discussed in more detail.

5.3. Communication and Public Relations

Communication is probably the most widely applied use of virtual social worlds. There are four trends in the ways business schools increase their advertising potential in SL: First, business schools can set-up virtual islands to present digital equivalents of their campuses in RL. The Business School Toulouse (ESC Toulouse, France), for example, completely replicated its physical buildings in SL.

Second, communication can be conducted by buying advertising space in virtual malls or radio stations. Companies such as MetaAdverse, the advertising network in SL, rent out virtual billboards and subsequently track who views them to provide information to advertisers similar to that obtained in the context of traditional online banners.

A third way of advertising in-world is the sponsoring of virtual events, as done by the Kelley School of Business (Indiana University, Bloomington, Indiana), which hosted a conference on "Virtual Worlds and the Future of Business Education" including representatives from IBM and Microsoft.

Finally, business schools are aware of the positive impact their activities within virtual worlds can have on RL press coverage. Conducting any form of activity within SL was arguably the best way to get positive business press coverage during the period of buzz around virtual worlds (2006–2007). Thus, Babson College's (Wellesley, Massachusetts) development of a virtual business incubator in SL gained them not only an award from the National Collegiate Inventors and Innovators Alliance (NCIIA) but also free RL press attention.

5.4. Virtual Education

Aside from the aforementioned communication purposes, virtual worlds also offer the possibility for holding in-world lectures complementary to or even substituting

RL lectures. In June 2007, the first virtual classes delivered by a European business school were hosted by IE Business School (Madrid, Spain) on the topic "Online Communities and Second Life." SDA Bocconi (Milan, Italy) makes use of its SL presence to enhance their top management education by simulating and explaining teamwork dynamics of virtual teams as well as testing virtual outdoor exercises. Also, the Erivan K. Haub School of Business (Saint Joseph's University: Philadelphia, Pennsylvania) reaffirms its interest in SL, stating:

> One of our goals is to use the medium [Second Life] as an aid in supplementing what's being taught in the classroom.

Besides virtual lectures, SL also offers potential for e-learning applications. Several business schools such as the Dallas School of Management (University of Texas: Dallas, Texas) have taken first steps in this direction. Given that virtual worlds offer much richer possibilities to present and interact, this approach is likely to be more successful than more traditional e-learning approaches. Finally, an approach was chosen by the Jenkins Graduate School of Management (North Carolina State University: Raleigh, North Carolina) and the Kelley School of Business (Indiana University: Bloomington, Indiana), whose students worked synchronously to learn about service innovation by using a combination of several social media, among them SL, where they held meetings and collaborated on team projects.

5.5. Internal Process Management and Student Recruitment

Another interesting opportunity for business schools is to use virtual worlds as a platform for organizing internal meetings and knowledge exchange. The Virtual Management School created by the University of Edinburgh (United Kingdom) offers a SL building in which staff, students, potential students, alumni, and anyone interested in the work of the school can discuss the activities of the school and its programs. Several rooms are available for formal or informal meetings. The University of Hamburg (Germany) hopes that their SL presence will bring faculty and students together across different departments and research areas by displaying an interactive project finder, helping faculty to get to know each other's current projects.

In addition to advertising, virtual worlds can also be used to recruit potential students. Up to now, no business school has actually led entire recruitment talks in SL. However, potential students can meet current students or alumni to obtain information about programs or campus life. This is offered on Toulouse Business School's (France) premises in SL. In the future, avatars themselves might be interviewed for potentially joining a business school. For several years, business schools have invested money and time in the building up of reliable video- and phone-conferencing systems for the recruitment of potential students dispersed all around the globe, but the extremely limited ways of interaction proposed by such media have been significant obstacles to their broad use. SL might provide a good alternative in the future.

5.6.   Scientific Research

Finally, business schools can also use virtual worlds for scientific research purposes. The Department for Strategic Management, Marketing and Tourism of the University of Innsbruck (Austria) plans to use SL for consumer behavior studies. According to department members, in comparison with often lengthy and rather expensive study designs in the real world, SL offers an inexpensive and non-bureaucratic alternative. But it is not only for cost-efficiency reasons that scientific researchers turn to SL: Professor Robert Bloomfield of the Cornell University Johnson Graduate School of Management (Ithaca, New York), for example, uses SL for his research since this virtual world offers him a more realistic economic environment to study than any laboratory-simulated environment could offer. Bloomfield points out that today's virtual worlds are very much like the US economy about a century ago, when there was almost no regulation, which makes SL an ideal opportunity for study purposes (Di Meglio, 2007b). Also, Edward Castronova, director of the Synthetic Worlds Initiative, a research center at Bloomington Indiana University for studying virtual worlds, posed the idea of creating multiple virtual economies to study the effects of different regulatory policies. Finally, SL and virtual worlds can also be used to inform about current scientific studies and their results, as is done by Ulm University (Germany), for example.

5.7.   How INSEAD Experiences Second Life's Potential and Challenges

To analyze INSEAD's SL presence as well as its experience with this new medium, a combination of literature research, observation, and qualitative interviews was used. Key insights and lessons learned will be presented here.

The case of INSEAD is of particular interest for at least two reasons: first, INSEAD is the first major business school to enter the online economy, instead of merely studying it. Second, and more importantly, INSEAD makes intense use of the virtual environment and is much more involved and advanced in their virtual experience in comparison to other business schools. With this case study, we are presented with close insights into the potential but also the limitations of a virtual campus.

INSEAD (Institut Européen d'Administration des Affaires – European Institute of Business Administration) is an international graduate business school and research institution founded in 1957 with campuses in France and Singapore. As one of the world's leading business schools (# 5 in the *Financial Times* Global MBA Ranking 2009), INSEAD's main differentiation factor lies in its global perspective and cultural diversity. This focus on cultural diversity makes SL particularly interesting for INSEAD. The school's SL team essentially consists of four persons: Miklos Sarvary, professor of marketing and the manager of INSEAD's SL island; Jill Huret, Assistant Director of the Learning Innovation Centre, responsible for the organization and communication of SL events at INSEAD; Joseph Lajos, PhD student in marketing and lead virtual research lab designer; and Balint Halasz, architecture student and technical and design manager of virtual INSEAD.

5.8. INSEAD's Three Virtual Campus Areas

In April 2007, INSEAD opened its virtual presence in SL. All four opportunities as described earlier on how business schools make use of SL are extensively applied to INSEAD's case. However, INSEAD structured its island not according to four but to three applications of virtual worlds (see Figure 5.1: INSEAD's virtual campus plan; also see Pictures 5.1–5.3 for screenshots of INSEAD's SL presence).

1. Public space and beach (public campus)

The public campus consists of a lounge, bar areas, and a beach where avatars of prospective students or potential employers can get in contact with INSEAD. Throughout the area users can ask questions to so-called chatterbots, artificial computer-controlled avatars designed to simulate intelligent conversations with human avatars through auditory or text methods. Furthermore, there are several information boxes where one can find information on the different programs offered at INSEAD, how to apply for them, lifelong learning programs, the alumni association, and so on. Interested avatars can then be connected to INSEAD's webpage. From time to time, special events are hosted here for applicants, companies, and everybody else interested in the school. Apart from the possibility of receiving information about INSEAD on the public campus, the school also uses this area for more direct advertising activities by handing out free INSEAD

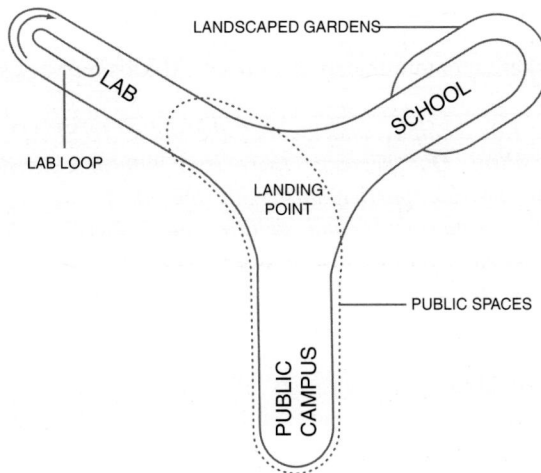

Figure 5.1: INSEAD's virtual campus

Picture 5.1: INSEAD's social interaction space and beach (public campus)

promotional T-shirts and other freebies. Finally, setting INSEAD's presence in SL is of course marketing communication in itself. Miklos Sarvary states:

> *The Second Life campus underscores the value INSEAD places on entrepreneurialism. Our presence there is a natural extension of our dedication to provide participants with the most current, real-time technological advancements and deliver top leadership development programs, whether it takes place on a physical campus or online digital world.* (Jensen, 2007).

2. School and library

The school and library area consists of public access areas (auditorium and library) and restricted access areas, accessible only to avatars belonging to INSEAD (e.g., meeting rooms, where one has to type in a code to enter). In the library, avatars can read for example scientific articles by INSEAD faculty members, the Linden blog, the SL Business Review or inform themselves about studies of virtual

Picture 5.2: INSEAD's virtual auditorium and virtual lectures

worlds and their results (interested avatars will usually be connected to respective websites). Generally speaking the "School" area offers a learning environment in which INSEAD students from around the world can learn together and collaborate with each other in real-time. SL is part of all major programs at INSEAD, including its MBA, Executive MBA, and general Executive Education. Classes held in SL such as lectures for MBA and EMBA students focus on the theme of virtual worlds; these classes complement in-person learning but do not substitute it. According to Miklos Sarvary, *"the idea is not to replace face-to-face meetings and classroom experiences but to make sure that we can extend the experience that our regular students are having"* (Baxter, 2008). However, Miklos continues, "SL certainly adds to the INSEAD offering in a significantly better manner than anything else that the school has tried so far in terms of the Internet and online tools". Finally, the school and library area also allow alumni or current students not able to attend an event in RL to join it in SL: for example, the 20th Alumni Sustainability Executive Roundtable (October 2008) was held at the INSEAD France campus, and simultaneously on its virtual campus in SL.

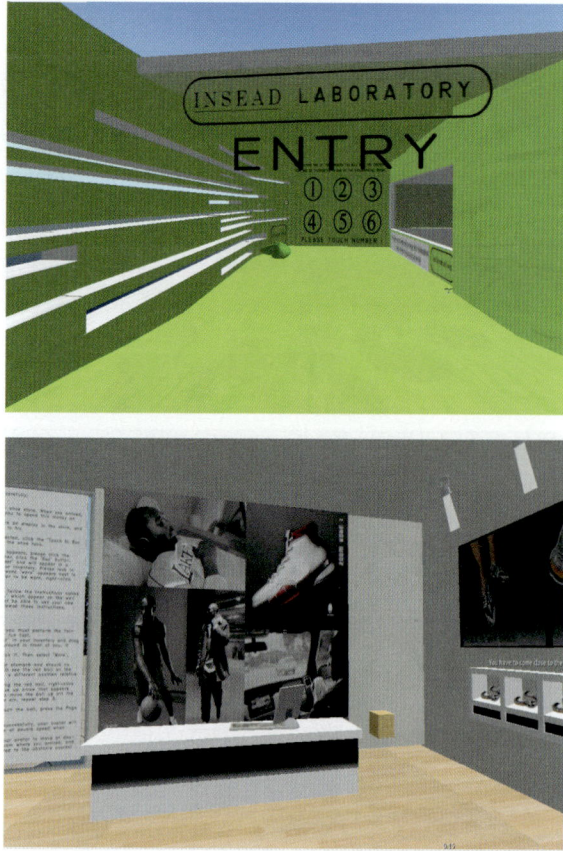

Picture 5.3: Entry to the laboratory and the experimental shoe store

3. Research lab

The "Lab" displays several laboratories for research purposes. Avatars can participate in scientific studies that "aim to enhance the quality of teaching at INSEAD" and are designated "purely for academic purposes" and not "directly for companies" as is specified on the SL presence. One of these studies was aimed at analyzing whether avatars embrace RL brands in SL, or whether they instead prefer smaller, specialty brands that exist only in the virtual world. To do so, participants were randomly assigned to one of three groups and given ten Lindens (official SL currency) to buy a pair of running shoes in the INSEAD experimental store. In the RL brand group, all the shoes in the store carried a very well-known brand logo of athletic shoes. In the SL brand group, all of the shoes carried a SL brand logo. In the no brand group, the shoes did not carry a logo. Furthermore, each of these groups was blindly divided into two subgroups: In the "accelerated speed" subgroups, the shoes gave avatars the ability to run faster than normal, whereas in the "normal speed" subgroups, the shoes did not have any effect on the speed with which avatars could run. After having purchased a pair of shoes avatars are asked to try the shoes by completing a brief obstacle course before filling out a questionnaire on an external website about the shoes that they chose. Avatars in each group were asked how much they liked the shoes that they purchased as well as their liking for and beliefs about RL branded shoes. After completion, avatars are compensated with 100 Lindens (around 40 US cents). Given that most items in SL still cost around 10 Lindens, this is a relatively high compensation. Finally, participating avatars are also informed about the predictions of study results:

> *We predict that participants in the accelerated speed subgroups will, on average, report liking the shoes that they purchased in our experimental store more than will participants in the normal speed subgroups. Furthermore, we predict that among participants in the real life brand group, those in the accelerated speed subgroup will report liking real life branded shoes more and thinking that branded shoes can increase a runner's speed more than will those in the normal speed subgroup. We are also interested to see whether participants like the RL branded shoes more on average than the Second Life branded shoes, or vice versa.*[2]

5.9. INSEAD's SL Presence Characterized by Informal Start-up Feeling

INSEAD's spirit of going into SL was much like that of a start-up company rather than that of a major business school. Miklos Sarvary had the original idea of entering a virtual world, and his principal motivation was driven by the opportunity of offering classes in the form of avatars. Miklos, who is also the Director of the INSEAD Learning Innovation Centre, saw INSEAD's efforts in virtual worlds as being part of its duty to explore and develop new learning technologies, methods, and ideas. Therefore, the setting up of INSEAD's virtual campus began with a small virtual lecture hall on a small lot of land in SL where INSEAD held a few experimental classes with then-MBA students. Since student feedback generated from this enterprise was excellent, INSEAD decided to buy a whole island and to build a virtual campus including all of the business school's activities, which went live in April 2007. The virtual research lab was the result of Miklos having offered the possibility of creating a behavioral research lab and in consequence doing scientific research in SL with Joseph Lajos, PhD student in marketing. Thus, the research lab, though not part of the original SL plans, is the result of a PhD student being interested in this immersive environment. Miklos Sarvary hired Balint Halasz, a Hungarian architecture student to

---

2. The results of this experiment have not yet been released.

act as research assistant and to build up the virtual INSEAD campus. Eventually the workload became too intense and Balint and two of his friends created their own company, Pixelbreeze (based in Budapest and Vienna), which still maintains the INSEAD island and regularly organizes events there.

This start-up-like process of the virtual INSEAD has been successful: INSEAD's virtual campus was selected as an example of the world's best SL architecture in a book called *Space Between People* (Doesinger, 2008), which published the results of the first architecture and design competition in SL.

Alongside offering virtual classes and eventually doing research in the virtual world, cost was another motivation for INSEAD to enter SL: As Miklos Sarvary pointed out in an interview (Di Meglio, 2007a) "Besides putting the INSEAD community at the forefront of new technology, [...] the plan is to help the school cut back on travel and physical building expenses." The costs of buying the land and building the campus are fairly low: The island cost €1000, to which a monthly fee of around €100 must be added. The cost of design and creation of the campus were another €10,000. These costs are small in comparison to RL building costs and maintenance. Compared with setting up virtual presence units and investing in state-of-the art videoconferencing, Miklos points out that designing a campus in SL was relatively inexpensive (Murray, 2008). Next to saving on travel and physical building expenses, INSEAD sees two additional cost-saving opportunities. First, the use of SL can reduce costs for companies whose executives are absent as a result of course work: INSEAD's virtual campus allows faculty to keep in touch with participants, helping them to instantaneously implement skills and knowledge learned from attending a program at INSEAD for a fraction of the cost. Second, the virtual campus also increases the extent of reaching alumni beyond their time as actual students: although INSEAD has historically used webinars (web-based seminars), as well as action learning programs to keep in contact with alumni, SL will prospectively take the lead at INSEAD for these purposes.

5.10.   Challenges and Limits of INSEAD's SL Island

Of course, INSEAD's presence in SL has had and still has its challenges. First, limitations are set by faculty members, students, and unaffiliated individuals simply visiting the public areas. So far, few faculty members other than Miklos have made use of SL's potential for offering virtual classes. Although around a dozen of professors have created avatars and participated in some of the virtual events organized by INSEAD, they are an exception. Also, students were not enthusiastic about investing in considerably significant learning costs to know how to behave, move, and simply survive as an avatar. Particularly in the early stages, it was difficult to persuade students and alumni to invest their scarce time for studying virtual worlds.

Also, outsiders can create challenges on the virtual campus. Not everybody on the INSEAD island is automatically a fan of the business school, is dressed appropriately, or necessarily knows what INSEAD is: for example, at one point in time one could find a prostitute avatar dressed in scanty clothes on INSEAD's island offering her services. In this real example, the avatar claimed to be on the INSEAD campus by accident, of course. Probably even worse than the preceding example, most of the time INSEAD's SL presence is completely deserted, which is not a positive message for those who are considering joining the INSEAD community in either virtual or RL. This is a major challenge that INSEAD shares with other corporations in virtual worlds (Kaplan & Haenlein, 2009d).

Furthermore, some technical problems have yet to be overcome. On the Internet, comments from participants in virtual events on the INSEAD campus mention technical issues leading to lag and computer crashes. Classes with more than 40 people become technically problematic and difficult to handle. Also, the chatterbots described earlier seem not to be technically mature yet: For example, whenever one asks the question: "Where is INSEAD?" the chatterbot answers: "Where the heart is. I haven't heard of INSEAD." This answer is certainly not the best way of advertising to a prospective INSEAD student! To partly overcome this last issue, INSEAD's real-life receptionists in Fontainebleau and Singapore are provided with avatars so that they can greet virtual visitors at the newly built SL reception desks. According to Jill Huret "Deserted spaces are still a challenge as our receptionists have real day jobs to do and cannot be focused primarily on the virtual campus, but it is especially useful when we host events as they can direct the visitors".

Finally, the research lab has also created several challenges. Although the virtual research lab is very efficient in terms of attracting participants, the set-up costs of a study are extremely high. According to Joseph Lajos, it would take 10–20 times longer to set up a study in the virtual lab as in a real world behavioral lab. Small details created numerous problems which can be illustrated in the aforementioned study concerning the branding of SL and RL shoe brands. Whenever subjects put on the fast shoes they had to put on two things, that is, the shoes plus the device for making the shoes faster-which is not easy from a programming point of view. Thus Lajos reports that "one extremely frustrating thing was that the part that would make the avatar run fast would often sort of fall off on the ground in a way that was difficult to pick up." Furthermore, problems were caused by difficulties when avatars had to pay for the shoes. Concerning these challenges, Lajos sees two issues researchers must face when doing research in SL: First, if one is not a programmer oneself, one is completely dependent on a third person. Second, and more importantly, since programming takes time, this might lead to publishing deadline issues. On a side note, Lajos mentions the fact that to obtain good data, one to two researchers in the form of avatars must be present in the research lab whenever the experiment is running: it is not possible to completely leave the lab and the test subjects on their own.

5.11. INSEAD's Future in SL

Although INSEAD's presence in SL creates challenges there have been numerous successes reported: virtual classes get good feedback. Alain Desvigne, MBA student at the Singapore campus, states:

> *It's very much like attending a normal course. You get the same sense of community that you do in a lecture theater, because you can see each other, you are all there in the same place. At the end of the course, I made my way over to the avatar of a student, who was actually in Paris, and we had a discussion, the relationship was very direct.* (Piovezan, 2007).

In the future, Miklos Sarvary would like to offer entire courses in SL, not just individual sections. A further objective is to get more faculty members interested in teaching in the SL world.

Moreover, the virtual research lab has a huge advantage: it is very efficient in terms of acquiring participants since it is very easy to ensure numerous test subjects with very short notice. In fact, Joseph Lajos suggests not posting announcements searching for study participants too far in advance since avatars tend rather to live in the present and therefore will show up immediately. For the study described earlier, it took only a few hours to get 60 participants. Additionally, there were many more avatars who wanted to participate in the study but who had to be turned down. Even with all the above-mentioned problems, Lajos is sure that he will certainly use the virtual research lab for some of his projects.

In the future, INSEAD intends to create links from the SL environment to all the services that one can find on its website, such as faculty presentations, research, databases, course information, etc. Says Miklos Sarvary: "there will be a snowball effect. As more and more users, whether alumni, faculty or the INSEAD community at large start using Second Life and talking about our virtual campus, the amount of users will rise dramatically" (Sarvary, 2007). At the moment, however, it remains difficult to conceptualize and explain a virtual world if one has not yet experienced it firsthand.

5.12. How Virtual Worlds Might Change in the Future

Virtual worlds are a rapidly changing environment and business schools are trying out many different ways of tapping the full potential of this new medium. Concerning future evolutions, there are five developments that are likely to be of specific importance for business schools that are in SL or are planning to be so in the next years (see also Kaplan & Haenlein, 2009d for a similar argumentation with regards to businesses).

5.13. Advances in Hard and Software

SL's hardware requirements such as a powerful graphics card are demanding; therefore, some business schools would potentially have problems running SL on their own computers in their computer labs. Indeed, whenever multiple avatars are at a same location, lag time is intense, making lectures with large groups a daunting task. Also the ease of use of the SL software still has room for improvement. In-world navigation is not as easy to learn as one might expect and avatar customization can take several hours if one wants to have an individualized look. Also, training is needed to use the voice application in SL, and it does not work perfectly yet. Additionally, as we saw in the example of INSEAD, faculty in particular but also busy executive education students are rather reluctant to invest time in learning how to use what to them seems to be not much more than an online game. All these drawbacks of SL are the reasons why several business schools are sticking to their old ways of doing distance education: IESE, for example, still prefers virtual presence software such as Adobe Connect and Webex (a fee-paid Cisco application) to have distance team meetings, host online conferences, or hold online discussions. Yet, as with all other technological innovations, experts expect substantial and rapid advances in this respect over time. Given the huge potential of three-dimensional virtual worlds compared to the traditional two-dimensional World Wide Web, some of them, among them Miklos Sarvary (2008), even assume that corporate presences within virtual worlds will take over the role of traditional Internet pages in 5–10 years time.

5.14. Evolution of Virtual Worlds to the Internet of Tomorrow

Be it through virtual distribution (virtual commerce/v-commerce), advertising, or other business functions, there is little doubt that the increasing growth of virtual asset trade within virtual worlds will evolve beyond their gaming roots to becoming a main contact channel between companies and consumers. By looking at the very active users of SL who spend several hours a day in world, stating that SL for them is not a game but an extension of their real lives (Kaplan & Haenlein, 2009a, 2009b, 2009c, 2009e), one rapidly grasps the full potential of virtual worlds. Of course, the virtual road is still long until this actually becomes reality for everybody, but since business schools should aim to be wherever companies are, incorporating virtual worlds into a school's strategy becomes logical. Only a few years ago the concept of a business school having an internet presence was highly disputed among faculty – there are few today who would argue that a business school's internet presence is superfluous. It is possibly the same when it comes to presence in virtual worlds. A good example of how business schools and companies in virtual worlds already work together is the ESC Toulouse's virtual business incubator, designed to accelerate the successful development of entrepreneurial ideas and to allow students a common area to present proposals for potential business projects to interested corporate actors.

5.15. Transformation toward Standardization and Interoperability

Social media are essentially all about user participation and co-creation. It is unlikely that virtual worlds will stay as they are, that is, managed by a few companies using proprietary software and protocols; instead, a similar transformation to the one that changed the Internet from a few interconnected military computers to the World Wide Web is expected shortly. This implies a transition toward open source, standardization and, ultimately, a connection between all virtual worlds that transforms them into one all-encompassing Metaverse, that is, not just into one virtual world but into a virtual universe. Several developments in this direction are already visible today. In January 2007, Linden Lab made the source code for the SL Viewer available to the public, allowing each Internet user to modify and improve the main gateway to the virtual world. Eighteen months later, in July 2008, Linden Lab and IBM showed that avatars could be transferred from the SL grid to an OpenSim virtual world server. This allows for the traveling of avatars from one virtual world to another and will probably lead to people maintaining and customizing one avatar that would be used in multiple environments, similar to the use of one main email account today. This would lead to two improvements for business schools using virtual worlds: First, one could host one's own virtual world in the same spirit as each business school hosts its own web presence, that is, schools would be independent of companies such as Linden Lab. Second, the fact that students could have one avatar – similar to them having one main email address – would make their identification easier. As a member of SL, you cannot choose your own last name but only your first name – the last name being given to you by Linden Lab. However, students want their professors to know them – especially when they participate frequently in class. Until now the only way to overcome this limit of SL is the creation of name tags floating above each student's head. Being able to choose one's own name will be an important improvement for the creation and identification of the self in SL.

5.16.   Interconnection between Reality and Virtual Worlds

One development agreed upon by experts is that over the next few years, innovation and creativity will lead to virtual worlds that will resemble more and more what one sees in reality (Hemp, 2008). Today, the graphical capabilities of worlds such as SL are still rather limited and avatars and virtual cities still look very different compared to their RL counterparts. However, the boundaries between virtual and real are already becoming more and more blurred, and this trend is likely to continue in future. Software giant Microsoft, for example, might transform its Microsoft Virtual Earth product into a virtual world that offers avatars the possibility of walking through a three-dimensional equivalent of Paris, New York City, or Munich. Combine this idea with avatars that closely resemble RL people (as characters in modern video games are only barely distinguishable from real human beings), and it becomes difficult to define the difference between virtual reality and reality. Or, to put it differently, if a user spends several hours a day working and meeting friends in a virtual world that completely resembles the real one, is it still possible to differentiate between what is virtual and what is real? Virtual worlds will be even more competitive in comparison to other ways of doing online courses such as using

Webex and other web-based interfaces. Miklos Sarvary stated: "Since there is no feeling of being in a classroom, participants easily get bored with just watching the screen with PPTs." Being in a SL classroom is already quite realistic but just imagine how it would feel if students had a real replica of a classroom within a certain institution, a replica of the institution, or even a real replica of the city where the institution is located.

5.17.   Setting up Law and Order in Virtual Worlds

Last but not least, to create a viable environment for business schools, law and order in virtual worlds need to be established, that is, there is a need to have them governed by similar legal rules and ethical norms as in the real world – which as yet is not the case. Although being legally bound to US and Californian law (as a result of Linden Lab being located in San Francisco) such regulations have just not yet been introduced into SL. However, the first steps in this direction are already visible today. In July 2007, Linden Lab (in reply to an FBI investigation) communicated a ban on in-world gambling and prohibited all betting on games of chance or games that rely on the outcome of an RL organized sporting event when they provide a payout in Lindens or an RL currency. Among others, this ban resulted in the collapse of a major virtual bank called "Ginko Financial," which led to severe liquidity problems for the rest of the virtual banks and halved the size of SL's economy. Similar to RL happenings, Linden Lab started to regulate the virtual banking industry in January 2008 and prohibited the offering of interest or any direct return on investment by all companies who were unable to prove an applicable government registration statement or financial institution charter. Evidently, such legislation does not come without problems in an environment that, as it seems, operates outside any legal boundaries existing in the real world. But improvements in law and order will be a necessary step to improve institutional trust and to transform virtual worlds into a relevant and trustworthy channel for business schools.

5.18.   Conclusions: Business Schools Using Virtual Worlds

Although nobody can say with certainty what role virtual worlds will play in 10, 20, or 30 years, many experts maintain that they have the potential to be of similar importance as the Internet is today. Gartner, Inc. (2008), for example, estimates that 70 percent of organizations will have established their own private virtual worlds by 2012 and predicts that these internal worlds will have greater success due to lower expectations, clearer objectives and better constraints. This is a strong argument for any higher education institution in general and business schools in particular to seriously consider the use of this new form of social media (Kaplan & Haenlein, 2010). Apart from the insights into virtual campuses given earlier, three further suggestions can be made, which any business school should consider when planning the implementation of a virtual extension of their RL school activities:

First of all, the considerable learning costs for faculty, administrative staff as well as potential students should be kept in mind. As explained earlier, only relatively few people already know how to operate in virtual worlds. Therefore, if a business school wants their faculty to teach virtual classes, incentives should be offered for them to become familiar with these new environments. This could reduce initial objections of lecturing in virtual worlds. For the same reason, it might not make sense to interview potential students for executive education programs through the virtual world. These target groups usually are pressed for time and might be reluctant to invest in proficiency with virtual worlds. However, whenever they start their classes, the program syllabus should ensure that students learn to navigate in the virtual environment. This offers the possibility to not only offer virtual classes to them but to stay in contact with them for lifelong learning after they have graduated.

Second, do not forget the negative effects of a deserted island. All the virtual campuses visited for this research were completely empty, apart from on the days of specific events. This is certainly not the best image an active business school wants to give to the outside world. To avoid such emptiness and apparent lack of activity, a business school should ensure constant traffic of at least some avatars belonging to the school. This could be achieved by regularly and frequently organizing events on the virtual campus in which faculty and students are interested. Another possibility would be to use the virtual environment as the business school's intranet or a sort of platform where students can download class material or hand in assignments. It must be ensured that only avatars belonging to the business school have access to certain areas, but equally that they can potentially get in contact with people not belonging to the school, since one of the aims is to avoid giving an image of a seemingly "abandoned" island.

Finally, be aware of the fact that SL is not the only option. There exist several other virtual worlds such as Active Worlds or There.com which might be more adapted for any specific business school's extension into the virtual sphere. Besides, it is possible to create a proprietary virtual world completely adapted to a school's preferences and needs. Obviously this would be a more cost intensive option but there might be opportunities to team up with companies or other sponsors. In the end, this would not be so different from business schools branding their buildings or auditoriums with corporate names or completely taking on the name of a donor (e.g., "The University of Chicago Graduate School of Business" rebranding itself the "University of Chicago Booth School of Business"). The bottom-up construction of a proprietary virtual world certainly has the further disadvantage of being disconnected from the big virtual environments such as SL, but as was explained before there is a development toward standardization and interoperability of the different virtual worlds.

Until now business schools are only a minority group of the around 200 universities and colleges present in SL, with institutions specializing in technology or social sciences taking the lead. However, considering the potential uses of virtual worlds such as SL for business schools, the possible future evolutions of virtual worlds in general, as well as the relatively minor set-up and maintenance costs discussed earlier, it is highly likely that there will be an increase of business schools extending their RL activities into the virtual sphere.

References

Baxter, A. (2008). A Second Life for classrooms with vision. *Financial Times*, March 3, p. 12.

Di Meglio, F. (2007a). I was a Second Life B-school student. *Business Week Online*, April 16. Accessed July 3, 2009, from http://www.businessweek.com/technology/content/apr2007/tc20070416_129266.htm

Di Meglio, F. (2007b). Theory meets practice online: Researchers and academics are looking to online worlds such as Second Life to shed new light on old economic questions. *Business Week Online*, July 24. Accessed July 3, 2009, from http://www.businessweek.com/bschools/content/jul2007/bs20070724_664068.htm

Doesinger, S. (2008). *Space between people: How the virtual changes physical architecture*. New York: Prestel.

Gartner. (2008). Gartner says 90 per cent of corporate virtual world projects fail within 18 months, Press release, May 15.

Hemp, P. (2006). Avatar based marketing. *Harvard Business Review*, *84*(June), 48–57.

Hemp, P. (2008). Getting real about virtual worlds. *Harvard Business Review*, *86*(10), 27–28.

Holzwarth, M., Janiszewski, C., & Neumann, M. M. (2006). The influence of avatars on online consumer shopping behavior. *Journal of Marketing*, *70*(4), 19–36.

Jensen, H. (2007). INSEAD establishes presence on Second Life, INSEAD press release, March 3.

Kaplan, A. M., & Haenlein, M. (2009a). Consumers, companies and virtual social worlds: A qualitative analysis of Second Life. *Advances in Consumer Research*, *36*(1), 873–874.

Kaplan, A. M., & Haenlein, M. (2009b). Consumer use and business potential of virtual worlds: The case of Second Life. *International Journal on Media Management*, *11*(3).

Kaplan, A. M., & Haenlein, M. (2009c). Flagship brand stores within virtual worlds: The impact of virtual store exposure on real life brand attitudes and purchase intent. *Recherche et Applications en Marketing*, *24*(3).

Kaplan, A. M., & Haenlein, M. (2009d). The fairyland of Second Life: About virtual social worlds and how to use them. *Business Horizons*, *52*(6).

Kaplan, A. M., & Haenlein, M. (2009e). Utilisation et potentiel commercial des hyperréalités: Une analyse qualitative de Second Life. *Revue française du marketing*, *222*, 69–81.

Kaplan, A. M., & Haenlein, M. (2010). Users of the world, unite! The challenges and opportunities of social media. *Business Horizons*, *53*.

Murray, S. (2008). Technology: Networking widens EMBA net. *Financial Times*, October 27.

Piovezan, S. (2007). Unis coming to grips with Second Life. Harvard and Stanford are using the virtual world for teaching. France is following suit, Le Monde Campus, March 13.

Sarvary, M. (2007). Professor Miklos Sarvary tells us about INSEAD's virtual campus, INSEAD Alumni newsletter, July 2007.

Sarvary, M. (2008). The Metaverse: TV of the future? *Harvard Business Review*, *86*(2), 30.

Schlosser, A. E. (2003). Experiencing products in the virtual world: The role of goal and imagery in influencing attitudes versus purchase intentions. *Journal of Consumer Research*, *30*(2), 184–198.

Schlosser, A. E. (2006). Learning through virtual product experience: The role of imagery on true versus false memories. *Journal of Consumer Research*, *33*(3), 377–383.

Author Biography

Andreas M. Kaplan (mail@andreaskaplan.eu) is Professor of Marketing at the ESCP Europe (Paris campus). His main research domain deals with analyzing social media such as virtual worlds, blogs, or social networking sites. Additionally, Andreas has carried out research in the areas of customer lifetime valuation, mass customization and public sector marketing. He did his PhD at the University of Cologne and HEC Paris. Andreas holds an MPA from the École Nationale d'Administration (ENA; French National School of Public Administration), an MSc from ESCP Europe, and a BSc from the University of Munich. Additionally, Andreas was visiting PhD at INSEAD.

Chapter 6

Online Instructor Immediacy and Instructor-Student Relationships in Second Life

Traci L. Anderson

6.1. Student Perceptions of Instructor Nonverbal Immediacy

Although the educational use of Second Life has grown exponentially, there still is not much scholarly research at this time regarding specific behaviors and practices that enhance the student's learning experience in Second Life. Over a decade ago, Horton (1997) argued that as technology grows and becomes more germane to education, educators will need to improve teaching effectiveness in technology-specific contexts. One abundant area of research regarding teaching effectiveness is nonverbal immediacy or "teacher immediacy." Nearly four decades of research have provided a wealth of evidence that instructor immediacy positively affects students. In 2001 Hoyt, Thomas-Maddox, and Evans argued that educators must work toward integrating a greater variety of immediacy behaviors when teaching in *online* environments [my emphasis] (Hoyt, Thomas-Maddox, & Evans, 2001). Second Life presents instructors with the opportunities to engage in immediacy behaviors online.

In the field of instructional communication, presence receives a great deal of scholarly attention. Central to the construct of presence is immediacy, conceptualized as a set of verbal and nonverbal behaviors that "enhance closeness to and nonverbal interaction with another" (Mehrabian, 1969, p. 203). In other words, immediacy behaviors bring about a sense of psychological and/or physical closeness between people. Mehrabian's (1971) "principle of immediacy" states:

> *people are drawn toward persons and things they like, evaluate highly, and prefer; and they avoid or move away from things they dislike, evaluate negatively, or do not prefer* (p. 1).

Higher Education in Virtual Worlds
Copyright © 2009 by Emerald Group Publishing Limited
All rights of reproduction in any form reserved
ISBN: 978-1-84950-609-0

Thus, when a person uses immediacy behaviors he/she positively affects the level of psychological distance with others, and instructors who engage in immediacy behaviors have a positive influence on students and learning outcomes. Thomas, Richmond, and McCroskey (1994) noted that nonverbal immediacy behaviors include moving around the classroom, making eye contact with students, smiling, gesturing, speaking without a podium, use of range of vocal techniques, and appropriate touching.

In educational settings, immediacy has been applied to interactions between teachers and students; if an instructor can increase the sense of psychological closeness with students through the use of immediacy behaviors, educational outcomes can be affected positively. Instructors who use certain nonverbal and verbal behaviors are perceived by students as more immediate (e.g., Andersen, 1978). Specifically, researchers have found a positive relationship between instructor immediacy and student motivation and affect. For example, Witt, Wheeless, and Allen (2004) conducted a meta-analysis of student learning and instructor immediacy in which they examined 81 studies conducted between 1979 and 2001. These 81 studies reported that instructor immediacy was associated positively with increased cognitive learning, positive evaluations of instructors, and increased student affect (e.g., liking the course material and the instructor).

Certain nonverbal immediacy behaviors, however, have been found to be most important for instructors when interacting when students; these are smiling, vocal variety/expressiveness, and having a relaxed body position (e.g., Gorham, 1988; Kelley & Gorham, 1988; Richmond, Gorham, & McCroskey, 1987). Andersen, Andersen, and Jensen (1979) argued that smiling is an essential component in creating a sense of immediacy. Paralinguistic factors such as vocal variety and vocal expressiveness also affect perceptions of immediacy. For example, research suggests that how a lecture is delivered significantly influences students' perceptions of the instructor, course, and material (Weineke, 1981) and increased vocal variety and expression is an important component in immediacy (Andersen et al., 1979). Also, an instructor's use of kinesics, or body movement, has been found to positively influence perceptions of immediacy (Andersen, 1979; Andersen et al., 1979). The positive influence of an instructor's relaxed body position is consistent with Mehrabian's (1971) initial assertion that when instructors increase their use of gestures, it will be associated with more cooperation and liking from the students.

6.2. Nonverbal Immediacy and Learning Outcomes

A number of studies over the past three decades have shown a positive correlation between instructors' use of immediacy behaviors and affective learning (e.g., Andersen, 1978, 1979; Andersen, Norton, & Nussbaum, 1981; Kearney, Plax, Smith, & Sorensen, 1988; Kearney, Plax, & Wandt-Wesco, 1985; Witt & Wheeless, 2001). In a 2004 meta-analysis, Witt, Wheeless, and Allen found more than 80 studies that showed the effects of immediacy on learning. Specifically, a wealth of research has linked instructors' use of immediacy behaviors to enhanced affective learning among students. Affective learning refers to the attitudes and predispositions that students have toward the course, material, and instructor.

Nonverbal immediacy is also linked to students' motivation to learn the course material. Motivation is conceptualized as the desire for students to study and involve themselves in the learning process (Gorham & Millette, 1997). Christophel (1990) examined the relationship between student motivation and instructor immediacy in college courses and found that instructor immediacy influenced student motivation. As a result of increased motivation, student learning increased. In addition, Christophel noted that nonverbal immediacy was the greatest predictor of student learning. This is likely due to students perceiving an instructor who is high in immediacy as someone who is enthusiastic about the material and teaching and who cares about his or her students' learning and success.

Source credibility is the degree to which a person perceives a source to be believable (McCroskey, 1998); therefore, instructor credibility is the degree to which a student perceives an instructor to be believable. Researchers have found that nonverbal immediacy is positively associated with higher perceptions of credibility (Johnson & Miller, 2002; Teven & Hanson, 2004). Because students may initially not consider a class in Second Life to be as rigorous or serious as a face-to-face class, perceptions of instructor credibility could be crucial to making the class a success.

6.3. Social Presence, Immediacy, Technology, and Education

Short, Williams, and Christie's (1976) social presence theory, which seeks to explain how a person's saliency during an interaction influences the saliency of the interpersonal relationship, is grounded in the concept of immediacy. Schroeder (2002) suggested that virtual world participants' avatars are used to increase a sense of presence (or telepresence). Schroeder said presence is the feeling of "being there." Research conducted by Gerhard, Moore, and Hobbs (2004) indicates that presence positively influences computer-mediated communication, social interaction, and education; thus, presence is an essential component of effective interaction online. Studying members Active Worlds, another virtual environment, Peterson (2006) reported that avatars enhanced perceptions of presence.

Instructors' use of nonverbal immediacy behaviors will bridge the psychological distance between themselves and their students. However, to what extent do these behaviors function, if at all, in a virtual environment such as Second Life? Can avatars display immediacy? Certainly, the need for psychological closeness is as important – if not more so – in virtual learning environments as in face-to-face learning environments. Although there is an abundance of research on immediacy in traditional face-to-face educational environments, minimal research exists that examines immediacy in online classes. Some scholars argue that immediacy can only exist in face-to-face settings, but this assumption seems short-sighted particularly given the continued growth of computer-mediated communication and increased use of distance and online education. Furthermore, research has shown that immediacy and presence influence outcomes in other types of technology-assisted learning. Instructors' immediacy behaviors have been found to positively influence students' perceptions of presence in televised classrooms (Hackman & Walker, 1990) and their perceptions of the class and instructor in videotaped classes (Guerrero & Miller, 1998).

6.4. Online Instruction, Immediacy, and Educational Outcomes

Researchers have begun to explore the role of immediacy in online, versus traditional face-to-face, classroom environments. Although there is not an abundance of research in this area at this time, preliminary findings suggest that immediacy plays an equally – if not more – important role in online instruction (e.g., Gunawardena, 1995; McAlister, 2001, Baker, 2000). For example, use of nonverbal immediacy in distance learning environments helps reduce the psychological distance between instructors and students in these settings (e.g., McAlister, 2001). In addition, immediacy was the most significant predictor of both affective and cognitive student learning in a study of online classrooms (Baker, 2000). More recently, Witt and Schrodt (2006) and Schrodt and Witt (2006) reported that regardless of the amount of technology instructors used in the class, students perceived instructors more positively if they were highly immediate. Similarly, Gunawardena and Zittle (1997) found that social presence predicts student satisfaction in online learning environments.

Because computer-mediated communication is in some ways unique versus face-to-face communication, students' perceptions may be influenced by technology-specific factors or, at the very least, behaviors that take on more meaning online. For example, in Second Life, communication and avatar actions may influence perceptions of presence, or emoticons – text-based icons that form an image through the use of standard keyboard characters – may take the place of some face-to-face nonverbal immediacy behaviors. Research examining how online interactants adapt to their environment to compensate for reduced cues shows that people include affect displays (such as the use of emoticons) when communicating online to increase psychological closeness (e.g., Gunawardena & Zittle, 1997; Rice & Love, 1987). Additionally, Turkle (1995) posited that, when used online, these keystroke characters can substitute for the facial expressions and gestures used in face-to-face settings to enhance immediacy. Thus, she claimed, online communication fits somewhere in between face-to-face oral communication and written communication. Also, research has found that when students participate in synchronous, text-based CMC, it can enhance their motivation (Kitade, 2000). Motivation may function as an especially important factor for student success in Second Life because students need to be willing to work through the learning curve necessary to become comfortable interacting in-world.

6.5. Research Questions

Because instructor nonverbal immediacy is related to multiple student outcomes and because it is not yet known if perceptions of nonverbal immediacy can translate to Second Life, the following research questions are posed:

RQ1. To what extent is perceived nonverbal immediacy of instructors in Second Life related to student motivation?

RQ2. To what extent is perceived nonverbal immediacy of instructors in Second Life related to students' assessments of instructor credibility (competence, character, and caring)?

RQ3. To what extent is perceived nonverbal immediacy of instructors in Second Life related to students' affective learning (affect for Second Life course and affect for the instructor)?

6.6. Method

6.6.1. Sample and Procedure

This study was designed to examine the effect of perceived instructor nonverbal immediacy in Second Life on student outcomes. As part of a larger study on student and faculty perceptions of teaching and learning in Second Life, a convenience sample of 203 undergraduate students in various disciplines (social science, physical sciences, business, arts, and humanities) completed an online survey designed to assess their attitudes about Second Life coursework and the instructors who use Second Life; of these, 188 surveys were usable. Participants were solicited in classroom announcements and emails; a request was made for students to visit and voluntarily complete a website survey if they met the requirement for participation, which was to have participated in Second Life with an instructor who used voice chat (versus text chat) as either part of a class or for an entirely virtual class within the past year. The types of coursework students completed in Second Life varied.

Projects included completing ethnographies of Second Life populations, using Second Life locations to better understand literary periods, and exploring virtual museums. As recommended by Plax, Kearney, McCroskey, and Richmond (1986), participants were asked to think about their most recent (Second Life) course and the instructor of that course when completing the survey. The participants' ages ranged from 19 to 47 with a mean age of 20.86 (Median $= 21.24$; SD $= 5.49$). 121 of the participants were female (64.36%) and 67 were male (34.64%). Regarding class rank, 11.17% (n $= 21$) were first-year students, 17.02% (n $= 32$) were sophomores, 27.66% (n $= 52$) were juniors, 20.21% (n $= 38$) were seniors, and 23.94% (n $= 45$) identified themselves as graduate students.

6.6.2. Measurements

Nonverbal immediacy: A modified version of McCroskey, Richmond, Sallinen, Fayer, and Barraclough's (1995) Revised Nonverbal Immediacy Measure (RNIM) was used to measure students' perceptions of instructor immediacy. The RNIM is a 10-item, 5-point Likert scale (ranging from 0 = never to 4 = very often), which is based on Andersen's (1978, 1979) Generalized Immediacy Scale and measures students' perceptions of an instructor's immediacy behaviors. Andersen (1978) demonstrated that student reports of instructor immediacy behaviors are a valid way to gather and measure data. Items were reworded to reflect instructors' possible behaviors in Second Life; for example, the item "Moves around the classroom while teaching" was rewritten to read "Avatar moves around the virtual environment while teaching class." Also, one item was omitted because it does not reference a behavior that is likely to occur in Second Life (see Table 6.1 for modified scale). Prior research has shown the scale to be reliable (e.g., Kearney, 1994). In this research the alpha coefficient for modified 9-item perceived immediacy measure was .86 (M = 21.6, SD = 8.31).

Motivation: Christophel's (1990) State Motivation Scale was used to measure students' motivation for the class. The scale includes twelve 7-point semantic differential items that require participants to rate their sense of state motivation toward the instructor and the course. Past research has shown this scale to be reliable (e.g., Myers & Rocca, 2000). In this research, the alpha coefficient for state motivation was .94 (M = 41.78, SD = 18.44).

Credibility: McCroskey and Teven's (1999) Source Credibility Measure was used to assess the degree to which students perceived instructors' levels of credibility. The 18-item, 7-point bipolar scale measures three dimensions of credibility, each with 6 items; these dimensions are character, competence, and caring. Prior research

Table 6.1: Modified revised nonverbal immediacy scale.

Scale items
1. Avatar gestures while talking to the class[a]
2. Uses monotone/dull voice when talking to the class
3. Avatar faces class while talking[a]
4. Avatar smiles at the class while talking[a]
5. Avatar appears to have a rigid body position while talking to the class[a]
6. Avatar moves around the virtual environment while teaching class[a]
7. Avatar appears to have a relaxed body position while talking to the class[a]
8. Avatar frowns at the class while talking[a]
9. Uses a variety of vocal expressions when talking to the class

Note: Item in the original scale that was excluded in this study: "Looks at the board or notes while talking to the class."
[a]Items were reworded to reflect instructors' avatar behaviors in Second Life.

has shown the scale to be reliable (e.g., Teven & McCroskey, 1997). In this research the alpha coefficients for each dimension were as follows: character a = .90 (M = 36.22; SD = 7.91); competence a = .88 (M = 54.87; SD = 6.29); caring a = .89 (M = 28.05; SD = 8.87).

Affective learning: McCroskey's (1994) Affective Learning Measure was used to assess students' perceptions of their affective learning. This scale includes twenty-four 7-point bipolar items that measure three dimensions of affect: (1) affect toward the course content; (2) affect toward the instructor; and (3) affect toward the behaviors taught in the class. Mottet and Richmond (1998) argue that only two of these dimensions specifically evaluate affective learning. Thus, for this study, only 16 items were used – those that measured the dimensions of affect toward course and affect toward instructor. Prior research has shown the measurement for both dimensions is reliable (e.g., Mottet & Richmond, 1998), as well as the reliability of a single composite measure (Ellis, 2000). In this research, the reliability for affect toward course content was .88 (M = 39.73; SD = 11.48) and the reliability for affect toward the instructor was .93 (M = 41.91; SD = 13.64).

6.6.3. Results

Table 6.2 reports the mean, standard deviation, and alpha coefficient for each scale used in the study. Research question 1 asked, "To what extent is perceived nonverbal immediacy of instructors in Second Life related to student motivation?" Perceived nonverbal immediacy was positively related to student motivation ($r = .43$, $p < .05$). As student perceptions of instructors' nonverbal immediacy in Second Life increased, student motivation increased.

Research question 2 asked, "To what extent is perceived nonverbal immediacy of instructors in Second Life related to students' assessments of instructor credibility

Table 6.2: Means and standard deviations for variables.

Variable	Mean	SD	Alpha coefficient
Perceived nonverbal immediacy	21.6	8.31	.86
Motivation	41.78	18.44	.94
Credibility			
Character	36.22	7.91	.90
Competence	54.87	6.29	.88
Caring	28.05	8.87	.89
Affective learning			
Content	39.73	11.48	.88
Instructor	41.91	13.64	.93

(competence, character, and caring)?" Perceived nonverbal immediacy was positively related to student perceptions of all three dimensions of instructor credibility. Specifically, nonverbal immediacy in Second Life was positively related to student perceptions of instructors' competency ($r = .64$, $p < .05$). Also, nonverbal immediacy was positively related to student perceptions of instructors' caring ($r = .31$, $p < .05$). Finally, nonverbal immediacy was positively related to perceptions of instructors' character ($r = .24$; $p < .05$). Thus, as student perceptions of instructors' nonverbal immediacy in Second Life increased, student perceptions of both instructors' competence and caring increased.

Research question 3 asked, "To what extent is perceived nonverbal immediacy of instructors in Second Life related to student affective learning?" Perceived nonverbal immediacy was positively related to affect for the instructor ($r = .47$, $p < .05$). As student perceptions of instructors' nonverbal immediacy in Second Life increased, students' affect for the instructor increased. However, no significant relationship was found for nonverbal immediacy in Second Life and students' affect for the course ($r = .19$; $p = .21$).

6.6.4. Discussion

This study examined the extent to which student perceptions of instructor nonverbal immediacy in Second Life was related to students' motivation, perceptions of instructor credibility, and affective learning. In general, the results indicate that nonverbal immediacy is conveyed by instructors to students in Second Life and that nonverbal immediacy does positively influence some student outcomes. Of specific note is the finding that, similar to research results from studies of face-to-face classroom interactions, instructors in Second Life can and do portray nonverbal immediacy behaviors through the use of avatar gestures and paralinguistic cues when using voice chat.

The first research question asked "to what extent does perceived nonverbal immediacy of instructors in Second Life influence students' motivation levels?" The results showed a significant positive relationship between the two, with student perceptions of instructor nonverbal immediacy in Second Life accounting for 18% of the variance. These findings suggest that instructors' use of nonverbally immediate behaviors is important and that there is a benefit to engaging in these behaviors; however, motivation is not affected to a large degree by nonverbally immediate behaviors as evidenced by the somewhat low amount of variance explained by immediacy. This may be due to students' motivation being driven by different factors that were not explored in this study. Students are likely to be driven by grades, desire to graduate, applicability of course material to their current circumstances, etc., whereas instructors may strive to motivate students through such means as encouraging students to read and assigning research papers. In other words, although student motivation was assessed in this study, the specific factors that motivate students were not. It is also worth noting that students' reported level of motivation was not particularly high in this study – an average of 3.48 of a 7-point scale. A very likely influence on student motivation in Second Life classes is the rather steep learning curve that is necessary when first entering Second Life and learning to use and navigate the virtual terrain. Undoubtedly, instructors who use Second Life are familiar with the software and provide rather detailed direction to help students adapt. Nonetheless, depending on the student's level of comfort and expertise with computer technology, online and/or video gaming, and willingness to engage with the software, the tasks of creating and editing one's avatar, learning to move about in-world, mastering voice chat and gestures, and other basic yet essential Second Life skills may be extremely daunting to some students. This, paired with the requirement of completing other "standard" class assignments, may – for some students –simply be too much and, thus decrease their motivation for the course. Relatedly, students' experiences in-world may affect their motivation. When a student has positive experiences in Second Life, such as meeting and having pleasant conversations with other users and discovering new and interesting virtual places to visit, then motivation could increase. Conversely, if a student has negative experiences in Second Life, such as an encounter with a griefer, then motivation could decrease. In addition, perhaps students perceive Second Life coursework as warranting less motivation (e.g., it is "just" an online class, it is "a game") than face-to-face courses.

The second research question asked "to what extent does perceived nonverbal immediacy of instructors in Second Life influence students' perceptions of instructor credibility?" The results showed significant positive relationships between all three dimensions of credibility and students' perceptions of instructor nonverbal immediacy. The dimension of caring was found to have a significant positive relationship with student perceptions of nonverbal immediacy, accounting for 10% of the variance. This finding suggests, again, that it is beneficial for instructors to portray nonverbal immediacy behaviors in Second Life. Considering that some students are new to Second Life and may feel somewhat overwhelmed initially, students who perceive their instructors as caring about them may adapt or be more willing to adapt to the learning environment. The character dimension of instructor credibility was found to have a significant positive relationship with perceived nonverbal immediacy, accounting for 6% of the variance.

Perhaps most interesting, this research found that the relationship between perceived nonverbal immediacy and instructor competence accounted for 41% of the variance and the relationship between perceived nonverbal immediacy and instructor caring accounting for 10% of the variance. This suggests that, in general, instructors' use of avatar gestures and paralinguistic cues in Second Life that portray nonverbal immediacy function similarly to instructors' nonverbal immediacy in traditional face-to-face classrooms (Johnson & Miller, 2002; Teven & Hanson, 2004). The amount of variance explained by the relationship between nonverbal immediacy and instructor competence is particularly interesting in the light of research that found highly immediate instructors are able to offset certain negative effects of technology use (Witt & Schrodt, 2006). Also, student perceptions of instructor competency in Second Life may likely be tied to how competent students perceive instructors' use of the technology. Because the software and in-world skills are such a necessary component to effective Second Life interaction, students may rate instructor competency largely based on how savvy the instructors are (or appear to be) in-world. This would suggest that, to some extent, an instructor's level of competency could be dependent on not only her or his own Second Life knowledge and skills, but also unexpected technological glitches (i.e., university computers not updated with the latest software when class begins, severe lag in-world, a bookmarked location in-world suddenly disappearing, etc.). It is also possible that some students may equate an instructor's use of Second Life as a function of laziness or inability to effectively teach a face-to-face class. This does not appear to be the case in this study as students rated instructor competency, on average, as 4.57 of a 7-point scale.

The third research question asked "to what extent does perceived nonverbal immediacy of instructors in Second Life influence student affective learning?" The results showed a significant positive relationship between perceived nonverbal immediacy and students' affect for the instructor; this relationship accounts for 22% of the variance. However, for perceived nonverbal immediacy and students' affect for the course, no significant relationship was found. This is consistent with the abundance of past research on instructor nonverbal immediacy and student affect for instructor in face-to-face courses (see Witt et al., 2004 for overview); thus, it appears that nonverbal immediacy of instructors' avatars functions similarly to instructors' face-to-face nonverbal immediacy. Of equal interest is the finding that student affect for the course was not related to instructor nonverbal immediacy because this is inconsistent with prior research that has shown a strong link between the two (see Witt et al., 2004 for overview). One explanation for this departure may be the technology-specific issues and Second Life learning curve noted above. That is, even though students may perceive their instructors as relatively immediate, this immediacy may not be enough to counteract the frustration some students may feel with a course in Second Life, particularly if they are new to virtual environments. This explanation is consistent with the research by Turman and Schrodt (2005) who state students prefer courses in which instructors make use of some technology but not use it to replace the traditional course.

For instructors wishing to bolster their own nonverbal immediate behaviors while teaching in Second Life, the recommendations for instructors teaching in Second Life are: (a) vocal expressiveness (using a good deal of vocal variety versus speaking in a monotone voice), (b) using one's avatar to gesture and smile (which requires the use of script in Second Life), (c) moving the avatar around the (virtual) location where the class is taking place (not standing in one location for the entire class period), (d) and positioning the avatar so that it is facing the students (giving the appearance of looking at the students, versus turning one's back on them). It is important to remember that, in world, the instructor's avatar represents that instructor and, as such, should mimic immediacy behaviors many instructors already use when teaching their face-to-face courses.

6.7. Limitations and Future Research

This study sought to provide a preliminary investigation of instructors' nonverbal immediacy when teaching in Second Life. The results suggest that nonverbal immediacy in Second Life functions similarly to immediacy in face-to-face contexts, yet also suggests other factors may mediate the effect of immediacy in Second Life. One limitation of the current study was the use of a nonrandom convenience sample of students who had participated in Second Life coursework. The participants who chose to complete the survey may have been those students who had a particularly positive – or negative – experience with the course content, instructor, or with Second Life itself. That is, self-selection might have been an issue.

Another potential limitation is the self-report measurement of nonverbal immediacy in this study. However, an experimental design – although possible – could prove to be difficult if data for students who took an entire semester-long course were desired.

Another possible limitation of this research is related to the conceptual and operational definitions of nonverbal immediacy used in this research. First, students may not hold the same expectations for instructor nonverbal immediacy in Second Life as they do in traditional face-to-face classes. In distance learning, research has shown that students expected less from their instructors in terms of nonverbal immediacy (Freitas, Myers, & Avtgis, 1998; Witt & Wheeless, 2001). Thus, nonverbal immediacy may need to be conceptually tweaked for use in studies of virtual environments. Second, it is highly likely that instructors show nonverbal immediacy in Second Life through some unique technology-specific or adaptive ways that are not measured by the RNIM. For example, instructors may portray immediacy in Second Life by sending a student an invitation to be friends, giving the student a free object, or offering to teleport a student to a location.

A final limitation was that this research focused only on students who had participated in Second Life classes in which voice chat was used. Because there may be instructors who prefer to use text chat or who choose to do so because students can keep a transcript of the class session, a comparison of immediacy in text chat versus voice chat classes may be useful. However, the focus on voice chat was due to the richer communication afforded by voice versus text-only chat.

Future research should also examine the effect of nonverbal immediacy on cognitive learning, which was not investigated in this study because some students were currently enrolled in the relevant course and did not yet have a final grade (which is commonly used to assess cognitive learning in related research).

Finally, educators would benefit from examining nonverbal immediacy in Second Life compared to face-to-face classrooms to examine what, if any, differences exist in student perceptions of immediacy in these two different contexts. Overall, the research findings in this study suggest that nonverbal immediacy is important for instructors who are currently teaching, or are planning to teach, in Second Life.

References

Andersen, J. F. (1978). *The relationship between teacher immediacy and teaching effectiveness.* Unpublished doctoral dissertation, West Virginia University, Morgantown, WV.

Andersen, J. F. (1979). Teacher immediacy as a predictor of teaching effectiveness. In: D. Nimmo (Ed.), *Communication yearbook* (Vol. 3, pp. 543–559). New Brunswick, NJ: Transaction.

Andersen, J. F., Andersen, P. A., & Jensen, A. D. (1979). The measurement of immediacy. *Journal of Applied Communication Research, 7,* 153–180.

Andersen, J. F., Norton, R. W., & Nussbaum, J. F. (1981). Three investigations exploring the relationships between perceived teacher communication behaviors and student learning. *Communication Education, 30,* 377–392.

Baker, J. (2000). *The effects of instructor immediacy and student cohesiveness on affective and cognitive learning in the online classroom.* Unpublished doctoral dissertation, Regent University.

Christophel, D. M. (1990). The relationships among teacher immediacy behaviors, student motivation, and learning. *Communication Education, 39,* 323–340.

Ellis, K. (2000). Perceived teacher confirmation: The development and validation of an instrument and two studies of the relationship to cognitive and affective learning. *Human Communication Research, 26*(2), 264–292.

Freitas, F. A., Myers, S. A., & Avtgis, T. A. (1998). Student perceptions of instructor immediacy in conventional and distributed learning classrooms. *Communication Education, 42*(4), 366–372.

Gerhard, M., Moore, D., & Hobbs, D. (2004). Embodiment and copresence in collaborative interfaces. *Human-Computer Studies, 61*(4), 453–480.

Gorham, J. (1988). The relationship between verbal teaching immediacy behaviors and student learning. *Communication Education, 17,* 40–53.

Gorham, J., & Millette, D. (1997). A comparative analysis of teacher and student perceptions of sources of motivation and demotivation in college classes. *Communication Education, 46,* 245–261.

Guerrero, L. K., & Miller, T. (1998). Associations between nonverbal behaviors and initial impressions of instructor competence and course content in videotaped distance education courses. *Communication Education, 47,* 30–42.

Gunawardena, C. N. (1995). Social presence theory and implications for interaction and collaborative learning in computer conferences. *International Journal of Educational Telecommunications, 1*(2/3), 147–166.

Gunawardena, C. N., & Zittle, F. J. (1997). Social presence as a predictor of satisfaction within a computer-mediated conferencing environment. *The American Journal of Distance Education, 11*(3), 8–26.

Hackman, M. Z., & Walker, K. B. (1990). Instructional communication in the televised classroom: The effects of system design and teacher immediacy on student learning and satisfaction. *Communication Education, 39,* 196–206.

Horton, L. A. (1997). *Face-to-face and computer-mediated learning: Differences in interactions, learning, and course satisfaction in a graduate class.* Doctoral dissertation, University of South Dakota, Vermillion, 2000.

Hoyt, B. R., Thomas-Maddox, C., & Evans, D. C. (2001). Addressing immediacy issues in online learning. *WebNet Journal, 3*(2), 14.

Johnson, S. D., & Miller, A. N. (2002). A cross-cultural study of immediacy, credibility, and learning in the U.S. and Kenya. *Communication Education, 50,* 280–292.

Kearney, P. (1994). Affective learning. In: R. B. Rubin, P. Palmgreen & H. E. Sypher (Eds), *Communication research measures: A sourcebook* (pp. 81–85). New York: Guilford Press.

Kearney, P., Plax, T. G., Smith, V. R., & Sorensen, G. (1988). Effects of teacher immediacy and strategy type on college student resistance to on-task demands. *Communication Education, 37,* 54–67.

Kearney, P., Plax, T. G., & Wandt-Wesco, N. J. (1985). Teacher immediacy for affective learning in divergent college classes. *Communication Quarterly, 33,* 61–74.

Kelley, D. H., & Gorham, J. (1988). Effects of immediacy on recall of information. *Communication Education, 37,* 198–207.

Kitade, K. (2000). L2 learners' discourse and SLA theories in CMC: Collaborative interaction in Internet chat. *Computer Assisted Language Learning, 13*(2), 143–166.

McAlister, G. (2001). *Computer-mediated immediacy: A new construct in teacher-student communication for computer-mediated distance education.* Unpublished doctoral dissertation. Regent University, Virginia Beach, VA.

McCroskey, J. C. (1994). Assessment of affect toward communication and affect toward instruction in communication. In: S. Morreale, M. Brooks, R. Berko & C. Cooke (Eds), *1994 SCA summer conference proceedings and prepared remarks* (pp. 55–71). Annandale, VA: Speech Communication Association.

McCroskey, J. C. (1998). *An introduction to communication in the classroom* (2nd ed). Acton, MA: Tapestry Press.

McCroskey, J. C., Richmond, V. P., Sallinen, A., Fayer, J. M., & Barraclough, R. A. (1995). A cross-cultural and multi-behavioral analysis of the relationship between nonverbal immediacy and teacher evaluation. *Communication Education, 44,* 282–291.

McCroskey, J. C., & Teven, J. J. (1999). Goodwill: A re-examination of the construct and its measurement. *Communication Monographs, 66,* 90–103.

Mehrabian, A. (1969). Some referents and measures of nonverbal behavior. *Behavioral Research Methods and Instrumentation, 1,* 213–217.

Mehrabian, A. (1971). *Silent messages.* Belmont, CA: Wadsworth Publishing Company.

Mottet, T. P., & Richmond, V. P. (1998). Newer is not necessarily better: A reexamination of affective learning measurement. *Communication Research Reports, 15,* 370–378.

Myers, S. A., & Rocca, K. A. (2000). Students' state motivation and instructors' use of verbally aggressive messages. *Psychological Reports, 87,* 291–294.

Peterson, M. (2006). Learner interaction management in an avatar and chat-based virtual world. *Computer Assisted Language Learning, 19,* 79–103.

Plax, T. G., Kearney, P., McCroskey, J. C., & Richmond, V. P. (1986). Power in the classroom VI: Verbal control strategies, nonverbal immediacy and affective learning. *Communication Education, 35,* 43–55.

Rice, R. E., & Love, G. (1987). Electronic emotion: Socioemotional content in a computer mediated communication network. *Communication Research, 14,* 85–108.

Richmond, V. P., Gorham, J. S., & McCroskey, J. C. (1987). The relationship between selected immediacy behaviors and cognitive learning. In: M. L. McLaughlin (Ed.), *Communication yearbook 10* (pp. 574–590). Newbury Park, CA: Sage.

Schrodt, P., & Witt, P. L. (2006). Students' attributions of instructor credibility as a function of students' expectations of instructional technology use and nonverbal immediacy. *Communication Education, 55,* 1–20.

Schroeder, R. (2002). Social interaction in virtual environments: Key issues, common themes, and a framework for research. In: R. Schroeder (Ed.), *The social life of avatars: Presence and interaction in shared virtual environments* (pp. 1–16). London: Springer.

Short, J., Williams, E., & Christie, B. (1976). *The social psychology of telecommunications.* London: Wiley.

Teven, J. J., & Hanson, T. L. (2004). The impact of teacher immediacy and perceived caring on teacher competence and trustworthiness. *Communication Quarterly, 52*, 39–53.

Teven, J. J., & McCroskey, J. C. (1997). The relationship of perceived teacher caring with student learning and teacher evaluation. *Communication Education, 46*, 1–9.

Thomas, C. E., Richmond, V. P., & McCroskey, J. C. (1994). The association between immediacy and socio-communicative style. *Communication Research Reports, 11*, 107–115.

Turkle, S. (1995). *Life on the screen: Identity in the age of the Internet.* New York: Simon and Schuster.

Turman, P. D., & Schrodt, P. (2005). The influence of instructional technology use on students' affect: Do course designs and biological sex make a difference? *Communication Studies, 56*, 109–129.

Weineke, C. (1981). The first lecture: Implications for students who are new to the university. *Studies in Higher Education, 6*, 85–89.

Witt, P., & Schrodt, P. (2006). The influence of instructional technology use and teacher immediacy on student affect for teacher and course. *Communication Reports, 19*(1), 1–15.

Witt, P. L., & Wheeless, L. R. (2001). An experimental study of teachers' verbal and nonverbal immediacy and students' affective and cognitive learning. *Communication Education, 50*, 327–342.

Witt, P. L., Wheeless, L. R., & Allen, M. (2004). A meta-analytical review of the relationship between teacher immediacy and student learning. *Communication Monographs, 71*, 184–207.

Author Biography

Traci L. Anderson's (PhD, University of Oklahoma) research focuses on computer-mediated interpersonal communication, specifically, the relationships among uncertainty, person-perceptions, and impression management and how these factors influence the development and maintenance of online social and personal relationships. She has taught courses in the area of computer-mediated communication on There.com and Second Life. Dr. Anderson's research has appeared in *Communication Research Reports, Communication Studies, Cyber-Psychology and Behavior,* and *Computers in Human Interaction.*

Chapter 7

Cross-World Branding – One World is Not Enough

Nina Belei, Gwen Noteborn and Ko de Ruyter

7.1. Introduction

Integrating virtual worlds into academic education bridges the apparent gap between theory and practice by providing opportunities for enriching the student experience, providing authentic context and activities for experimental learning, as well as for simulation and role play. To provide students with a playground for real business experience, we decided to integrate Second Life into an undergraduate brand management course. The course is positioned in the marketing major of an International Business program and is designed to provide students with in-depth knowledge about various branding concepts as well as several important aspects of marketing communication. With the Second Life project, we sought to exemplify the importance of letting students experience first-hand the practical consequences of theoretically driven efforts and activities (Picture 7.1).

This chapter analyzes the prospects and perils of using Second Life as an educational tool by drawing on the insights and feedback provided by students during and after the course. Analyzing data collected in a questionnaire at the end of the course adds value to both academics and practitioners, as experiences gained will be translated into concrete recommendations for future projects similar in content and scope.

7.2. Marketing Theory in Traditional Academic Curricula

Aimed at providing knowledge to contemporary businesses in various industries, marketing education draws upon economic principles, psychological concepts, and

Higher Education in Virtual Worlds
Copyright © 2009 by Emerald Group Publishing Limited
All rights of reproduction in any form reserved
ISBN: 978-1-84950-609-0

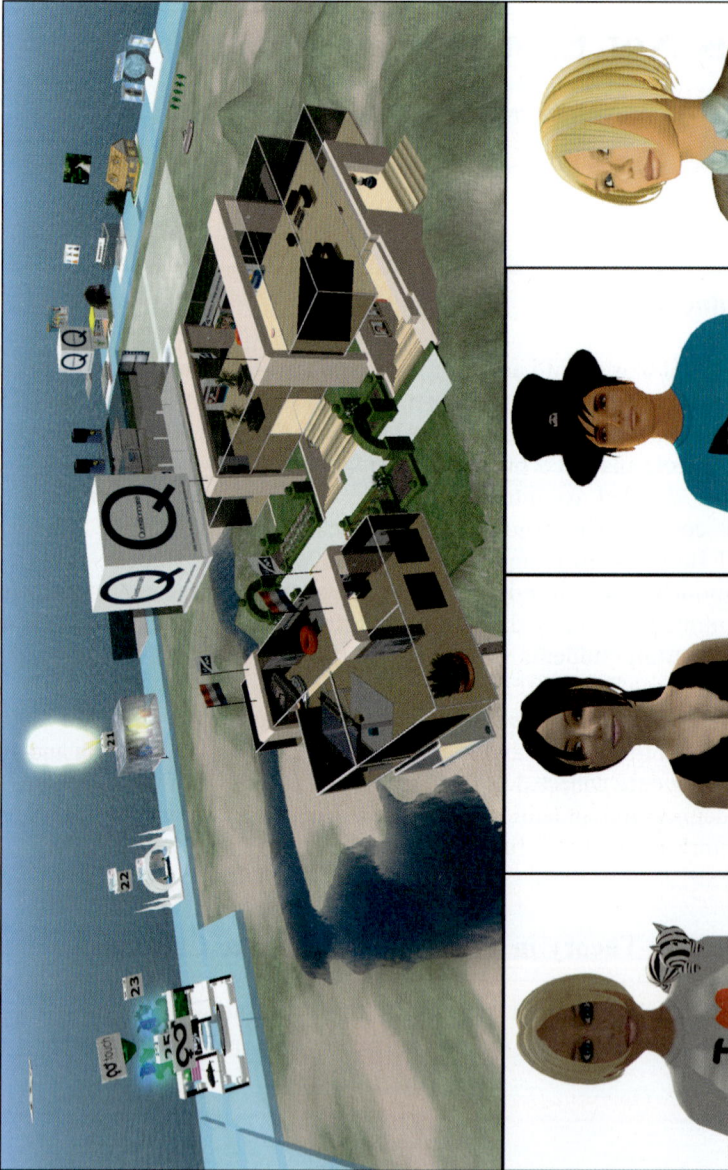

Picture 7.1: Maastricht University Campus Island in Second Life

sociological and cultural insights for building a strong and valuable theoretical foundation. Although marketing can be considered an applied discipline, the role of theory in the decision-making processes at an individual or organizational level must not be underestimated. The important cross-disciplinary function marketing theory plays is best illustrated by examining some principles and mechanisms related to managing brands.

The management of one of a company's most valuable assets – its brand – is very prominent in marketing practice and themes. Since products are increasingly becoming more standardized, the only difference between them is their brand label. Strong brands simplify consumer decision-making, serve as a signal of quality, and reduce risks associated with product purchases (Keller, Aperia, & Georgson, 2008). Thus, to excel in markets characterized by fierce competition and high consumer expectations, it is imperative to have an outstanding branding strategy and a strong marketing orientation rooted in a firm's core business principles.

But brands are no manna from heaven. It takes serious effort to build, maintain, and exploit a brand, and a thorough understanding of the underlying mechanisms, marketing models, and branding tools is crucial. For example, without a proper understanding of the fundamental linkages between brand management and consumer behavior, the plan to create a strong and successful brand will perish from the outset.

The often diverse needs and wants of groups of consumers and different organizations must be satisfied by the companies targeting them, for which sound theoretical knowledge about how people think and create meaning of their environment is essential.

In terms of input, students are usually provided with a selection of relevant book chapters and academic articles that they are required to study. During regular class meetings, the material is discussed and real-life examples are used to illustrate the theoretical concepts. To further deepen their knowledge, and to increase the level of practical relevance, students are often asked to write a paper on a (hypothetical) brand-related problem in which they can "apply" their branding skills. A prominent example is to let students write an Integrated Marketing Communication plan (IMC plan) for a particular brand. Although an IMC plan is a suitable means for students to demonstrate that they have studied the key branding concepts and principles discussed in class, it has several limitations.

As the name suggests, an IMC plan focuses on the marketing tools suitable to communicate the brand value to its target group. It ignores, however, all the concepts related to the actual brand-building process. Thus, the task to write an IMC plan assumes that a brand is already successfully developed, which leaves out all the steps related to effective brand creation. It is the steps of brand-building that are inherently difficult to implement. Consequently, the application of theoretical knowledge by means of an IMC plan does not allow any feasibility check or real-life experience with the practical implications of theoretical strategies. Whether students' communication strategies would work in reality remains unknown as the emphasis of academic attention is on input rather than process and output. The traditional course design points at several challenges faculties face when planning and coordinating marketing courses. Two of them are outlined below:

First, the ability of textbooks to illustrate the dynamic nature of external factors[1] influencing a theoretical principle is rather limited. Without ever experiencing the challenges real (business) life imposes on marketing managers, students will be completely unprepared for the many situations real-life presents in which a straightforward application of a theoretical concept simply does not work.

Second, students would have to engage in activities that provide them with practical knowledge and skills to bridge this gap between theory and practice. Ideally, practical knowledge and skills are gained by means of "real-life experiences," for example, by doing an internship in a marketing department of a firm or by actually being responsible for the sales of a branded product. The problem, though, is that those options are time consuming and in practice do not always provide students with the practical insights they were hoping to gain. Besides that, by engaging in these kinds of activities, students are most likely to end up with a study delay, a situation often backfiring on them when applying for a job.

Returning to the previous example of teaching brand management, the opportunity of real-life experiences related to strategic branding decisions would be invaluable to students. Students following a brand management course should be able to experience first-hand the effects that their developed branding strategies produce. Consequently, there is a strong need to provide students with a learning environment stimulating authentic context and activities for experimental learning.

7.3. Role of Simulations in Contemporary Academic Curricula

A very promising approach to narrow the gap between theory and practice relates to the usage of simulations in class. Milligan (1998) argued that knowing relevant theory is not enough if it cannot be put into practice. Other authors (e.g., Frederiksen, 1984; Tillema, Kessels, & Meijers, 2000; Biggs, 1996) stress that the ultimate goal of education is to enable the practical application of the information acquired. Simulation or role play can play an important role in achieving this ultimate goal. Simulation relies on the principles of behavior modeling for influencing performance (Murthy, Challagalla, Vincent, & Shervani, 2008). Bolt, Killough, and Koh (2001) find that behavior modeling is superior to lecture-based training for complex tasks, and Murthy et al. (2008) provide evidence that behavior modeling is effective in teaching a wide range of skills and competences. Typically, simulation is used to provide students with "real-life" experience by taking advantage of the ability of simulation to mimic reality. The so-called existence of realistic context has been found to lead to more elaborate processing enabling access to declarative and procedural knowledge. This, in turn, results in superior transfer of skills and behaviors

---

1. External factors refer, for example, to the unpredictability of competition and the volatility of consumer responses to marketing stimuli

(Anderson, 1995; Yi & Davis, 2003). Furthermore, the presence of built-in feedback has been shown to accelerate the learning process by means of vicarious learning (Murthy et al., 2008). Providing students with feedback in simulation games facilitates cognitive organization and knowledge retention and establishes connections to previously learned skills and competences (Murthy et al., 2008). Besides that, simulation offers students a paced learning experience: it provides learners with the opportunity to go through the learning process at their own pace. Consequently, simulations seem to be a promising and effective means to bridge the gap between theory and practice and should therefore be integrated into academic curricula.

7.4. Simulating Brand Management

How brands can be built and managed is the primary topic of the course "Brand Management." Third-year bachelor students participating in this course study what a brand is, which elements constitute a brand, and which (strategic) aspects need to be considered in the actual management of brands. For building brands, marketing communication (e.g., advertising) is perhaps the most important instrument and therefore deserves explicit attention in a course on branding. Marketing communication seeks to influence consumer behavior; hence, understanding the basic aspects of that topic is important for thoroughly studying brand management. Although students tend to believe that advertising is a synonym for marketing communication, it is only one of the communication opportunities companies have at their disposal. Increasingly, attention is shifting from pure advertising to holistic marketing communication, and this course reflects this trend by discussing the "Integrated Marketing Communication Model" as the linking pin to consumer behavior.

Considering the different theoretical themes in the course "Brand Management," and taking into account the previous discussion on the importance of explicitly linking branding theory to practice, the main objective of this course is to provide students with a solid theoretical framework by means of extensive in-class discussions of the learning material, while simultaneously offering a learning environment stimulating rich experiences and realistic context. Thus, students taking this course should end up having a solid knowledge on the various brand management principles, practices, and processes in considerable breadth and depth. Moreover, they should be able to apply this knowledge in a context mimicking reality in the best possible way to experience what it means to being responsible for a brand in its totality.

The latter was achieved by integrating Second Life into the course, which was expected to make learning more interactive and interesting. Allowing students to implement a branding strategy within a virtual 3D platform such as Second Life allows the simulation of a complete branding experience through role play. The avatar-based virtual world education of Second Life is highly interactive, while providing a richer, more effective, and more enjoyable experience compared to written assignments. Jarmon, Traphagan, and Mayrath (2009) indicate strong experiential learning benefits from using Second Life to facilitate graduate students' learning of interdisciplinary communication strategies.

Other advantages of employing Second Life as an educational support tool for a branding course are the representation of real-life companies in the virtual community, which is especially interesting for marketing students. The presence of other firms and shops in Second Life provides students with insights into the branding opportunities existing in a virtual world. Furthermore, the online environment of Second Life holds the potential of offering students the unique experience of a full-scale consumption incident, including the selection of the brand of interest, the actual brand purchase, the usage of the branded product, and finally the chats with friends about this special consumption experience. Hence, although emphasis is placed on providing students with the basic concepts and principles of branding and IMC, an essential course goal regarded the active application of the knowledge students gained during the semester.

7.5. The Second Life Branding Project

What is a better way for students to test their skills in branding than to let them brand, promote, and sell their self-branded products? The idea of the Second Life branding project was that teams of four to five students would develop a branding strategy for an existing product from the personal care category, which was to be promoted and sold in Second Life. Teams could choose between three different products: shampoo, deodorant, and shower gel. The fact that the product was "real" implied that it had certain attributes that enabled it to be used – at least hypothetically – in the real world by real people. Students were asked to brand the product they selected and to design a proper marketing communication strategy taking into account the fact that the hypothetical brand had to be promoted first and foremost in the context of Second Life. Students were allowed, to cross the border between Second Life and the real world to support their campaign with additional/complementary advertising. Thus, it was important for them to keep in mind that each avatar was representing a real person and that the characteristics, wants, and needs of those persons defined the target group.

It was deemed helpful for students to think of the project in such a way that they were representing a company in the real world deciding to make use of a new communication or even distribution channel – Second Life – to take advantage of the fact that the target group is well represented there. So, instead of merely using a medium such as the Internet to promote a brand, students were asked to take the marketing of the brand into a new "world" in which different situational factors shaped the boundary conditions for their strategy.

Students soon realized that some "traditional" marketing tools were very difficult to implement in Second Life because of the virtual character of the marketplace. On the other hand more "fancy" marketing methods became feasible, and students created virtual experiences with the products for their customers. Students had to be creative in achieving their goal of selling their product to their target group while

Picture 7.2: Student avatar promoting her product

keeping a close eye on the core elements of a theoretically sound branding strategy, as this was what students had to defend in their final presentation (Picture 7.2).

The success of the branding strategies was measured in terms of how many of a branded product teams had sold at the end. Each individual student received an amount of Second Life money (Linden Dollars), which he/she had to spend on the brands created by the other student teams. That is, all teams were sellers, but every student was also a buyer. To ensure fair competition, students were neither allowed to spend the money on their own brands, nor outside the community.

Students were given six weeks to work on their projects while simultaneously following regular class meetings. During this period, students were provided with additional guidelines, deadlines, manuals, and small assignments to improve their Second Life skills. For example, to relieve the technical burden on students, they were all provided with 150 Linden Dollars (41 Euro cents) for "building" purposes. The building money was intended for students to buy items needed for their stores that were too complex to build or script themselves. The money was also used to upload images or textures for their individual branding activities. All teams were free to use this money as they wanted; all money left, though, had to be paid back to the Maastricht University Donation Box before a predefined deadline.

Seeking to create value for their target market (the entire student group in this course; $N = 160$), students' brand management creativity was only limited by their own imagination. At the end of the six-week period, teams were required to launch their hypothetical brand and make their products available in Second Life for the others to purchase it.

At this stage of the project, the actual shopping experiment started. Students began to spend their personal Linden Dollars on the brands offered by their competitors. It was possible to shop for products on two consecutive days. One day after the shopping experiment, information was collected from each team regarding the number of products sold and dollars earned with the selling of their brand.

It is important to note that the financial success per se did not have an impact on the final grade for this project; the grading was based on the quality, argumentation, and creativity of student's branding strategy, all of which they were able to demonstrate in the final presentation at the end of the course.

Even though the money students made with selling their brands was not taken into account for grading purposes, the team that was able to acquire the most money was rewarded with a basket of personal care products donated by Henkel.[2] At the end of the shopping experiment, a list with the individual rankings of each team in terms of how much money had been made was published on the course site, indicating to students how well they did with their branding activities relative to their competitors.

In their final presentations, students had to be able to justify all branding action taken by supporting their decisions with high-standard academic literature. Not only the study material was used to provide tutors[3] with a sound argument; the fact that their branding efforts were also evaluated by their fellow students was used actively by teams to reflect on each strategy's effectiveness and thus had a double learning effect: on the one hand, the teams benefited by gaining feedback on their marketing actions, which in essence revealed whether a strategy had worked, whereas on the other hand, each individual student benefited by providing the feedback, as they had to have a critical look at the branding efforts of their colleagues for which it was essential to take the brand management literature into account.

Overall, students indicated at the end of their presentations that they perceived this way of grading the project as fair, as it did not penalize those student teams with less computer-based experience or technical savvy. This is because the conceptual aspects of branding instead of the technical acquisitions achieved in Second Life were put at the core of the evaluation.

7.6. Technical Support

For students to be able to work in Second Life, all technical aspects were introduced to them in an interactive lecture given by an expert in Second Life and Education

---

2. Henkel is a globally operating company covering the following business sectors: Laundry and home care, cosmetics and toiletries, and adhesive technologies.
3. "Tutor" refers to an academic in charge of the tutorial sessions for students. For more information see http://www.maastrichtuniversity.nl/web/Main/Education/EducationalProfile/ProblemBasedLearning.htm

from the company Eduverse[4] at the beginning of the course. In this two-hour lecture, each student team entered Second Life and was granted access to the Maastricht University Campus Island, which was open for students participating in this course only. Here, the instructor taught them the basics of building by means of small assignments. Moreover, a Second Life section was made available on the course website in which students could find all information relevant for this project. All questions they encountered during the process could be sent to a specially created email address and were dealt with by two faculty members with Second Life expertise. These two faculty members also provided extensive "in-world support" for students by being present in Second Life with their avatars. This made the project very realistic and resulted in a very positive relationship between tutors and students. Finally, students had access to technical support in two computer rooms on several days for the duration of the course.

7.7. Deliverables

Despite the apparent success of the project, which could be observed both in the course evaluations and students' enthusiasm with the project, one of the core questions related to evaluating its effectiveness was the following: Did the Second Life project really facilitate the application of student's branding knowledge?

To answer this fundamental question, an online questionnaire was developed in which students were asked to reflect in nine open-ended questions on their specific individual experiences with Second Life as an educational tool. Moreover, they were required to answer a set of 10 closed questions designed to get a general overview of the effectiveness of using Second Life for the course from a student perspective. Areas that were addressed related to students' learning experiences, their perceptions of the effectiveness of using Second Life in this particular course and in general, as well as their thoughts regarding future opportunities and potential constraints in using Second Life as an educational support tool. Students were granted access to the questionnaire through a hyperlink placed in Second Life at the end of the shopping experiment.

In the following sections, we outline some of the key insights regarding the theoretical and practical value experienced with the Second Life branding project. Findings of the online survey will be integrated accordingly, which will result in an assessment of the project's educational value.

7.8. Quantitative Analysis

A first analysis of the quantitative data collected at the end of the course ($N = 139$) yielded a very positive picture about the usability of Second Life in higher education.

---

4. The Eduverse foundation is a company that stimulates virtual education (www.eduverse.org).

In relation to our core question of whether Second Life facilitated the application of student's branding knowledge, we asked students in one statement to indicate their perceptions of Second Life as a nice way to apply the knowledge gained during this course. 72.7 percent agreed that indeed Second Life was perceived to be appropriate to translate knowledge into practice The results of a one-sample t-test ($M = 5.02$; $p < 0.001$; 7-point Likert scale with $1 =$ totally disagree and $7 =$ totally agree) support this finding. Likewise, it was found that 81 percent of the students would rather do the Second Life project than a written report ($M = 5.67$; $p < 0.01$; 7-point Likert scale with $1 =$ totally disagree and $7 =$ totally agree), as the related workload was perceived to be fair ($M = 4.95$; $p < 0.01$; 7-point Likert scale with $1 =$ totally disagree and $7 =$ totally agree) and students seemed to enjoy working on the Second Life project ($M = 5.19$; $p < 0.01$; 7-point Likert scale with $1 =$ totally disagree and $7 =$ totally agree). Interestingly, although we found that 59.1 percent of the students were unlikely use Second Life again in the future privately ($M = 3.14$; $p < 0.01$; 7-point Likert scale with $1 =$ totally disagree and $7 =$ totally agree), 72.7 percent of the students agreed that they would recommend the project again for next year's course ($M = 5.20$; $p < 0.01$; 7-point Likert scale with $1 =$ totally disagree and $7 =$ totally agree).

7.9.   Qualitative Analysis

7.9.1.   The Shopping Experiment

The shopping experiment was designed to provide student teams with the opportunity to launch their individual brands. During the shopping experiment, the teams were confronted with the results of their branding efforts, which were reflected in the amount of products sold and the written evaluations they received from their competitors.

In contrast to a traditional IMC plan, here students received clear and unveiled feedback about whether their branding strategies had been effective. This peer feedback, which is central to behavior modeling training, served as a correctional function helping to reduce the discrepancies between ideal branding strategies and the individual students' actions (Davis & Yi, 2004; Decker & Nathan, 1985). In addition, the detailed feedback helped students to develop procedural knowledge on the topic, to gain a complex cognitive understanding of the task, and to strengthen their cognitive organization and retention (Kraiger, Ford, & Salas, 1993; Robertson, 1990; Simon, Grover, Teng, & Whitcomb, 1996).

To buy or not to buy was the essential question driving student's shopping behavior. For the duration of the shopping experiment, every student acted as an individual buyer and was expected to spend the entire amount of Linden Dollars he/she was provided with. Each student carefully selected those brands for purchase which he/she considered to be most attractive. Students later said that the brand selection process was heavily influenced not only by the physical appearance of the virtual shops, but especially by the various marketing campaigns they have been confronted with during the previous weeks:

> *This brand got my attention from the beginning since I was looking around a bit in second life while starting to build on our own platform. I was really surprised by the changing-colors floor! When I received a message about a party in second life I knew directly that it was of the group with that floor I had previously seen. I also saw a flyer in my tutorial room. I was amazed by how flashy and really good designed this flyer was! I found the idea of glowing hair very creative and I think that the design in second life and the design of the flyer was one of the best. It really attracted me.* (Simone, Dutch student)

> *This team had the best online advertising of all. They made two youtube videos and I loved them; I almost thought the 'day in the life of a student' video was made by a pro; great commitment, they clearly put a lot of effort into this and deserve to be rewarded for it.* (Christian, German student)

The fact the students were asked to provide clear arguments to explain why they purchased a certain product allowed the selling teams to truly understand which aspects of their branding efforts turned out to be the driving forces for product sales. Those teams that barely sold any products were provided with insightful feedback as to why their branding efforts had not been successful:

> *I did intentionally not purchase from group 15 because I found the whole concept, idea, and advertising not appealing. To be honest, I perceived the email-flood they spread as really annoying.* (Moritz, German student)

> *I did not buy from this store, because the name DRAMA, in my opinion, conveys the image that your hair becomes a drama after washing it.* (Jeroen, Dutch student)

The shopping experiment allowed students to really experience the effects of their branding and marketing campaigns and the detailed "peer-to-peer" evaluations enabled students to fully understand why some concepts that work perfectly in theory are sometimes difficult to execute in "real-life" (Picture 7.3).

7.9.2. *Experiencing Competitive Intensity*

One of the core benefits of using Second Life for executing branding strategies was the fact that students were constantly confronted with the real-life issues a brand manager faces on an everyday basis.

Already in the second week of the course, students were faced with the brutal logic of competition. As noted earlier, at the very beginning of the course, teams were

Picture 7.3: Student store: NITELITE, buy your glow-in-the-dark shampoo!

asked to select one of three products (a shampoo, a deodorant, or a shower gel). Ensuring an equal distribution of product types, the following situation emerged:
    33 student teams in total

- 11 teams working on a branding strategy for a shampoo
- 11 teams working on a branding strategy for a deodorant
- 11 teams working on a branding strategy for a shower gel

This situation reflected realistic competition between the individual products about which some of the students had previously been unaware of. It was not sufficient for students to only concentrate on product-related attributes for distinguishing themselves from their competitors, but students realized the necessity of drawing on their entire set of branding skills to come up with a unique brand positioning which in the end would result in products sold.

Students were reminded that when starting to think about the positioning of their hypothetical brand, they should keep in mind that 10 other teams were doing exactly the same. To avoid a scenario in which, for example, all of the shampoo teams ended up with exactly the same brand positioning, it was decided that all teams of all products had to disclose their positioning in week three of the course. This again reflected first-life reality, as in real-life companies do not define their branding strategy out of the blue, but instead, they do so by keeping a close eye on the activities of their competitors. As a consequence, students had the chance to gain insight into what their primary competitors were doing, and thus to adapt their strategy accordingly. A list of all brand positioning statements was published for one day on the course website and it was up to the teams to decide how they would use this information.

> *We could have a look at the competition and had to adjust our ideas accordingly. This felt like a real life situation.* (Verena, German student)

Having decided on their individual brand positioning which, to a large extent, took into account competitive positioning statements, students started to build their shops in which the branded products were to be sold. During that phase, teams were closely watching each others' building activities. To prevent their creative ideas from being copied, groups were forced to think of alternative ways to "protect" their branding efforts. This resulted in teams building virtual fences that others could not look through, or student groups building their stores high up in the air to pretend they were not present yet.

7.9.3. *Experiencing Financial Constraints*

By restricting the building money for each team, students were financially challenged as well. Whereas a written IMC plan does not provide students with a financial feasibility check, the execution of a branding strategy in a virtual world does. The financial limitations established by a limited amount of building money challenged students to be innovative. Groups that were spending all their building money on only one special item were forced to find alternative ways to supply the rest of their store, resulting in very creative actions. Some students earned extra money by "camping" (getting paid for staying in a certain virtual place), by dancing, or by having a virtual job. Other students asked teams with excess money for donations, and by doing so obtained the missing building money they still needed.

> *We had the perfect idea but we soon realized that we had to make trade-offs about what to actually implement → we only had a limited amount of money we could use for building.* (Ina, Belgian student)

> *Budget constraint was pretty strict…though it made you think about how to improve on costs, so that was good.* (Sam, Dutch student)

Other financial constraints related to the pricing of the products. As mentioned earlier, all teams were sellers, but every student was also a buyer equipped with a certain amount of money (20 Linden Dollars per student). Whether it made sense to follow a premium branding strategy implying high unit prices or an everyday low prices (EDLP) strategy had to be decided upon. Thus, students were forced to carefully analyze their target market with its specific needs and financial possibilities to increase the future success of their branding efforts. Deciding on a pricing strategy certainly had implications for the marketing of the different brands:

> *We decided to go for a premium pricing strategy. In the beginning, we were really unsure whether this would be a wise decision, but the feedback by people that bought our brand showed us that the pricing and the marketing actions were in sync. That was nice to see.* (David, Dutch student)

7.9.4.   *Experiencing Marketing (Challenges)*

During the building phase of the project, students were invited to launch marketing campaigns for their brands, while being allowed to cross the borders between real-life and Second Life. Students could carry out practically any marketing campaign they desired and considered appropriate. Thereby, the challenges a real brand manager faces became obvious while simultaneously stimulating the fun of experiential learning:

> *The SL project actually was a very quick and fun overview of a lot of challenges a brand manager faces. A brand manager accompanies a product from founding to the shop. He needs to come up with a name, place it in its portfolio. He needs to come up with an advertising and selling strategy. He needs to use the IMC tools. I think SL contained all this.* (Nienke, Dutch student)

The way you produce a brand and a whole strategy around it, e.g., advertising, packaging, pricing, is quite realistic. We really used the CBBE model and the 4P's to structure the project for ourselves-I think, that is close to real life! (Kathrin, German student)

The actual application of theory makes constraints in terms of what is feasible, what is coherent, clearer. You actually are RESPONSIBLE, like in real life, and have to bear the consequences. (Thomas, German student)

Early on in the course, student groups started to distribute brand flyers both in Second Life and in real life. Posters and flyers of their projects were vividly present around the premises, distributed through e-mail or avatars in Second Life. Some student groups even set up websites or web-blogs to promote their products. Furthermore, word-of-mouth played an important role in students' marketing campaigns; some student teams were almost constantly present in Second Life informing their fellow students about their amazing products. Other teams did so in real-life, creating effective awareness for their products.

By crossing the border between real-life and Second Life, students were continuously forced to think "outside the box" to break through the increasing clutter of brand information. A very effective tactic was implemented by one student group. This team had T-shirts with their brand logo printed and all team members wore their customized T-shirts both in Second Life and in real-life during the tutorial meetings. Thereby, not only brand awareness was optimized, but also the team's devotion to their brand was expressed.

For me the best campaign of all 33 teams! They invented an awesome idea to make other people curious […]. The store was built in Old Greek style, and the product name is OLYMP. Finally, I bought 2 products from them to show my 'loyalty' to them (my appreciating for their work). (Lena, German student)

Hence, the Second Life project enabled students to get a clear understanding of the marketing theories and principles they had learned in class. They experienced the challenges and opportunities a brand manager faces in his job. The concept of brand awareness now certainly "got a face," competition was taken to a complete different dimension, and their creativity was challenged like never before (Picture 7.4).

All things considered, it can be concluded that the Second Life project was successful for all parties involved. It was a brand-new, innovative way for students to apply their branding skills obtained in the course and has proven to be a lot of fun for both the students and the faculty members involved.

Most importantly, though, the fundamental quest of finding a way to narrow the gap between theory and practice has been resolved by integrating a virtual world into the academic curriculum. Following the results of the online survey, the question whether Second Life can be used to properly assess students understanding of

Picture 7.4: Student store: OLYMP: "*Heavenly, why settle for less?*" shampoo

theoretical concepts and their ability to apply these theoretical principles to real-life scenarios can be affirmed.

7.10. Looking Back and Ahead: Lessons Learned

As with any other project, the Second Life branding project should be viewed in light of its limitations. These limitations were mostly of a practical or technical nature.

7.10.1. General Remarks

Most of the general remarks mentioned by students included to some extent a technical aspect hindering them from using Second Life to its full potential. Examples of technical issues were "slow laptops," "malfunctioning internet connections," and the fact that Second Life could not be installed in computers at the library. Moreover, the technical constraints correlated highly with timing issues and several students mentioned time in combination with the technical restrictions:

> *Time and money constraints; in my group we split the tasks as the program didn't run properly on all computers, the actual construction after the planning was tricky and time consuming, and some of us had other time intense courses.* (Berit, Dutch Student)

> *The technological aspect was one limitation in executing our strategy. There were some things we wanted to do in our strategy, yet were unable to because we did not have the technical know-how.* (Yen, Chinese student)

Indeed, many remarks focused on the technical aspects related to Second Life. Future educational projects which integrate Second Life into the academic curriculum should prepare for the technical constraints involved in using advanced (3D) metaverses. It is important to avoid having technical issues interfere with project-related aspects, as students tend to be very critical on "external" constraints and often do not differentiate between technical and project related factors.

7.10.2. Second Life as a Branding Tool

A second limitation regards the usage of Second Life as a branding tool. Here, comments were focusing primarily on a few issues related to the project's boundary conditions. For example, several students indicated that the selection of the product category (personal care products) was unfortunate and that the fact that the products had to be sold in a closed circuit was too restricting:

> *I think that the main restriction was the product, I mean that 'personal care products' is something that an avatar would really not need so they*

> *won't evaluate the product efficiency, just the looks or the campaign.* (Milagros, Brazilian student)

> *We would have liked to target a different market.* (Judith, German student)

Furthermore, it was mentioned a couple of times that for some students it was difficult to clearly distinguish between what to do in real-life and which aspects were clearly subject to Second Life:

> *That it is hard to draw a distinction between are we trying to advertise and market via second life conditions or by real life conditions.* (Charlotte, German student)

> *I was once confused about whether our branding strategy is focus on only second life, the virtual world, or should include the real world (and second life is a communication channel of our branding strategy.* (Chen, Chinese student)

Compared to the analysis of the first limitation concerning general technical constraints, the entire set of different factors mentioned regarding the usability of Second Life in a branding course was closely related to the project regulations rather than to the platform *per se*. This implies that students approved and liked the idea of working with a virtual 3D platform for applying their branding skills which is further reflected in the following comments:

> *I think that through a project like this it is easier to know and realize if we actually have learned something. Because with SL we have applied everything that we have learned so far from the course.* (Gayoso, Dutch student)

> *The second life project gives you an opportunity to put "in practice" what you have learned in theory.* (Shajayra, Italian student)

7.10.3. *Second Life as an Educational Support Tool*

These comments point toward the crucial question of whether Second Life can be viewed as an appropriate support tool for academic education in general. When asking students about the limitations of using Second Life as an educational tool, they again mainly mentioned time management issues as well as issues related to a fair distribution of pre-knowledge students have about Second Life. Getting familiar with Second Life in such a short time span was perceived to be rather challenging for students:

> *If you are good in programming you have a huge advantage and it's not really fair. I'm good in marketing but not in computers!* (Theo, Dutch student)

> *Lack of prior knowledge about second life.* (Marie Germans student)

Yet, most of the remarks express a very favorable attitude toward Second Life as an educational tool, as it is primarily seen as great means to link theory with practice:

> *I think that the second life project was a great way of applying and "playing around" with the knowledge we gained during the course.* (Moritz, German student)

> *The Second Life project is more lively and active. It allows for greater creativity. It is not only about one's own efforts but the results of the other teams are visible, too → better personal benchmark and more interesting/exciting.* (Annemarie, Belgian student)

> *Second Life is really interactive, better way to learn (applying, not just writing), FUN, good way to test marketing skills in a controlled environment, simulates a real marketing situation.* (Adelina, Chinese student)

Finally, we believe it is helpful to emphasize the importance of carefully designing and structuring a project in which Second Life or any other virtual 3D platform is used, already early on. Providing students with precise and clear manuals and offering them enough time to get acquainted with the technicalities related to using such as program is deemed to be essential by both tutors and students:

> *More information from the beginning. Because in the first lecture it was clear for me that a lot of time was going to be needed to master this program.* (Max, German student)

> *More lectures about the use of second life and more information before the course about what second life actually is.* (Martine, Dutch student)

> *Give an extensive training, so that you really are motivated to participate, since you know you have the knowledge necessary to achieve the objectives.* (Jeroen, Belgian student)

The importance of a proper structure and early implementation of the Second Life project was also expressed by student comments to the open question: What would you recommend to students that will take the course next year for being optimally prepared for the Second Life project? According to students, the key to successfully master the Second Life project is time management. The following comments are illustrative of the significance of good time management for the project:

> *Start early! Stick to your time plan…if you don't have one…MAKE ONE!!!* (Luca, German student)

> *Start living your "second life" in advance of the course.* (Rob, Dutch student)

> *Start playing around with the program before the course starts. That's the only way you will learn how to work with SL… by practicing with it!!* (Annemarie, Dutch student)

Apparently, students believed that when taking into consideration the advantages good time management entails, the course indeed had the potential to be a lot of fun:

> *To have fun and see the project as a real opportunity to express their creativity and their ideas as if they were managers.* (Caroline, French student)

> *Enjoy the project!* (Lars, German student)

> *Just practice, after a while if you understand how to build, and how to move, it is a lot of fun.* (Maarten, Dutch student)

> *Use it as a fun way to illustrate the brand strategy of your product.* (Victor, Dutch student)

7.11. Conclusions

Using a 3D metaverse such as Second Life for educational purposes holds the promise of effective and enjoyable instruction for both students and tutors. The research reported here is one of the first to provide a concrete basis for educators on how to implement this platform effectively, as well as to evaluate (both monetary and non-monetary) investments regarding Second Life as a course enhancement.

The analysis of both qualitative and quantitative data collected at the end of our Second Life branding project yields important insights regarding the opportunities and challenges involved in virtual teaching environments. In particular, the close resemblance of Second Life with the real world allows students to experience the many challenges brand managers face in their daily activities in a very realistic manner. In response to these challenges, students can draw on newly acquired branding skills, which make the learning of theoretical concepts and branding principles not only more effective but also more enjoyable.

We believe that especially in today's competitive environment, students need to be equipped with both theoretical and practical knowledge and skills. Simulating reality by means of a virtual world can narrow the gap between theory and practice, thereby providing a competitive advantage for students. With the ongoing emergence of Internet-based technologies and the current demands companies and technology-savvy students impose on educational institutions; the use of simulation in education will become an imperative. Having a "second life" in an educational environment will be inevitable in the near future if the trend toward virtual worlds continues at its current pace. Educators will need to be better prepared and able to set the stage for high-quality academic education when they use virtual worlds in a didactic manner. This results not only in a competitive advantage in attracting good students, but ultimately provides a whole new dimension to the present teaching and learning environment.

References

Anderson, J. R. (1995). *Learning and memory: An integrated approach.* New York: Wiley.

Biggs, J. (1996). Enhancing teaching through constructive alignment. *Higher Education, 32,* 347–364.

Bolt, M. A., Killough, L. N., & Koh, H. C. (2001). Testing the interaction effects of task complexity in computer training using the social cognitive model. *Decision Science, 32*(1), 1–20.

Davis, F. D., & Yi, M. Y. (2004). Improving computer skill training: behavior modeling, symbolic mental rehearsal, and the role of knowledge structure. *Journal of Applied Psychology, 89*(3), 509–523.

Decker, P. J., & Nathan, B. R. (1985). *Behavior modeling training: Principles and applications.* New York: Praeger.

Frederiksen, N. (1984). The real test bias. Influences of testing on teaching and learning. *American Psychologist, 39,* 193–202.

Jarmon, L., Traphagan, T., & Mayrath, M. (2009). Understanding project-based learning in Second Life with a pedagogy, training, and assessment trio. *Educational Media International, 45*(3), 157–176.

Keller, K. L., Aperia, T., & Georgson, M. (2008). *Strategic brand management: A European perspective.* Harlow, England: Financial Times/Prentice Hall – Pearson Education.

Kraiger, K. J., Ford, K., & Salas, E. (1993). Application of cognitive, skill-based, and affective theories of learning outcomes to new methods of training evaluation. *Journal of Applied Psychology, 78*(2), 311–328.

Milligan, F. (1998). Defining and assessing competence: The distraction of outcomes and the importance of educational process. *Nurse Education Today, 18,* 273–280.

Murthy, N. N., Challagalla, G. N., Vincent, L. H., & Shervani, T. A. (2008). The impact of simulation training on call center agent performance: A field-based Investigation. *Management Science, 54*(2), 384–399.

Robertson, I. T. (1990). Behavior modeling: Its record and potential in training and development. *British Journal of Management, 1*(1), 117–125.

Simon, S. J., Grover, G., Teng, J. T., & Whitcomb, K. (1996). The relationship of information system training methods on cognitive ability to end user satisfaction, comprehension, and skill transfer: A longitudinal field study. *Information Systems Research, 7*(4), 466–490.

Tillema, H. H., Kessels, J. W. M., & Meijers, F. (2000). Competencies as building blocks for integrating assessment with instruction in vocational education: A case from the Netherlands. *Assessment & Evaluation in Higher Education, 25*, 265–278.

Yi, M. Y., & Davis, F. D. (2003). Developing and validating an observational learning model of computer software training and skill acquisition. *Information Systems Research, 14*(2), 146–169.

Author Biographies

Nina Belei is a PhD candidate in the Department of Marketing and Supply Chain Management at the Faculty of Economics and Business Administration at Maastricht University. She received her MSc in February 2007 with her final thesis titled "Massclusivity – The paradox of affordable luxury." Before she started as a PhD candidate at the Department of Marketing and Supply Chain Management in April 2007, she was working as a Junior Lecturer for her Department. Her PhD project deals with health-perception spillover effects and the resulting product consumption consequences. It is supervised by Prof. Dr. Jos Lemmink, dean of the Faculty of Economics and Business Administration. In 2008, she coordinated the 3rd year bachelor course "Brand Management" in which the virtual world Second Life was implemented as an educational support tool.

Gwen Noteborn is Innovation Manager at the Department of Marketing and Supply Chain Management at the Faculty of Economics and Business Administration at Maastricht University. Within her job she is constantly looking for interesting educational innovations and is responsible for the technical aspects of Second Life implemented in the course "Brand Management." Gwen received her MSc in August 2007 with her thesis titled "You only live Twice, about the affects and antecedents of co-creation self efficacy within the metaverse Second Life." Currently Gwen is following a Master of Arts in Conflict Management at the Faculty of Law of Maastricht University, for which she is finalizing her thesis at the Court of Roermond.

Ko de Ruyter is Professor of Marketing and Head of the Department of Marketing at Maastricht University, the Netherlands. He has published six books and numerous scholarly articles in among others the *Journal of Marketing, Management Science, Journal of Consumer Research, Journal of Retailing, Journal of the Academy of Marketing Science, International Journal of Research in Marketing, Decision Sciences, Organization Science, Marketing Letters, Journal of Management Studies, Journal of Business Research, Journal of Economic Psychology, Journal of Service Research, International Journal of Service Industry Management, Information and Management, European Journal of Marketing and Accounting, Organisation and Society*. His research interests concern international service management, e-commerce, and customer satisfaction and dissatisfaction.

Appendix

Second Life Evaluation Questionnaire – Closed-Ended Questions[5]

1) Second Life was a nice way to apply your knowledge.

Totally disagree	Disagree	Somewhat disagree	Neutral	Somewhat agree	Disagree	Totally agree
1	2	3	4	5	6	7

2) I would rather do the Second Life project than a written report.

Totally disagree	Disagree	Somewhat disagree	Neutral	Somewhat agree	Disagree	Totally agree
1	2	3	4	5	6	7

3) The workload of the Second Life project was fair.

Totally disagree	Disagree	Somewhat disagree	Neutral	Somewhat agree	Disagree	Totally agree
1	2	3	4	5	6	7

4) I enjoyed the Second Life project.

Totally disagree	Disagree	Somewhat disagree	Neutral	Somewhat agree	Disagree	Totally agree
1	2	3	4	5	6	7

5) I enjoyed building in Second Life.

Totally disagree	Disagree	Somewhat disagree	Neutral	Somewhat agree	Disagree	Totally agree
1	2	3	4	5	6	7

6) I enjoyed watching other avatars and buying from them.

Totally disagree	Disagree	Somewhat disagree	Neutral	Somewhat agree	Disagree	Totally agree
1	2	3	4	5	6	7

7) The Second Life support (manuals, helpdesk etc.) was sufficient.

Totally disagree	Disagree	Somewhat disagree	Neutral	Somewhat agree	Disagree	Totally agree
1	2	3	4	5	6	7

---

5. The online questionnaire was answered by 69 women and 70 men.

8) I could manage to use Second Life after a few weeks.

Totally disagree	Disagree	Somewhat disagree	Neutral	Somewhat agree	Disagree	Totally agree
1	2	3	4	5	6	7

9) I would recommend to do the Second Life project again next year.

Totally disagree	Disagree	Somewhat disagree	Neutral	Somewhat agree	Disagree	Totally agree
1	2	3	4	5	6	7

10) I would use Second Life again in the future.

Totally disagree	Disagree	Somewhat disagree	Neutral	Somewhat agree	Disagree	Totally agree
1	2	3	4	5	6	7

Second Life Evaluation Questionnaire – Open-Ended Questions

11) What are the benefits of using Second Life compared to a written report?

12) How could Second Life be used more efficiently in next year's Brand Management course?

13) What limitations do you see for using Second Life as an educational tool?

14) What factors constrained the use of Second Life as an educational tool?

15) Which factors limited the execution of your branding strategy in Second Life?

16) In the context of implementing a branding strategy, which factors did limit the execution of your strategy?

17) In what way does the Second Life project resemble the challenges a brand manager in real life faces?

18) What would you recommend to students that will take the course next year for being optimally prepared for the Second Life project?

19) Do you see other possibilities for using Second Life in education?

Chapter 8

Literary Analysis as Serious Play in Second Life

Mary McAleer Balkun, Mary Zedeck and Heidi Trotta

8.1. Introduction

The study of literature has changed dramatically in the past twenty years, in large part as a result of technological advances that have made research materials more accessible, has led to digitization of texts, and has enabled exhaustive searches of documents of all kinds. These changes have been felt in the literary profession as well. Traditionally a solitary pursuit, literary scholarship is becoming a more collaborative endeavor, with scholars sharing insights and posing questions through listservs or posting their musings and work-in-progress on blogs. Theoretical approaches to texts such as Cultural Criticism, New Historicism, and Postcolonialism emphasize the importance of interdisciplinarity and contextuality in literary analysis, modes that are more easily accommodated using the wide variety of resources and tools available online.

Such developments have had a corresponding impact on the teaching of literature, with technologically enhanced instruction, whether this takes the form of a simple PowerPoint presentation or more sophisticated use of multi-media and online materials, and with more courses that are learner-centric as opposed to instructor-centric. No longer residents of the ivory tower, today's teacher-scholars realize that they must provide students with more than just a set of literary terms and the ability to parse a sentence, although these remain important skills. They must also help prepare students for a world in which collaboration is becoming the norm, where the ability to adapt to new technologies is an advantage, and where the practical application of knowledge is expected. And, in addition to all this, they must find ways to motivate students and engage them in material that can seem dated and even irrelevant. The changes are evident in such things as the use of wikis for whole-class

Higher Education in Virtual Worlds
Copyright © 2009 by Emerald Group Publishing Limited
All rights of reproduction in any form reserved
ISBN: 978-1-84950-609-0

projects, online discussions that extend conversations about literature beyond the class period, and course management systems and word processing tools that facilitate online peer review and collaborative writing assignments. The shift can also be observed in the ongoing stream of books and articles on everything from active learning in the college classroom to cooperative learning to ways of using various forms of technology for college teaching in all disciplines.

Given its collaborative nature and its ability to incorporate other forms of media, Second Life is a natural corollary to the aforementioned tools and one that can be used to enhance the study of literature in ways that are not only creative but also are not easily achieved otherwise. There is already a strong literary presence in Second Life, with such sites as Literature Alive![1] which, according to its blog, "seeks to provide quality content to SL residents by focusing on the creation, development, and dissemination of literary resources in Second Life."[2] It features "builds" based on literary texts such as the novel *Mama Day* and the works of Edgar Allan Poe, among others. In addition, one of the most interesting developments in Second Life has been the increasing number of venues where people can share their written work. Although this is primarily creative work at the moment, it is only a matter of time before formal literary scholarship also makes an appearance, especially given the increasing obstacles to publishing in the real world. At sites such as Book Island Publishing Village – which is described on the Second Life site as a space "[f]or books, magazines, publishers, publishing, editors, printers, writers, media, authors, books, writing, thinc, events, literary, political discussion, hangout, discussion, printing and more!" (Second Life, 2008, n.p.) – members can view a range of exhibits, chat with authors and publishers, and visit a book fair. Publishers such as Macmillan and Penguin have an in-world presence, and there are author events, open readings of original work, and other evidence that literature is alive and well in the virtual world. [Second Life itself is supposed to have been inspired by the cyberpunk novel *Snow Crash* by Neal Stephenson (2000).] Given these resources, the question then becomes how to harness the unique characteristics of Second Life for the formal study of literature in a way that is meaningful and thoughtful. Lloyd P. Rieber (2009) contends that "it can be very difficult to arrange one's own learning environment in order to learn something new at a deep level" and that this is one of the fundamental problems with education as now know it (p. 1). Second Life provides a learning environment that can be shaped both for and by students into a place where deep and engaged learning can occur. It is also a place where the role of instructor is transformed. As Cynthia M. Calongne (2008) observes, "In virtual worlds, the instructor's role shifts from being the 'sage on the stage' to being the domain expert-the authority who stimulates and supervises exploration while providing structure, guidance, feedback, and assessment" (n.p.). This new perspective also requires

---

1. http://literaturealive.wikispaces.com/ and SLURL: http://slurl.com/secondlife/Eduisland%20II/181/237/23
2. http://literaturealive.blogspot.com/

preparation, since students expect the instructor to know as much about Second Life as about any other content area.

Over the course of two years, we have engaged students in three different classes, two undergraduate and one graduate, in projects on Seton Hall University's Pirate Island in Second Life. What has come to be known as the House of 7 project began with the graduate class in the fall 2007 semester as a recreation of the Turner-Ingersoll mansion, better known as the House of the Seven Gables made famous by Nathaniel Hawthorne in the novel of that title. The goal for that group was to create a site where students could explore the novel in depth, along with its historical and cultural contexts. It has since expanded to become a site for the exploration of the Gothic and the grotesque. Rather than simply participating in an existing environment, students develop projects that apply critical analysis in practical and creative ways, both to learn and to help others understand the texts they have chosen to examine. Although the thematic focus of each course – a graduate course on the American Renaissance and material culture, a senior seminar on American Gothic literature, and a Women and Literature course with the theme "Woman as Witch" – was slightly different, three elements created a common thread: a cultural approach to literary analysis, specifically material culture; an insistence on student-generated or found objects and learning materials; and an emphasis on close reading and comprehension. The result in all three cases has been a collaborative and creative experience not replicable in a traditional literature class.

The House of 7 in Second Life is an interactive environment in which visitors can understand what it might have been like to be an American woman in the early nineteenth century, or what a garden of the period would have looked like and contained in the way of flowers and plants, or about the prison reform movement in the nineteenth-century and its relation to a text like *The House of the Seven Gables*. It is also an evolving site, one to which students in subsequent classes can continue to add, thus extending and expanding the collaborative nature of the experience.

The House of 7 is one of several builds on Seton Hall's island, which also includes a virtual marsh, a Welcome Center, and various meeting spaces. The university is an active member of the New Media Consortium (NMC), to which over 300 learning-focused organizations belong, and Seton Hall's Pirate Island is part of that larger space within Second Life. Because NMC space is academic in orientation, having the island and project under that umbrella means the environment is more private and secure than the typical Second Life space, since only members of NMC and their guests can gain access. This is especially important when working with students nervous about being in a virtual world for the first time. However, the private nature of the NMC site also means that those projects are not available to the Second Life population at large, either for use or feedback.

The House of 7 was initially funded by a Faculty Innovation Grant (FIG) from Seton Hall's Teaching, Learning, and Technology Center (TLTC); the award included the support of two Instructional Designers, one of whom had worked on several projects in Second Life. The primary goal of the project was to determine whether a hands-on approach to the analysis of literature, in particular one emphasizing material culture theory, would engage students on a deeper level with texts and literary theory. A scan of other literature sites in Second Life revealed that most of the development had been done by the instructors working with in-world builders. Students entering the site click on objects and receive a notecard with information, are asked to make choices about certain aspects of the text, and then take a quiz or write an essay to assess their understanding of the work. However, they are not the architects of the various projects. The experiences are immersive and interesting, but not student generated. Rather than repeat what had already been done, we decided to take a completely different approach, one that put students at the center of the process. Although the basic site for their work would be developed by us, the students would furnish the house and its environs and create all the projects it contained.

Preparatory work for the course and the site began in the summer of 2007, and even this stage involved extensive collaboration as well as interaction with and interpretation of the Hawthorne novel. First, the house shell had to be designed and built, something that proved much easier said than done given the discrepancies between the house as it appeared in the novel and the actual house in Salem, Massachusetts. Because of time constraints, an independent Second Life "builder," Eloise Pasteur (her SL name), was hired to "construct" the house. Detailed plans were developed to determine cost and feasibility and to ensure the house was constructed as close to its description in the text as possible. This process started with an actual visit to the original house in Salem and a close reading of the text by the Instructional Design staff. Pictures, both present and historical, were taken or obtained, and a paper 3D model of the house was found and constructed. All this was done to guarantee the correct placement of the gardens, the seven gables, and the house in reference to the street. The design and building of the house was a crucial step in the process because the student projects would be developed in relation to the actual spaces in the novel. Thus, some students would recreate the Cent Shop, others would recreate bedrooms in relation to specific characters, whereras others would work on the kitchen, the parlor, and the garden.

The first conflict between the real and the virtual surfaced as detailed blueprints for the house were developed and it became apparent that the rooms in the house described in the novel did not match the floor plan of the actual house, causing the designers to research and compare architectural changes made to the house over time. Another problem was the cost estimate of the initial version of the house, which exceeded what we had budgeted (approximately $500). To simplify the design and save money, the interior walls were removed, with the expectation that the projects themselves would define the spaces. As it turned out, the students became very creative about this, arranging furniture and erecting transparent panels to demarcate their areas. As with most recreations, the resulting House of the Seven Gables that stands on Seton Hall University's Pirate Island[3] is a compromise between the fictional representation in the text, historical accuracy, as well as practical, monetary,

---

3. http://slurl.com/secondlife/Seton%20Hall/128/128/25

and in-world limitations. One benefit of this process was that it foreshadowed the kinds of choices the students themselves would have to make as they developed their projects.

We also made some early decisions about how work would proceed. During the final weeks of summer, everyone in the class was emailed and told what we would be doing and why. They were encouraged to join Second Life, create an avatar, and do some exploring on their own, although they were also told this was not mandatory (given our awareness that not everyone would have easy home access to SL and that some students would join the course right before the start of the term). One advantage of this approach was that communication between the instructor and the students began even before the official start of the semester. In addition, most students came to the first class session – scheduled for a computer lab in the university's TLTC – already prepared to join us in the virtual environment. The few students who did not have avatars yet were set up in Second Life that first evening.

Seton Hall uses the Blackboard course management system, so we created a Blackboard course site specifically for the House of 7 project and included various resources to help students get started: links to YouTube videos, an introduction to Second Life skills, links to some sample builds, tutorials, and project proposal guidelines. That first evening, students toured the newly constructed house and viewed some of the online resources; they were then to send an email in the next few days identifying the space in the house they most wanted to work on, providing a second and third choice. They were later partnered with someone based on the space in which both were interested.

The students had also been asked to read the Hawthorne novel by the first night of class so we could talk about the text and projects in some detail. The full discussion of the novel was scheduled for the second class session, although we spent just half that time on the text itself on the theory that we would actually be discussing the novel throughout the term; the other half was spent discussing project ideas.

The actual assignment for this initial group of projects had three parts: to "furnish" the space appropriately for the period; to decide how the space functioned thematically in the novel and to create something that would convey that theme to others; and, finally, to develop an activity of some kind to engage a visitor to the space, preferably one that also made the visitor an active participant. Working with a partner, students submitted formal project proposals to the course wiki, explaining what they were planning to do in their "space" and why, providing an overview of what they would need to do and find, and outlining a possible activity. These proposals evolved in various ways over the course of the semester as students discovered the possibilities and limitations of Second Life and as they became more deeply familiar with their topic. For example, although everyone has the ability to build in Second Life, it takes time and skill to be able to create more than simple shapes with textures. Some groups also found that the materials they wanted – whether a particular type of plant or piece of furniture – were either not available or were cost prohibitive (even using Lindens).

The original plan for the project had each group posting a weekly update in the course wiki; however, it soon became apparent that, given the work load of most graduate students, this would have been seen as an impediment rather than a benefit. Instead, we agreed that each group would schedule three working sessions with the Instructional Designer to whom they had been assigned, either face-to-face or in-world, enabling us to chart and guide their progress. Each class session began with a brief update on the projects, which gave students a chance to hear what others were doing as well as to offer solutions and assistance. The semester ended with in-class presentations in-world; each pair of students showed their completed project, explained the rationale, as well as where they thought they had succeeded and what they had struggled with.

Although the projects had been visible while they were under construction, the completed versions were impressive by any standard and exceeded anything we might have anticipated. The students who worked on the Cent Shop decided to use it as venue to explore the rise of industrialism in the early nineteenth century, in particular the emergence of the railroad. Not only did they fill the space with appropriate objects and furnishings but they also included a model railroad, images from the period, and a quiz visitors can take. The kitchen became a site for understanding the Cult of Domesticity and True Womanhood, complete with a Thincbook (a Second Life object that looks like an actual book, but can contain text and images, as well as URLs to Internet sites) that contains recipes and advice for the housewife of the period, an open fireplace and wood-burning stove, and a table set with late-eighteenth/early nineteenth century utensils and dishware. For their activity, this group included links at the end of the Thincbook to websites with additional information about domestic life. Visitors visit a website, create a notecard with information they would like to add to the book, and leave the notecard in a "drop box."

In Hepzibah Pyncheon's room, a visitor is led through various activities that would have made up her early morning routine, including saying her prayers and writing at her desk. A harpsichord plays music, just like the one in the novel. Clifford Pyncheon's room is far less realistic than the others. The pair who developed this space decided they did not want to create yet another bedroom, so they opted for a less representational approach: since Clifford has just been released from prison when the novel opens, his room is designed as a jail cell, complete with torture devices, rats, and information about the prison reform movement in the nineteenth century. An essay assignment asks students to write about how this historical development might have influenced Hawthorne's writing of the novel.

The garden behind the house is a space where plants and flowers were chosen for the meanings they convey (loyalty, hope, love), as was true for gardens of the period; this information is delivered on a notecard when a visitor clicks on various plants. There is also a Hawthorne tree, a flock of chickens (which play a small but significant role in the novel), and Maule's Well. A stroll through the garden in period clothing offers an opportunity for the kind of "embodied and perspectival empathy for a system" that Gee argues is an aspect of gaming:

> *Many games let gamers easily switch between the two perspectives, either seeing and acting from one place or looking down on the whole world...This dual perspective, the ability and encouragement to flip*

*between an inside (situated) and an outside (global) perspective, is
potentially an extremely fruitful way to think about complex systems.
People can learn to see what things in a system look like from a given place
in the system and, at the same time, how that place looks from the
perspective of the system as a whole.* ("21st Century Survival Skills," p. 7)

Thus, a visitor can begin to understand why Phoebe Pyncheon prefers this space
above all others in the house; reading the materials provided, one can also be
introduced to the garden as female space.

The graduate students took advantage of one of the more unique qualities of
Second Life, the ability to create and have an immersive experience. Ben Salt, Claire
Atkins, and Leigh Blackall address this aspect of virtual worlds in their literature
review about teaching in Second Life, observing that:

*The immersiveness of Second Life itself is a rich source of learning
activities. The content and process of engagement boast a wealth of
opportunities to construct knowledge and activities can be embedded
across curriculum. Both synchronous and asynchronous, Second Life has
the flexibility to accommodate diverse learning styles and cultures.
Potentially, it gives the learner a great deal of autonomy, which is likely
to increase the all-important motivation to participate, especially if it is
seen as fun and meaningful.* (p. 20)

The element of fun or "play" should not be underestimated when considering the
value of Second Life as a forum for teaching and learning. Over the years, numerous
studies have been done examining the value of play and how it can be used to
motivate students. As Suzanne de Castell and Jennifer Jenson (2003) observe, "Such
work is often psychoanalytical in orientation, and is typically restricted in scope to
elementary and, mostly, early childhood education," citing classic studies by Axeline
(1947), Winnicott (1971), BrougPre (1999), and Corbeil (1999) (n.p.). In their article
about the ways educational games can be developed to be more like the kinds of
games students play for fun, such as video games, de Castell and Jenson call for a
return to "the classical connection between 'learning' and 'playing'" (n.p.). James
Paul Gee develops a similar argument in *Why Video Games Are Good for Your Soul*:

*good games create deep learning, learning that is better than what we
often see in our schools. Pleasure and learning: For most people these two
don't seem to go together, but that is a mistruth we have picked up at
school, where we have been taught that pleasure is fun and learning
is work, and, thus, that work is not fun (Gee 2004). But, in fact, good
video games are hard work and deep fun. So is good learning in other
contexts.* (p. 4)

Although Second Life is most definitely not a game, de Castell and Jenson's description of the virtual game environment is also reminiscent of the world of Second Life and why it is so intriguing as a place for learning that is seriously playful:

> *Entering an immersive environment means being willingly engulfed, enfolded, contained, and yet at the same time free of familiar worldly, ideological, and even bodily constraints. On entering a virtual place in a virtual body, what becomes important is motion through time and space, rich perceptual possibilities, both auditory and visual, illumination that renders some areas more and less visible, the patterning of zones within the environment, the ways both objects and activities define the organization of that environment, and the fact that all of these are navigable, so that player agency is paramount.* (n.p.)

The ability to control the environment was something that intrigued the graduate students, although some of them were also overwhelmed by the considerable possibilities available to them. Others not only flourished in this environment but also continued to explore it once the course was over. Their projects appeal to the visual, the auditory, and even the sensory, whether it is the podcasts, the torture devices in Clifford's room, the photography equipment in the attic that visitors can use to take pictures of themselves in front of a backdrop and post them, or the harpsichord that plays a tune in Hepzibah's room. In an article about their Literature Alive! site, Beth Ritter-Guth, Laura Nicosia, and Eloise Pasteur (2008) specifically address the relationship to one's avatar body in Second Life, where

> *[t]he sensation of embodiment-of moving around, of bumping into things, of seeing what is around the next corner-is made more real for most users. Many or all of the students have the sensation of being there: they get tired if they stand too long, they feel cold and wet in the rain, and so forth.* (Ritter-Guth et al., 2008, n.p.).

Because they were created by experienced and overall more intellectually advanced students, the projects in this first group have a sophisticated level of content that was generally not seen in the work of the subsequent groups. There was evidence of the success of this first iteration of the project besides the actual quality of the work. For example, several of the students chose to write their research papers about the same topic as their Second Life project, and the weekly written analyses and class discussions exhibited an increasingly nuanced understanding of the importance of material culture in the study of literature. There was also a deeper understanding of the ideas and events that inform both Hawthorne's novel and the period, such as Transcendentalism, the Cult of Domesticity and True Womanhood, and the emergence of an urban and industrial economy.

There were challenges, of course, as with any new tool. The graduate students struggled with the technology more than we had anticipated, primarily because they did not have equal access to up-to-date equipment. Although Seton Hall has committed to ubiquitous computing, this is not extended to graduate students. Many of the students in this group were teaching assistants in the English department and thus had university-distributed laptops; however, those using their own computers sometimes found that they were unable to accommodate Second Life, which requires a great deal of bandwidth, memory, and a powerful video card. We had tried to anticipate and compensate for this by making lab time available, but graduate students generally have less time to spend on campus than undergraduates, and not being able to work easily from home was frustrating for some. In addition, this first group was less comfortable with the collaborative nature of the work, and they were more inclined to say, both in conferences and in the end-of-course evaluations they completed, that they would have preferred a traditional approach to the class presentation, which this had replaced.

Despite these difficulties, most of the students indicated that they enjoyed working in this new way and saw the potential of virtual worlds to change the way one interprets and engages with works of literature. They observed that the project considered different types of learners, while the multimedia aspect reinforced key concepts in the course. Others acknowledged that doing the necessary research gave them greater familiarity with the material culture of the period. Finally, the students enjoyed being able to see the work in progress and knowing that the completed projects would remain available to others. Their observations and the challenges they encountered while doing the projects provided us with the feedback we needed to improve our approach in the next iteration.

On the basis of our experiences with the graduate class, we made a number of modifications to our work in Second Life with the next group, senior English majors taking a required seminar class. The topic for the course was American Gothic Literature, chosen specifically for its links to the existing work at the House of 7. Whereas we had required the graduate students to work with a partner, partly to provide support and partly to limit the number of projects we would have to supervise, the seminar students were given the choice of whether to work alone or in groups. We had discovered that some students simply prefer to work on their own on a project (partly the result of years of bad group-work experiences), whereas others had difficult schedules and other obstacles with which to contend. Since there were plenty of opportunities for collaboration in the labs and with the Instructional Designer, we decided this was a preference we could afford to indulge. It also generated good will early on, something not to be underestimated when asking students to do something so different from their normal learning routine.

Another change we instituted was a more detailed project proposal template that asked students to provide an overview of the project and a clear objective, to identify the purpose and significance of the project, to explain what they thought they would need to complete the project, and a literature review of articles, sites, and other materials they had examined. Before this, we provided them with a list of possible project ideas and several examples of each as a way to present the myriad possibilities of Second Life, as well as to try to vary the types of projects contained in the site. The options included interviews with an expert in Second Life that would then be recorded and posted, a panel session on Gothic literature, a book discussion group, a role play or dramatization, an interactive exhibit, a video, a digital story, a Second Life webquest, and an in-world blog. Students were also invited to look at the existing projects in the House of 7 and propose changes, additions, and further developments. Finally, this group had the option to develop a project based on any of the texts we were reading or on American Gothic literature in general.

The students received detailed feedback on their proposals, with an eye toward what could reasonably be accomplished in the time allotted. For this group we also returned to our original concept of having three updates posted to the course wiki, since there were more projects to oversee; we gave feedback on these as well. We established a clear set of deadlines and scheduled several working sessions throughout the semester in a computer lab. Two graduate students from the previous class agreed to serve as assistants to the project, and they worked with students both in-world and at the lab sessions. Since just one Instructional Designer was now assigned to the project, this additional assistance was crucial. On the basis of our experience with the graduate students, the seminar students were actively encouraged to connect their Second Life projects to their research papers, and nearly half did so. In general, the process was much more focused and controlled in this iteration, while still allowing for student creativity. One example of this was our decision to have the second group of students use avatars that had been created by the graduate students. At the end of that first course, anticipating this need, we had asked the students to "donate" their avatars to the project (which meant providing their SL name and password).

Not only did this give us access to everything that had been purchased or created by those avatars, but it also cut down on preparation time before the course. Students were still able to change the appearance of their avatars (although not the name), and many of them already had Lindens associated with the avatar they received, as well as a well-stocked SL inventory of objects, landmarks, and scripts.

One of the significant changes in this second stage of the project was the degree of cooperation and collaboration on the part of the students, who more obviously became a community of learners over the course of the semester. Although the seminar students had university laptops and better technology skills overall, most of them regularly attended the labs as well, which became active collaboration sessions as more advanced students helped those who were struggling and students shared information and resources with one another. This sense of community carried over into class sessions, where we again had weekly updates. What was different this time, however, was the spirit of camaraderie and peer support that prevailed.

One reason for this may have been that a number of the students knew one another already and were in other classes together; they also simply had more time to work together than the graduate students. Finally, we believe the more relaxed and cooperative atmosphere was a result of our own growing confidence. Rather than representing the Second Life project as something exceptional, it was introduced as a useful and meaningful substitute for the typical in-class presentation, as a project that could provide the students with new and important skills and knowledge, and as an item they could include on their resumes to demonstrate their experience with technology, whether they were planning to go on to teach or to enter the business world (see "A Second Look at Second Life" on using virtual worlds in a business environment).

As had the graduate students, some of the seminar students created immersive experiences for the House of 7: one group built a graveyard, complete with podcast "interviews" with both living and dead authors, whereas another pair developed a horse and carriage murder mystery that carries participants around the island to gather clues at each stop; they also learn about Gothic literature along the way. A scavenger hunt leads visitors throughout the house and grounds as they answer questions about American Gothic literature, and a group of crows perched across the fence in the back of the garden are the triggers for a Jeopardy-like trivia game on American Gothic texts.

Other students exploited some of the other unique features of Second Life: one coordinated a panel discussion that took place in-world, contacting several experts who agreed to talk about literature in Second Life, including the builder of the house, Eloise Pasteur. Another student created a role-play of Temple Drake, one of the characters in William Faulkner's novel *Sanctuary*, for which he wrote the script, then acted in and filmed. Another student recreated a scene from Henry James' *The Turn of the Screw*, in which Miss Jessell seems to appear and disappear, depending on the angle of vision. This set of projects more fully exploits the playful aspects of Second Life, asking visitors to participate in games and using humor more often.

The seminar students were generally more open to and excited about the Second Life experience. They appreciated that it replaced the in-class presentation and that they were able to work with someone else. Students also commented on the variety of projects available and that it was relatively easy to find one that met their technology skill level. The student who created the project blog had initially struggled to find a project she felt she could complete, and the blog proved to be a perfect vehicle for her. She was able to report on the activities of other groups and make resources more widely available.

The third group of students who have worked to date in Second Life, those in the Women and Literature: Woman as Witch class, pursued a few new project forms and went beyond the course texts in ways the earlier groups had not. For example, one team of students created an activity based on fairy tales featuring witches from cultures we had not studied; another group created a "Witches in the Media" image gallery, which also contains links to audio and video clips from various shows and movies.

One student created a menagerie containing animals that typically serve as familiars; she included podcasts she had recorded for several of the animals in which she explained both their historical role and their function in the texts we had studied. The students in this course again submitted project proposals, had the opportunity to work with others or alone, and were expected to provide three wiki updates during the semester. They also had the option to work with any texts from the course or something more broadly about the course theme.

One of the most significant differences between the third class and the first two was the number of students who chose to expand their Second Life project into full-length research papers, an integration that was quite common with the traditional in-class presentation format. This meant that the project had become an integral part of the course work, generating enough research and ideas about a topic to continue to engage students for the duration of an eight- to ten-page formal paper. Face to face meetings with each student about the proposal, as opposed to just written comments, also provided an opportunity to help them develop project ideas that were complex enough to provide the foundation for a full-length paper.

By the start of the third course, we were able to anticipate many of the difficulties we might face, but we were also encouraging students to incorporate other forms of technology into their projects, such as digital storytelling and the creation of external web sites. This group showed the greatest creativity in the development of their avatars (which were again those created for the first course), several of them choosing to reflect the theme of the course, "Woman as Witch," in their appearance. (One student even came to the final presentation dressed as Elphaba, the main character in Gregory Maguire's novel, *Wicked.*) These students were also the most confident in their approach to Second Life. One reason for this may have been the variety of projects they were able to see before they began. On the first evening of class we took them through the House of 7 as well as the rest of the Seton Hall island, showing them various works both completed and in progress. They also had access to a "sandbox" where they could practice building small objects, as well as a rich store of resources such as links, scripts, and video and textual materials stored in the Blackboard course.

We also received help from another Seton Hall instructor, Wendiann Sethi (SL: Panda Jishnu) who has been working to develop the Seton Hall site, and her SL colleague, Stuart Warner (SL: Stuart McCaw), an experienced Second Life builder. Finally, the very specific theme of the course led to a more focused as well a more interconnected set of projects.

Beyond whatever else it offers students, the House of 7 project is focused primarily on literary study and improving students' analytical and critical thinking skills. To create the projects, whether a role play between various characters or an interview with a real or fictional author, students must choose a specific issue, do the appropriate research, distill information to its most salient points, and convey that information in a way that is accessible and interesting. In addition, the Second Life projects demand that the abstract be made concrete, which has had the ancillary result of making the writing and thinking students do for the course more concrete.

Gary Stager's elements of a good project – "purpose and relevance, time, complexity, intensity, connected, access, shareable, and novelty" (p. 1) – provide a template for analyzing the results of the House of 7 projects:

Purpose and Relevance: Students in advanced English courses are generally responsible for an in-class presentation, which is intended to show their knowledge of a topic or text. The Second Life projects have the same purpose and relevance to the coursework, but they are interactive and permanent. Since the students designed their own projects, they chose subjects meaningful to them as opposed to being assigned a topic, which is what often happens with presentations.

Time: Students were given a full semester to do the work, although there was a clear schedule of deadlines for various steps. Some class time was given over to Second Life work, both at the very start of the semester and at the start of class once each week.

Complexity: Students had to draw on whatever prior knowledge of technology they had, as well as writing and research skills, close reading skills, their knowledge of various literary theories, and what they learned in class about the period, the topic, and the texts.

Intensity: Students spoke frequently about the projects in ways that suggested the intensity of the experience: they frequently mentioned going in-world to work on something for an hour or so and being so engaged that they soon found they were there for several hours. This phenomenon, which Mihaly Csikszentmihalyi refers to as "flow," "a subjective state that people report when they are completely involved in something to the point of forgetting time, fatigue, and everything else but the activity itself" (p. 600). The students also showed an interest in the work beyond their own projects, volunteering for the mock interviews, attending the panel discussion even though it was outside of class time, and attending the workshops, most of which happened in the evenings. The pair of students who created the murder mystery programmed a horse and carriage they purchased to make various stops on their "mystery tour." This type of engagement is a perfect example of the concept of "grit" Gee (2005) refers to in "Games, Learning, and 21st Century Survival Skills" (2009):

> *To achieve mastery and high respect on in these communities requires "grit" (Duckworth, Peterson, Matthews, & Kelly, 2007). "Grit" means a passion shared with others around which the Pro-Am [professional-amateur] community is, in fact, organized and perseverance or persistence to put in the many hours of practice (with failure and feedback) required for mastery in any worthwhile endeavor.* (p. 12)

The greatest challenge in many cases was to ensure the Second Life project did not detract from their other course work, especially the research paper; this is one reason later groups of students were strongly encouraged to think about a project that could then be turned into a paper.

Connected: The atmosphere in the workshops, the willingness to assist one another and share resources, all testify to the enhanced sense of collaboration in these classes. Friendships developed between students who had not known one another before and students worked together who would never have had any reason to do so otherwise. The projects became a common topic of conversation both in and out of class, with students from other courses also showing an interest in what we were doing.

Access: Beyond technological access, the value of Second Life is that it gives students access to materials and resources that would be difficult to have in the real world. These projects could not have been done as easily or as well outside of Second Life, and many would not have been possible at all in the same way. Students do not typically have access to experts in their field or the wherewithal to get them together for one hour on a college campus to talk about literature. Similarly, the student who created the Temple Drake film would have needed access to expensive equipment, some experience with filming and editing, and a real person to play the part. The taped interviews with authors could have been done using a digital recorder and then played for the class at some point (these recordings are podcasts, hosted online and accessed through the graveyard at the House of 7), but they would not have been readily available again, as they are in Second Life. (Not to mention that the podcasts are launched from the headstone for each author, a touch of the macabre that is in keeping with the House of 7 itself.) Similarly, they could have been done using tools such as Audacity or Skype and made available as podcasts, but then they would not have had the context of the other projects, nor would visitors have been able to comment on them as they can through the notecard feature in Second Life. And while one could create a "book" showing various visual images of the House of the Seven Gables, this would have required resources for printing and copying that Second Life mitigates. In-world events can also be accessed by students in other courses at Seton Hall or other universities, allowing for course to course access and university to university access.

Shareable: Unlike traditional projects, in Second Life students have access to anyone's project at any time, both during and after the process. This will be true for future cohorts, who can see what their predecessors did and create projects that complement or build on existing ones.

Novelty: No one in any of the classes had ever been in Second Life before, although one or two had heard of it. Having to recreate a space so that it is as true as possible to an early nineteenth century kitchen in a house dating back to the late seventeenth century is a hands-on experience with material culture. Short of creating dioramas in grade school, which is not the kind of activity students expect to find themselves doing again for a college class, and especially in a graduate seminar, they had not had an analogous educational experience. Part of the excitement, in fact, seemed to be that they were doing something they were not doing in all their other classes. In addition, each project was unique and the result of an individual or group learning process. No project has been repeated, although some of the tools have been used again (the Thincbook, for example), and since the creativity is coming from the students, the instructor does not have to rethink the project each time.

There are numerous advantages to having students create projects in Second Life besides those already mentioned. These include the ability to meet and talk with the instructor and their partners about their work in-world, as well as having easy access to experts from every walk of life. Given the growing development of the Seton Hall island and its membership in NMC, the students find themselves part of a broader community engaged in similar activities. They like the fact that their work is part of a larger whole and something that will endure (at least as long as Second Life does). Although they were skeptical about their ability to be creative, the final projects testify to hidden skills and potential, and their satisfaction and pride was palpable during the presentations.

There are also, of course, practical considerations that should be addressed by anyone planning to undertake a similar project in Second Life. It is important for the instructor to spend time in Second Life, getting comfortable moving around and even making simple objects. Students are far more comfortable with technology than most of their instructors, and that knowledge can be useful. It is also important, especially for the more skeptical students, to establish clear learning objectives and reasons for using Second Life as opposed to another approach. For all three groups of students, many of whom were either Education majors or teachers already, we stressed the acquisition of technical skills their own students will expect them to have and the pedagogical value of the activity they were asked to develop.

Providing lab time and making technical experts available gives students the support they need, even if they do not use either extensively (although many will). This is especially important at the outset. As students become more comfortable in Second Life, they can also reach out to experts in the Second Life community, who are almost always happy to participate. Although there is a monetary system in Second Life, and many objects are for sale, there are also enough free items for students to get what they need in most cases. Some Second Life residents will even donate an item or sell it at a discount if they know it is being used for educational purposes. As happened in the building of the house, the students also become very creative in their search for solutions.

Ultimately, the benefits of taking on such a project far outweigh the drawbacks. For example, it is not necessary to construct an actual building or site, as we did; the recreations and other materials students create can be part of an open space, with visitors moving freely between them. In addition, these can be as simple or as sophisticated as the instructor and students decide. For all the time and effort involved, the occasional technological glitches, the initial student resistance, and the limitations of Second Life, there now exists a simulated, primarily student-generated environment that not only can be used again and again but can also inspire and engage others.

Future students who visit the site will also be able to bring their own perspective to bear on the project. The current guideline is that students can change an existing scenario if they can demonstrate that it is flawed or incomplete. In addition, they can add those items they believe are important to understanding a particular text, period, or genre. This is certainly better than presentations that fade from memory and research papers that end up in desk drawers.

Working both face-to-face and in-world, all of those involved in the House of 7 had to find new ways to think, talk, and write about literature. This struggle was part of the learning process. As with the educational game de Castell and Jenson created and describe in their article "Serious Play" ("Ludus Vitae"), we were interested in developing

> *a resource in which centralized and dispersed design and development, face-to-face and computer-mediated interaction are interwoven in lived cultural practices,...what Illich (1973) called a "tool for conviviality", a place to meet and work and imagine and create.* (n.p.)

As instructors, one of our responsibilities is to try new things: new texts, new pedagogical approaches, and new ideas. It is also our responsibility to prepare our students for the workplace and for the significant changes happening in English and other disciplines. Second Life will not be for everyone, and whether it improves learning is still a matter for debate since there is little hard data so far. However, our experience in three English classes is that it is a rich environment for facilitating student collaboration and fostering creative engagement with ideas, problems, and issues. It is certainly a space that merits further exploration by those interested in improving student engagement and extending learning beyond the walls of the traditional classroom.

References

Axeline, V. M. (1947). In: L. Carmichael (Ed.), *Play therapy: The inner dynamics of childhood.* Boston, MA: Houghton Mifflin.

BrougPre, G. (1999). Some elements relating to children's play and adult simulation/gaming. *Simulation & Gaming, 30*(2), 134–146.

Calongne, C. M. (2008 September/October). Educational Frontiers: Learning in a Virtual World. *Educause Review,* 43.5. Available at http://www.educause.edu/EDUCAUSE + Review/EDUCAUSEReviewMagazineVolume43/EducationalFrontiersLearningin/163163. Retrieved on July 3, 2009.

Corbeil, P. (1999). Learning from the children: Practical and theoretical reflections on playing and learning. *Simulation & Gaming, 30*(2), 163–180.

De Castell, S., & Jenson, J. (2003). *Serious Play* (Available at http://faculty.ed.uiuc.edu/westbury/JCS/Vol35/decastell.html (retrieved on July 3, 2009). Taylor & Francis Ltd.

Gee, J. P. (2005). *Why video games are good for your soul.* Australia: Common Ground.

Gee, J. P., Games, Learning, and 21st Century Survival Skills. Pedagogy, Education and Innovation in 3-D Virtual Worlds. 2.1 (April 2009), pp. 4–12.

Rieber, L. P. (2001). Designing learning environments that excite serious play. Available at http://www.nowhereroad.com/seriousplay/Rieber-ASCILITE-seriousplay.pdf.   Retrieved on July 3, 2009.

Ritter-Guth, B., Nicosia, L., & Pasteur, E. (September/October 2008). Literature alive! *Educause Review, 43*(5). Available at http://connect.educause.edu/Library/. Retrieved on July 3, 2009.

Salt, B., Atkins, C., & Blackall, L. *Engaging with second life: Real education in a virtual world.* (pp. 1–99). Available at http://slenz.files.wordpress.com/2008/12/slliteraturereviewa1.pdf. Retrieved on March 10, 2009.

Second Life – Book Island. Linden Research. (2008). Available at http://world.secondlife.com/place/5d4dad3e-63d4-9001-f9db-5dd2003bf430. Retrieved on March 13, 2009.

Stager, G. What makes a good project? Eight elements to guide great project design. Creative educator. Available at http://www.thecreativeeducator.com/v05/stories/What Makes a Good_Project. Retrieved on March 11, 2009.

Stephenson, N. (2000). *Snow crash.* New York: Spectra.

Winnicott, D. W. (1971). *Playing and reality.* London: Tavistock.

Author Biographies

Mary McAleer Balkun is Professor of English at Seton Hall University. She is the author of *The American Counterfeit; Authenticity and Identity in American Literature and Culture,* as well as articles on Phillis Wheatley, Sarah Kemble Knight, Walt

Whitman, F. Scott Fitzgerald, and William Faulkner. She is currently at work on a study of the grotesque in early American literature. She has given presentations on her work in Second Life at the Educause Learning Initiative, Ed-Media, and NJEdge conferences. Mary is a member of Seton Hall University's Virtual Worlds Collaboration Group as well as the Digital Americanists group.

Mary Zedeck is an Instructional Designer with Seton Hall University's TLTC. She is an active participant in the investigation of virtual worlds, primarily Second Life, as a resource for teaching and learning in both face-to-face and distance learning courses. She volunteers for the Discovery Educator Network (DEN) in Second Life in the effort to acclimatize new residents to the virtual environment and train others in the benefits of this exciting emerging technology. She has given presentations on her work in Second Life at MARC, NJEdge, and other conferences.

Heidi Trotta is an Instructional Designer with Seton Hall University's TLTC. She has been an active participant in Second Life for several years, winning the 2008 New Media Consortium Learning Prize for creating, a virtual online endangered ecosystem learning environment based on a salt water marsh. She also developed and supported the Virtual Worlds Initiative to assess possible uses of online virtual educational environments in the classroom. She has an MA in Adult Education, Instructional Media and Design, and is completing an EdM in Instructional Technology/Media at Columbia University.

Chapter 9

Second Life – a Context for Design Learning

Ning Gu, Leman Figen Gul, Anthony Williams and Walaiporn Nakapan

9.1. Introduction

Integration of communication and information technologies into design curricula offers significant potentials for design schools. This potential is achieved through their capacity to facilitate designing in new learning environments, as well as advancing research and development in learning theories. There have been significant changes in architectural curricula to accommodate new demands, opportunities, processes and potentials provided by virtual environments and digital media (Kvan, Mark, Oxman, & Martens, 2004). With the introduction of these technologies, students find themselves in distributed, synthetic learning environments, collaborating and gaining experiential learning (Dede, 1996). Learning becomes most effective when students work in groups, share their thoughts, challenge each others' ideas and collaborate in the process of solving given problems (Pallof & Pratt, 1999; Johnson, Johnson, & Stanne, 2000). Collaborative learning, which is a specific form of group work, offers many benefits to learners and a technique founded on a constructivist learning philosophy (Yukselturk & Cagiltay, 2008). In design education, web-based tools (Craig & Zimring, 2000), virtual design studios (Maher, 1999; Kvan, Schmitt, Maher, & Cheng, 2000) and 3D virtual worlds (Gu, Gül, & Maher, 2007; Gül, Gu, & Maher, 2007) have been widely used, especially in the form of online and collaborative design studios.

Since 2008, a collaborative architectural studio has been established for undergraduate students of the University of Newcastle, Australia, and Rangsit University, Thailand. In this collaborative design studio, a total of 45 architecture students, geographically separated, collaborated on a joint-design project in Second Life. Students were asked to explore the design potentials in 3D virtual world, collaboratively explore the concept of a virtual home and complete the implementation of their collaborative design in Second Life.

Higher Education in Virtual Worlds
Copyright © 2009 by Emerald Group Publishing Limited
All rights of reproduction in any form reserved
ISBN: 978-1-84950-609-0

In addition to the design in a virtual domain and learning new design protocols are the skills of collaboration with design students of a different culture. This experience of confronting collaboration across international boundaries is aligned with the Graduate Attributes of the architectural profession as well as with the internationalization of the curriculum. Second Life can be utilised as a design platform, which provides for effective synchronous collaborative design and learning activities as well as opening up the opportunity for enhanced creativity in design.

This chapter presents the collaborative architectural design studio supplemented with the design outcomes from the studio, and comprehensive evaluations of the collaboration. On the basis of our teaching experience in Second Life and research into the pedagogies that best support this form of learning, the chapter will conclude with a set of strategies for course design that underpin the quality learning experiences in 3D virtual worlds. Our proposed strategies will assist design educators in understanding and achieving (1) a clear definition and implementation of course aim and objectives and how they are related to learning outcomes, (2) development of effective course content and tutorial sessions and (3) assessment strategies that support the collaborative nature of the design submissions.

9.2.   A Rationale for a Constructivist Approach in Design Education

Broadly, the educational approaches for various design disciplines fall into three groups: those evolving from a fine-arts background and generally conforming to a studio-based Beaux Artes educational model; those evolving from a technology background and generally conforming to an applied science educational model; and those that have sought alternative approaches, generally being combinations of Beaux Artes and scientific models.

Interest in alternative educational approaches to design education have been gradually increasing since the Bauhaus experiments of the 1930s in Germany and their "migration" to America in the post-war years and then to design education institutions throughout the developed world. The "Reflective Practitioner" philosophy (Schön, 1983, 1987) focused particularly on architectural and engineering education, was developed from Bauhaus principles and led initially to the introduction of "Problem-Based Learning" by Donald Woods (1985) for undergraduate engineering design education. Woods' approach was a form of experiential learning focused on integration of diverse knowledge and skills and problem-solving praxis to meet "real world" relevance expected by employers, all brought together through reflection.

A variation on a combination of Schön's and Woods' themes was a "cognitive apprentice" model (also called "Problem-Based Learning") developed by Howard Barrows (1986) for medical education. Problem-Based Learning is widely used across the discipline of architecture, which embraces constructivist theory encouraging students to create their own knowledge as they solve complex problems (Savery & Duffy, 1994), thus empowering the students to take charge of their own learning.

Some design educators reacted against these innovations and entrenched themselves in "scientific" design education approaches based on rigorous analytical design routines. A majority, however, adopted various combinations of scientific and studio-based approaches, with studio-based tutorials and master classes for some parts of their programmes, and analytical, procedural approaches for the other parts, often using parts of Schön's and Woods' theories to justify existing conventional design teaching practices.

As an ongoing process, constructivism can be employed as a design teaching approach which includes the facilitation of the emerging information and communication technologies. Constructivism characterizes how individuals construct their own understanding and knowledge of the world, through experiencing things and reflecting on those experiences (Mahoney, 2004; Huitt, 2003). According to the constructivist view, the learning process involves the following: knowledge is obtained and understanding is expanded through active (re)constructions of mental frameworks (Abbott & Ryan, 1999; Bransford, Brown, & Cocking, 2000), and learning is an active process involving deliberate progressive construction and deepening of meaning (Spady, 2001). An awareness of these patterns helps to anticipate and respond to students understanding (Brooks, Attree, Rose, Clifford, & Leadbetter, 1999).

Cognitive constructivism focusing on the cognitive processes people use to make sense of the world (Riegler, 2005), and social constructivism focusing on learning as a social process wherein students acquire knowledge through proactive interaction with significant others (Snowman & Biehler, 2000) both primarily impact the "competent, creative, mindful, collaborative and constructive dimensions" of learning (Spady, 2001). The social version of constructivism emphasizes how students can gain new strategies through peer collaboration by interpersonal discourse (Forman & Cazden, 1985). The influential psychologist Bruner (1966) makes the case for education as a knowledge-getting process-teaching and learning takes place in problem-solving situations and constructive learning is considered essential in effective design education.

9.3. Approaches to Construct Knowledge in Computer-Supported Education

Winn (1993) identified four different approaches in educational computing. The first one is based on behavior theory that gave rise to traditional approaches to instructional design (Dick & Carey, 1985; Gagne et al., 1988) that includes:

- Predicting students' behaviour (Reigeluth, 1983).
- Reducing necessary knowledge and skills by using appropriate analytical techniques (Landa, 1983).
- Following a set of procedures to ensure that instruction developed by their systematic application will work effectively without further intervention from designers or teachers (Winn, 1993).

A second approach is based on how information is presented to students (Fleming & Levie, 1993). The emphasis in this approach is on how students process information and has a greater impact on what they have learned rather than on the accuracy of task reduction and prescription of instructional strategies on the basis of content (Winn, 1993).

The third approach that is based on cognitive theories arose from the belief that the nature of the interaction between the students and the instruction is a determinant of learning equal to, if not of greater importance than content or how information is presented (Winn, 1993). For example, Anderson's ACT cognitive theory (Anderson, 1983, 1976) formed the basis of "intelligent" computer-based tutors, which included the following principles:

- Identifying the goal structure of the problem space.
- Providing instruction in the context of problem-solving.
- Providing immediate feedback on errors.
- Minimizing working memory load.
- Adjusting the "grain size" of instruction with learning to account for the knowledge compilation process.
- Enabling the student to approach the target skill by successive approximation.

The fourth approach relies on an understanding of how students interact with courseware, the assumption being that knowledge is constructed by the students themselves, not through the delivery of the courseware (Winn, 1993). In this constructivist view, the knowledge is constructed, not transmitted, and the students learn actively (Jonassen, 1999). To enhance learning, students should be given opportunity for exploration and manipulation within the environment as well as opportunities for discourse between students (Dickey, 2007). Within this context, students have opportunity to apply new knowledge and skills in collaborative environments (Gül et al., 2007). In learning as constructivist activities, the role of teachers is "to help and guide the student in the conceptual organization of certain areas of experience" (Glasersfeld, 1983).

In our development of designing and applying 3D virtual worlds for design education, we maintain the last two approaches of Winn's to emphasize the use of 3D virtual worlds as design and learning environments, providing structured lectures and tutorials, immediate feedback and the opportunities to interact within the environments during design development and implementation as well as other collaborative group activities.

9.4. Design Learning in Virtual Worlds

There are approaches that employ emerging fields in design education including employing parametric design, interaction design, experience design, graphic design, product design, and so on. Our research distinguishes from these studies by exploring the potential of 3D virtual worlds as constructivist learning environments.

Furthermore, we teach courses that regard 3D virtual worlds as a new design discipline in its own right.

Research of educational use of Virtual Reality (VR) provides compelling evidence of the potential of the emerging 3D virtual worlds to facilitate constructivist learning activities (Dede, Salzman, & Loftin, 1996; Dede, 1995; Winn, 1993). One of the main advantages of 3D virtual worlds identified is that students are able to view an object or setting from multiple perspectives (Dede, 1995), and virtual environments also offer many benefits including opportunities for experimentation without real-world repercussions, opportunities to "learn by doing" or "experiential learning," and ability to personalize an environment.

Another consideration is that virtual worlds offer those who are not readily able to access design studios, because of distance or physical incapability, to access and fully participate in the design activity. From the mid-1990s, virtual design studios (Kahneman & Tversky, 1996; Kvan et al., 2000; Maher, 1999; Schnabel, Kvan, Kruijff, & Donath, 2001) have been established in architecture and design schools internationally. These virtual design studios aim to provide a shared "place" where distant design collaboration especially synchronous design and communications can take place. The forms of virtual design studios vary from the early approach of digital design data sharing to the more recent 3D virtual world approach where the designs as well as the designers and learners are simulated and represented in the virtual worlds allowing "design and learning within the design". This new phenomenon has caught the attention of many design academics. Kvan (2001) argues that while design education has traditionally focused on the product, virtual design studios allow students to learn more about the design process. Dickey (2005) suggests 3D virtual worlds can provide "experiential" and "situated" learning. Clark and Maher (2005) examine the role of place in virtual learning environments which encourages "collaboration and constructivism." Wyeld, Prasolova-Forland, and Chang (2006) identify the potential of the use of virtual learning environments in supporting social awareness among design students where students from different cultural backgrounds design collaboratively.

9.5. Virtual Worlds for Enhancing Creativity in Design

In this chapter we use the term "design education" to describe the development of the ability to design, through processes of structured formal learning and formal assessment, across the whole range from very pragmatic to very aesthetic design types. Considering each level of design can have the components of creativity, conceptualization, schematization and realization, we can now consider them in terms of three differing levels of design complexity (Cowdroy & Williams, 2006):

Basic design: In many designs, the design process requires only minimal analysis of alternative design types. The design process here will only require actualization thinking (decision on design type) and realization thinking (production of drawings, models and a prototype), with a primary focus on realization through development of production drawings and models, etc.

Moderately complex design: Other designs (the majority of professional and commercial designs) involve a combination of three thinking types (and associated crafting types): schematization thinking to develop the initial overall design idea within a set of conventions, actualization thinking to decide on the final form of the design and realization thinking to control the articulation of the design idea into production drawings and models. The dominant thinking type here is schematization, which involves extensive reference to (past) experience and data, consideration of alternative design possibilities (through various schematic drawings and diagrams) and extrapolation to a new application. Design in these examples does not involve radical departure from previous designs.

Highly complex design: Some design processes, however, involve radical departure from previous designs, to make a "break-through" innovation to a new design type or benchmark, that addresses multiply complex constraints in a new way. Design involving this level of innovation and inventiveness and departure from conventional design rules require all four types of design thinking (and related crafting) to be engaged.

What is important for curriculum planners is to provide students with a diversity of design experiences that will allow them to develop experience and skills across a range of design contexts (Cowdroy & Williams, 2005). The opportunities and challenges presented in Second Life provide for students to extend their experience to designing in a totally new design context with alternative supports for design and collaboration and thus strengthen their experience and design skills.

9.6.   Case Study: A Collaborative Architectural Studio in Second Life

Our collaborative architectural studio was established in August 2008. The studio was the result of an on-going international collaboration between the University of Newcastle, Australia, and Rangsit University, Thailand. "NU Genesis," a virtual island in Second Life was set up as the studio place as well as the site for designing and implementing the collaborative project.

Besides the use of Second Life as the main collaborative design and learning platform, students were introduced to a wide range of synchronous and asynchronous design and communication tools and were encouraged to adopt them in supporting their group collaboration as needed. Each group was required to maintain a weekly group log to serve as a tool for monitoring their group collaboration and for self-reflection.

Aims: The aim of this studio was for students (1) to understand and develop the essential skills of collaborative design and modelling using 3D virtual worlds and (2) to develop the understanding and hands-on experience of 3D virtual worlds as an extension of conventional architectural design. The course content has two major components: (1) understanding collaborative design in 3D virtual worlds and (2) developing the essential skills for collaborative design in 3D virtual worlds. For students to develop the understanding of collaborative design in 3D virtual worlds, first, relevant theories such as the development of core skills for teamwork as well as design and collaborative cases in 3D virtual worlds were introduced and discussed. Second, students were guided to inhabit and critically assess a wide variety of design examples, as well as various design and communication features in Second Life. For the students to develop and practise the design and collaborative skills for 3D virtual worlds, a remote collaborative design project was used as the major assessment item.

Structure: The collaboration attracted 36 Newcastle students from the second year undergraduate architecture program. They were divided into groups consisting of three to four individuals. Each group was then allocated a remote collaborator from Rangsit University, who were enrolled in their third year undergraduate architecture program. Students from both universities remotely collaborated over the period of five weeks on a design project titled "Virtual Home." The weekly studio included a one-hour lecture/instruction and a two-hour design/discussion. Students were also encouraged to collaborate after these scheduled studio hours.

Collaborative project: Supplemented by tutorials for technical skill development, the collaborative design project provided opportunities for students to both experience and practise collaborative design in Second Life and develop and apply design principles and technical skills for virtual world design. The design brief required each group to design and implement *a place* in Second Life which demonstrated their concept of a virtual home and challenging the boundaries of a physical home (developed by students in an earlier traditional architectural studio). The design outcomes of the virtual home and the collaborative experiences of each group were documented in a slide presentation.

9.7. Collaborative Design Outcomes

Second Life as a potential platform for collaborative design learning remained challenging to some design students, as discussed in the following Evaluation and Discussion section. To extend the use of 3D virtual worlds in design education will require further consideration. However, our experience of applying 3D virtual worlds in the collaborative studio has shown a wide range of opportunities for enhancing student learning. Students demonstrate strategic approaches to adopting various communication and collaboration features of Second Life for design development, and they also widely explored new design potentials in virtual worlds, as demonstrated in the outcomes of the collaborative studio below.

Exploring creative design: The potential of 3D virtual worlds as an alternative means for exploring creative design is promising. For example, to plan and divide the "NU-Genesis" island for the collaborative project, an in-class design competition was conducted. The winning proposal excelled in its novel concept of the "Three Worlds" layout and was adopted for the zoning development of the virtual island. This winning design effectively addressed the conflict between the limitation of the virtual island's buildable surfaces and the large number of enrolled students, to incorporate the sites in a vertical structure on the island. As a result, the island has been used to its full capacity because the designs can utilise three different layers: under the "water," on the "ground" and in the "sky." This also provides many unusual sites to enable the emergence of innovative design solutions. As demonstrated below, many groups were very interested in selecting an unusual site, for example, an "underwater" site or a floating site in the "sky," which they are unlikely to confront in a conventional architectural studio.

Selected designs of virtual homes are shown in Figure 9.1, each of which represents a different design approach. The virtual home designs are analyzed from the following three perspectives and the classification of each design concept is listed in Table 9.1.

- Degree of realism in form: the designs applying dominantly the simulated physical world forms are classified as "realistic." The designs adopting mainly forms that are imaginative are classified as "non-realistic." Finally the ones using a combination of both are classified as "semi-realistic."
- Degree of abstractness in concept: the design having a profound meaning or concept behind its implementation is classified as having a high degree of abstraction. For example, a design that aims to simulate gardens literally is considered as non-abstract, whereas a concept depicting different "emotions" in a home environment is considered as abstract.
- Design approach: whether it is form-based or concept-based.

The selected designs can be summarized as:

- "Sky Garden" (for a site suspended in the sky): the group explores the idea of a virtual home as series of relaxing gardens. This design is most similar to designs in the physical worlds.
- "Archi-Bio" (for a site on the ground): this design is inspired by bio-mechanisms and transforms those dynamic and growing attributes into their virtual home in Second Life.
- "Metamorphosis" (for a site under the water): the concept mainly revolves around Krishnamurti's philosophy of "Living without Conflict" where materiality of the physical world conflicts with a person's inner self. The group emulates different levels of sub-consciousness through the creation of ambient environments that depict different "emotions."
- "Floating Cubes" (for a site suspended in the sky): the group represents home as series of floating cubes that shift the occupants from one activity to another and from one mind-set to another.
- "Zero Gravity" (for a site suspended in the sky): virtual worlds have no physical constraints such as gravity but still support various activities. This design uses (zero) gravity as the design trigger to challenge the constraint of gravity.

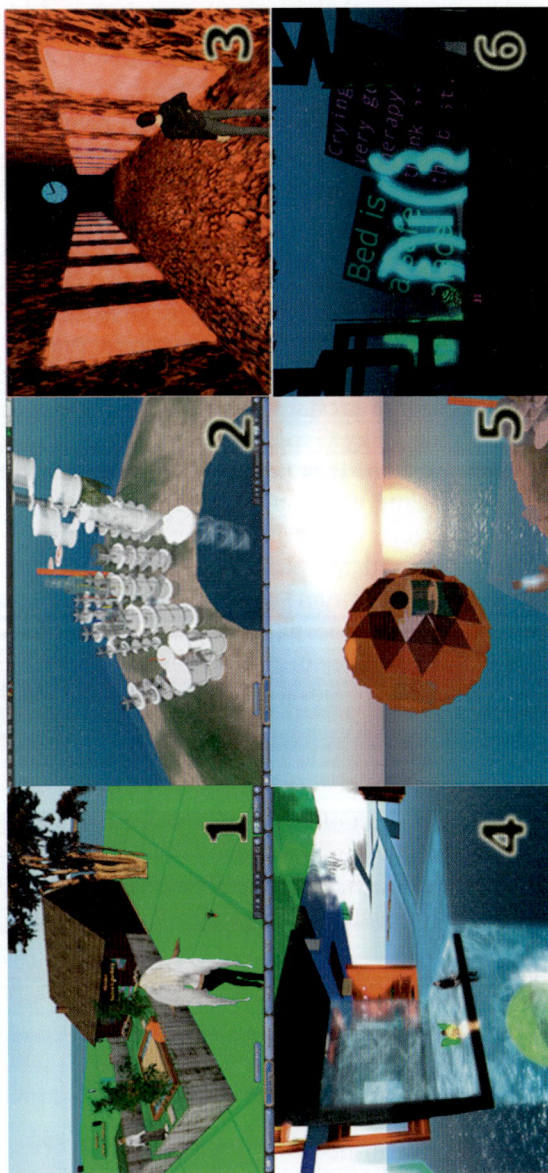

Figure 9.1: Six selected virtual home designs

- "})i({"(for a site under the water): The name of the design is a representation of a butterfly – a symbol of "freedom" – that you cannot verbally "say" it. The virtual home here is a place of communication inspired by poetry.

A combination of "degree of realism in form" and "degree of abstractness in concept" assists us in understanding and evaluating different designs evolving from the collaborative studio.

Non-realistic and abstract designs often receive higher recognition in the studio as they often represent a novel approaching to design and break from conventional designs with innovative and challenging solutions. They also often lead to more interesting outcomes and encourage students to explore different design possibilities during the collaborative process other than repeating what they have already learnt in the conventional architecture studio.

On the basis of the classifications of the designs as listed in Table 9.1, we can identify two different design approaches emerging from the collaborative design studio in 3D virtual worlds. The first one is the form-based approach where students start with the exploration of interesting forms, then adopt or sometimes even "create" a concept afterwards. "Sky Garden" and "Floating Cubes" are among the designs that follow this approach. It is noted that these groups can often quickly reach certain design solutions and move on to detailed design and documentation, as their design collaboration begins with form making and detailed modelling.

The second is the concept-based approach, in which students first explore, develop and agree on certain concepts at a quite deep level, and then realize the concepts through 3D models. "})i({", "Metamorphosis" and "Zero Gravity" are among the designs that adopt this approach. They progressed slowly especially in the early stage of the collaboration compared to the groups that have adopted the form-based approach. However, their design outcomes can often be sophisticated and interesting, if they can successfully reach a shared understanding of the concepts and implement them afterwards.

As discussed earlier, the prospect of virtual worlds for enhancing design creativity can be understood as the facilitations for three levels of design, basic, moderately complex and highly complex design. In this collaborative studio, the complexity of the design tasks and the requirements for the design outcomes have been modified to

Table 9.1: Classifications of the selected designs.

Design	Degree of realism	Degree of abstractness	Design approach
Sky Garden	Realistic	Non-abstract	Form-based
Archi-Bio	Semi-realistic	Non-abstract	Form-based
Metamorphosis	Semi-realistic	Abstract	Concept-based
Floating Cubes	Non-realistic	Non-abstract	Form-based
Zero Gravity	Non-realistic	Abstract	Concept-based
})i({	Semi-realistic	Abstract	Concept-based

suit the background of the students (second and third year undergraduates), and the timeframe of the collaboration is limited (five weeks). Nevertheless, as discussed earlier, most designs demonstrate the characteristics of moderately complex design, with some designs demonstrating various characteristics of highly complex design through the concept-based design approach.

Supporting collaborative design development: Students were able to explore and adopt a wide range of aids from 3D virtual worlds in assisting their group communication. In Figure 9.2, the left-hand-side image shows a "group photo" captured directly from Second Life. The individual identity in 3D virtual worlds during collaboration appears to be an essential factor, for example, students not only spend a considerable amount of time in customizing their avatars to reinforce their virtual identities, they also use avatars as the reference points when referring to design elements and 3D models during collaboration, for example, they often made statements such as "the floor above YOU."

We also observe that Second Life can enable people to become "immersed in the experience" of interacting with the design representations. "The sense of immersion" is defined as the level of fidelity that virtual environments provide to the user's senses (Narayan, 2005), which can be enhanced with the use of avatars. In some designs, avatars also become an important part of the virtual home. In most of the design presentations produced by the groups, avatars were used to help present the experience of inhabiting the virtual home.

In addition, students imported 2D scanned sketches, as shown in the Figure 9.2 middle image, into 3D virtual worlds for synchronous communication. They also exported screen shots, (Figure 9.2 right), captured from 3D virtual worlds for asynchronous communication such as email attachments.

Some groups demonstrated a very high level of competency in applying and adopting different features in 3D virtual worlds during different design phases. For example, in the "Archi-Bio" project, students successfully demonstrated how the group members strategically used different features in 3D virtual worlds to develop the design from initial concept, in the form of a scanned image, to inspire their design (Figure 9.3 left) through to the abstract 3D volumes that assisted their conceptual development (Figure 9.3 middle) and to their final detailed implementation of the virtual home (Figure 9.3 right).

9.8. Evaluation and Discussion

As discussed earlier, we adopted Winn's (1993) teaching approach, which relies on an understanding of how students interact with the courseware. The assumption of this approach is that the students play an active role in learning by not only receiving what has been delivered to them but also constructing the knowledge themselves through interactions in 3D virtual words during design development and implementation, as well as other collaborative group activities. Second Life provides an excellent platform with which the students construct their knowledge and gain

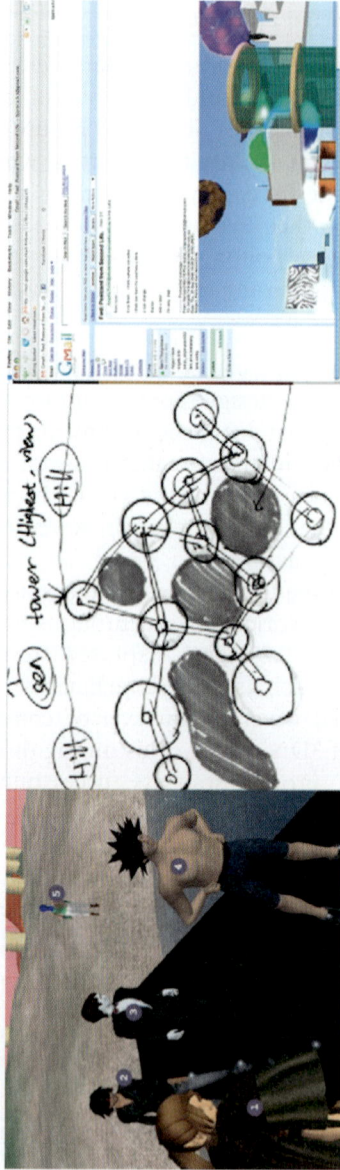

Figure 9.2: Different aids used during design collaboration

Figure 9.3: The design development of the "Archi-Bio" project in Second Life

creative design experiences. We have evaluated Second Life as a new kind of design-learning platform based on how it provides for several aspects of design. Gül (2008) points out those different virtual environments provide different affordances, which have an impact on designers' and learners' behaviors.

Design and modelling: Second Life supports the parametric modelling method, which comprises a set of 3D models whose forms are determined inside the virtual design environment by selecting geometric types and manipulating their parameters. The models can also be freely adjusted at a later stage. Most 3D virtual worlds also support different viewpoints such as first-person view and third-person view during modelling. Therefore, Second Life well supports the understanding of the spatial arrangement of the design elements; and the development of students' spatial abilities.

In terms of constraints, although 3D virtual worlds enable students to start designing/modelling from the very early conceptual stage using basic geometric forms, this can be challenging and inadequate for some students as the students comment that they often have to sketch the design on paper to understand the overall design concept and layout, before modelling in Second Life.

Collaboration and awareness: most 3D virtual worlds support synchronous collaboration. They often have a text-based chat channel for communication. Most virtual worlds afford the presence of designers/learners and their collaborators (the awareness of self and others) through the chat channel and the representation of the avatars; the use of place metaphor (the awareness of the design/learning environments) and the use of navigational and orientation aids.

In terms of constraints, monitoring collaboration and coordinating each other's design/modelling activities can become very difficult. In Second Life, more awareness is provided through so-called consequential communication and feed-through during the collaboration. In "consequential communication," the characteristic movements of an action (e.g., typing includes hand movements or walking includes legs and body movements) communicate its character and content to others (Segal, 1995). In "feed-through," the feedback produced when objects are manipulated provides others with clues about the manipulations (Dix et al., 1993). For example, in Second Life, when a student is modelling/manipulating a 3D model, these design actions and processes are visible to the collaborators. This is an example of "feed-through" behaviors that support awareness in the collaborative design environment.

9.9. Student Perceptions

At the end of the collaborative architectural studio, students who completed the studio were asked to answer a questionnaire. The questionnaire consisted of three parts with a total of 34 questions.

- Part one of the questionnaire aims to evaluate the performance of various technical features in Second Life for supporting collaborative design and learning activities, in relation to other synchronous and asynchronous communication tools.

- Part two of the questionnaire focuses on surveying students' awareness and perception of teamwork skill development in Second Life.
- The questionnaire ends with a set of open questions to develop more in-depth understanding of students' perception and expectation of 3D virtual worlds in supporting collaborative design learning. Participating students reported and discussed the evaluation, preference and expectation of various key issues, ranging from communication, design representation, design documentation, project management, to conflict resolution and other teamwork skill development in 3D virtual worlds.

The sample size of the study is 32 from a class of 36 students responding. 56% of the participated students are male. 70% of the students have two to three years design experience. 22% of them have only one year design experience. All students have at least one year experience in using general CAD tools. 100% of the students have a personal computer and only 17% of them do not have Internet connection at home, which implies that the students are computer literate. However, a majority (96%) of the students experienced Second Life for the very first time during the collaboration. The students are therefore considered as both novice designers and novice virtual world users. We summarize the questionnaire results indicating students' perception of Second Life for collaborative design learning in the following sections.

Design support: Students were largely divided regarding their level of satisfaction with Second Life in supporting decision-making and the design outcomes. 39% of the students rate their experiences as neutral, and 39% of the students were "dissatisfied/very dissatisfied." As shown in the following direct quotes from the students, their opinions are often conflicting, reflecting on both the strength and weakness of Second Life from their collaborative experience, and in relation to features of general CAD applications that are familiar to them.

> *3D collaborative modelling … instantaneous and easy to relay … I like that the group could see objects being made instantaneously … could discuss … dislike that it was hard to meet at the same time.*

> *is not compatible with other rendering software and has basic modelling technologies. But application of textures and lighting is excellent … very easy and quick for modelling.*

> *(in) 3D (it) is easier to understand the concept of the design and gives an impression of how it looks/behaves … Second Life was an entertaining, novel mode of communication, but was not often helpful, as it required every group member to be online.*

Communication: 32% of the students consider Second Life for communication as being "effective/very effective." 42% of the students consider the synchronous communication mode in Second Life as neutral when compared to asynchronous communication tools such as email. Once again, students' perception has been largely divided, indicating significant differences among students, even when they have similar background and experience.

- Students are divided about comparing synchronous communication in Second Life with other asynchronous web-based communication technologies such as blogs and wikis. 35% of the students consider the synchronous chat channel in Second Life as "effective/very effective," as a tool to communicate design ideas. Whilst 33% of the students rate "not effective/very not effective". Selected comments from the students include:

  > *Synchronous (communication) was most effective when meeting however asynchronous (communication was most effective) when organizing meetings and giving group information.*

  > *Text-based chat was the most appropriate. Audio can be a helpful tool but depends on the connection.*

- 45% of the students consider that other popular web-based communication tools such as MSN messenger is a more effective synchronous communication tool than Second Life. 42% of the students rate as neutral.

Teamwork: Teamwork skill development remains as the most challenging aspect in applying 3D virtual worlds for design collaboration. Students indicate that it was difficult to work together as a group due to the inability of having group members meeting face-to-face. 51% of the participants "agree/strongly agree" with this statement as they consider "Face-to-face meeting was the most productive," and 25% of them "disagree/strongly disagree." Furthermore:

- 51% of the students consider managing team activities difficult in remote design collaboration.
- 55% of the students fail to establish a plan or procedure collectively within their groups for working together.
- Nevertheless, 40% of the students do "agree/strongly agree" that teamwork tasks encourage collaborative learning. 42% of the students are not sure as they rate neutral. 48% of the students also believe that they gain knowledge and skills from their group members during the collaborative project.
- Commenting on the use of 3D virtual worlds for coordinating team activities in relation to other means, some students consider

  > *Email was good because we did not need to coordinate meeting times. Second Life, face-to-face (meeting) and phone call were good to get fast responses…*

- Some students indicated that their group did not prefer email for design communication because "people don't regularly check their emails and therefore it slowed down (the) progress," and the reason they prefer Second Life is because they "could communicate instantly whilst exploring options and activities."

Summary: The above results of the questionnaire indicate polarisation among students over the user perception and tool preference during the design collaboration in Second Life. The results together with our observation of and discussion with the students unveil some challenging aspects, especially regarding the issues relating to introducing new technologies and the management of teamwork. They have also directly impacted on the overall satisfaction of students.

The outcomes of the collaborative project as shown in the earlier section clearly indicate that the students are able to develop collaborative approaches and implement designs in Second Life to a very satisfactory level. However, the questionnaire results show that students were at times frustrated with various issues emerging from the collaboration including: lack of design support in Second Life compared to mainstream CAD applications; inability to manage the team; delay in responses from collaborators; language barriers; cultural differences; lack of shared design understanding and lack of a common goal for the collaboration. Students' answers also highlight the following virtual world features that require future development:

- More comprehensive features for 3D design development: the 3D mode of design representation allows clearer and more effective design communication among group members, compared to 2D sketches. The 3D representation provides an instant visual feedback of design creation and modification. There is a need for better support of collaborative 3D modelling including: referencing and virtual "pointing" of design models, more complex 3D modelling and model sharing including version control, compatibility and compliance with general CAD applications and professional CAD standards. Students also suggest possible add-ons to customize virtual worlds for design collaboration in specific design disciplines and to import and export more design and modelling resources for collaboration (e.g., direct information flow with other CAD applications), to enhance collaborative 3D design and modelling.
- More support for teamwork: tools that support collaboration are necessary, for example, it is very difficult to keep track of design development in a group collaborative session in Second Life. Effective monitoring of group design activities will increase the level of engagement for the remote team and encourage participation.

9.10. Recommendations

9.10.1. *Clear Aims and Objectives*

What was evidenced in the students' response to this studio was the need to be very clear when articulating to the students the aim and outcomes of the collaboration, and the relevance to the context of their own design disciplines. Students indicated that they could not always see the relevance of the activities such as learning new design and collaborative technologies and developing core skills for teamwork, when they consider the direct relevance to their design disciplines. It is important to provide them with a longer-term view of collaborative design to the technological issues they will confront as practitioners and the benefits of virtual design skills. Also students need to be made aware of the importance of the design activity set in new contexts, the opportunity to challenge design boundaries being important to their design skill and career development.

9.10.2.   *Strategies for Effective Course Content and Tutorial Sessions*

As shown in the evaluation, adopting 3D virtual worlds as a constructivist and collaborative learning platform in design education remains very challenging for many students, both technically and perceptually. When introducing students to a new learning experience that challenges the boundaries of their learning to date, it is important to scaffold their learning, especially at the early stages. The tutorial sessions are the primary opportunity to achieve this when the students are in a "hands-on" environment. Tutorials at the start of the module need to be highly structured and provide the elementary knowledge and skills to engage students in the virtual design domain. All students at times will feel challenged and self conscious in new learning environments so providing basic knowledge and skills is important to support their learning needs. Tutorial topics would include basic skills of inhabiting virtual worlds, 3D modelling (an appropriate level of) virtual world scripting/programming and digital communication. Once the students grasp these basic knowledge and skills and become more familiar and comfortable with 3D virtual worlds, the structure of the tutorials can then be more flexible and responsive to accommodate higher-level design activities such as design development, consultation and critique.

It is interesting also to see that students are not always able to transfer core skills such as communication or project management to new environments. As with the rationale for structured tutorials above, this highlights the importance of revisiting these skills and aligning them with design skills in the course content development. Also this is an opportune time to reinforce these skills in the context of their professional education overall.

Of significance in a collaborative design project such as this is the importance of introducing students to the concept of internationalization through the development of knowledge, skills and more importantly attitudes for effective cross-culture design collaboration. Generally these are new concepts to students and ones that need support in the initial stages of the project and an effective meta-cognitive phase in supporting students to think about the experience and draw from it.

9.10.3.   *Strategies for Collaborative Assessment*

Assessment of group work or collaborative exercises is always difficult but when it includes a new learning environment and cross-cultural collaboration this difficulty is compounded. Because of the "novelty" of this learning experience students will need extra support through formative assessment feedback as well as strategies such as:

- Guiding the groups to formalizing both the collaborative and individual tasks and following up on the quality of the delivery of the tasks.
- Monitoring closely the design activities at both group and individual levels, for example, through a group reflective blog or log. Assessing the collaborative process (not only the final outcome) and providing specific formative feedback.
- Encouraging active participation of group members by reflecting individual contributions (not only their group performances) in the assessment, for example, through self and peer reviews.

References

Abbott, J., & Ryan, T. (1999). *Constructing knowledge, reconstruction schooling.* http:// www.21learn.org/publications/edleadership1999.php(access:12 September 2009)

Anderson, J. (1976). *Language, memory and thought.* Hillsdale, NJ: Erlbaum Associates.

Anderson, J. (1983). *The architecture of cognition.* Cambridge, MA: Harvard University Press.

Barrows, H. S. (1986). A taxonomy of problem-based learning methods. *Medical Education, 20,* 481–486.

Bransford, J., Brown, A., & Cocking, R. (Eds). (2000). *How people learn: Brain, mind, experience and school.* Washington, DC: National Research Council.

Brooks, B. M., Attree, E. A., Rose, F. D., Clifford, B. R., & Leadbetter, A. G. (1999). The specificity of memory enhancement during interaction with a virtual environment. *Memory, 7*(1), 65–78.

Bruner, J. (1966). *The process of education: Towards a theory of instruction.* Cambridge, MA: Harvard University Press.

Clark, S., & Maher, M. L. (2005). Learning and designing in a virtual place: Investigating the role of place in a virtual design studio. In: J. P. Duarte, G. Ducla-Soares, & A. Z. Sampaio (Eds), *Proceedings of eCAADe 2005,* Technical University of Lisbon (pp. 303–310).

Cowdroy, R., & Williams, A. P. (2005). Aligning teaching and assessment: The key to greatly improved graduate quality and sustainable reaching efficiency. In: *The first international conference on: Enhancing teaching and learning through assessment,* Hong Kong.

Cowdroy, R., & Williams, A. P. (2006). Assessing creativity in the creative arts. *Art, Design and Communication in Higher Education, 5*(2), 97–117.

Craig, D. L., & Zimring, C. (2000). Supporting collaborative design groups as design communities. *Design Studies, 21*(2), 187–204.

Dede, C. (1995). The evolution of community support for constructionist learning: Immersion in distributed virtual worlds. *Educational Technology, 35,* 46–52.

Dede, C. (1996). Emerging technologies and distributed learning. *American Journal of Distance Education, 10*(2), 4–36.

Dede, C., Salzman, M., & Loftin, R. B. (1996). The development of virtual world for learning Newtonian mechanics. In: *Multimedia, hypermedia and virtual reality* (pp. 87–106). Berlin: Springer.

Dick, W., & Carey, L. (1985). *The systematic design if instruction.* Glenview, IL: Scott Foresman.

Dickey, M. D. (2005). Three-dimensional virtual worlds and distance learning: Two case studies of active worlds as a medium for distance education. *British Journal of Educational Technology*, *36*, 439–451.

Dickey, M. D. (2007). Teaching in 3D: Pedagogical affordances and constraints of 3D virtual worlds for synchronous distance education. *Distance Education*, *24*, 105–121.

Dix, A., Finlay, J., Abowd, G., & Beale, R. (1993). *Human-computer interaction* (3rd ed.). Spain: Prentice Hall.

Fleming, M. L., & Levie, W. H. (1993). *Instructional message design: Principles from the cognitive and behavioral science*. Hillsdale, NJ: Educational technology publications.

Forman, E. A., & Cazden, C. B. (Eds). (1985). *Exploring Vygotskian perspectives in education*. Cambridge: Cambridge University Press.

Gagne, R. M., Briggs, L. J., & Wager, W. W. (1988). *Principles of instructional design*. New York: Holt Rinehart & Winston.

Glasersfeld, E. V. (1983). Learning as constructive activity. In: J. C. Bergeron & N. Herscovics (Eds), *Proceedings of the 5th annual meeting of the North American Group of PME*, Montréal: PME-NA.

Gu, N., Gül, L. F., & Maher, M. L. (2007). Designing and learning within the design: A case study of principles for designing and teaching 3D virtual worlds. In: *Proceedings of CAADRIA 2007*, Nanjing, China (pp. 127–132).

Gül, L. F. (2008). Affording embodiment in collaborative virtual environments: What is the role of presence in collaborative design? In: A. Spagnolli & L. Gamberini (Eds), *Proceedings of Presence 2008*, Padova, Italy (pp. 297–304).

Gül, L. F., Gu, N., & Maher, M. L. (2007). Designing virtual worlds: A case study of design education in and of 3D virtual worlds. In: *Proceedings of CONNECTED 2007*, Sydney.

Huitt, W. (2003). Constructivism. *Educational Psychology Interactive*, Valdosta State University. Accessed September 12, 2009, from http://teach.valdosta.edu/WHuitt/index.html

Johnson, D., Johnson, R., & Stanne, M. (2000). *Cooperative learning methods: A meta analysis*. The Cooperative Learning Centre at the University of Minnesota. http://www.co-operation.org (access: 12 September 2009).

Jonassen, D. H. (1999). Designing constructivist learning environments. In: *Instructional design theories and models* (pp. 215–239). Mahwah, NJ: Erlbaum Associates.

Kahneman, D., & Tversky, A. (1996). On the reality of cognitive illusions. *Psychological Review*, *103*, 582.

Kvan, T. (2001). The problem in studio teaching-revisiting the pedagogy of studio teaching. In: *Proceedings of the 1st ACAE Conference on Architecture Education*, National University of Singapore (pp. 157–166).

Kvan, T., Mark, E., Oxman, E., & Martens, B. (2004). Ditching the dinosaur: Redefining the role of digital media in education. *International Journal of Design Computing*, *7*. http://wwwfaculty.arch.usyd.edu.au/kcdc/ijdc (access: 12 September 2009).

Kvan, T., Schmitt, G. N., Maher, M. L., & Cheng, N. Y.-W. (2000). Teaching architectural design in virtual studios. In: R. Fruchter, F. Pena-Mona, & W. M. K. Roddis (Eds), *Computing in civil and building engineering* (pp. 162–169). Stanford.

Landa, L. (1983). The algo-heuristic theory of instruction. In: *Instructional design theories and models*. Hillsdale, NJ: Lawrence Erlbaum Associates.

Maher, M. L. (1999). Variations on a virtual design studio. In: *Proceedings of the 4th international Workshop on CSCW in design*, Universite de Technologie de Compiegne (pp. 159–165).

Mahoney, J. (2004). What is constructivism and why is it growing? *Contemporary Psychology*, *49*, 360–363.

Narayan, M. (2005). Collaboration and cooperation: Quantifying the benefits of immersion for collaboration in virtual environments. In: *Proceeding of VRST 2005*. California: ACM Press.

Pallof, R., & Pratt, K. (1999). *Building learning communities in cyberspace: Effective strategies for the online classroom*. San Francisco: Jossey-Bass Publishers.

Reigeluth, C. M. (1983). *Instructional design: What is it and why is it?* Hillsdale, NJ: Lawrence Erlbaum Associates.

Riegler, A. (2005). Editorial; The constructivist challenge. *Constructivist Foundations*, *1*(1), 1–8.

Savery, J. R., & Duffy, T. M. (1994). Problem Based Learning: an instructional model and its constructivist framework. In: *Constructivist learning environments: Case studies in instructional design*. Englewood Cliffs, NJ: Educational Technology Publications.

Schnabel, M. A., Kvan, T., Kruijff, E., & Donath, D. (2001). The first virtual environment design studio, architectural information management. In: *Proceedings of eCAADe 2001*, Helsinki, Finland (pp. 394–400).

Schön, D. A. (1983). *The reflective practitioner*. New York: Basic Books.

Schön, D. A. (1987). *Educating the reflective practitioner: Towards a design for teaching and learning in the professions*. San Francisco: Jossey-Bass.

Segal, L. (1995). Designing team workstations: The choreography of teamwork. In: P. Hancock, J. Flach, J. Caird & K. Vicente (Eds), *Local applications of the ecological approach to human-machine systems* (pp. 392–415). Hillsdale, NJ: Lawrence Erlbaum.

Snowman, J., & Biehler, R. (2000). *Psychology applied to teaching*. Boston: Houghton Mifflin Company.

Spady, W. G. (2001). *Beyond counterfeit reforms: Forging an authentic future for all our learners*. Lanham, ML: The Scarecrow Press.

Winn, W. (1993). *A conceptual basis for educational applications of virtual reality*. Human Interface Technology Laboratory, Washington Technology Center, University of Washington.

Woods, D. (1985). Problem-based learning and Problem-solving. In: D. Boud (Ed.), *Problem-based learning in education for the professions* (pp. 19–42). Sydney: Higher Education Research and Development Society of Australasia.

Wyeld, T. G., Prasolova-Forland, E., & Chang, T.-W. (2006). Virtually collaborating across cultures: A case study of an online theatrical performance in a 3DVCE spanning three continents. In: *Proceedings of the 6th international conference on advanced learning technologies* (pp. 1076–1078).

Yukselturk, E., & Cagiltay, K. (2008). Collaborative work in online learning environments. *Critical Issues, Dynamics and Challenges*, *1*, 114–140.

Author Biographies

Dr Ning Gu is a lecturer in the School of Architecture and Built Environment at the University of Newcastle, Australia. He researches in the broad areas of design computing, particularly in generative design systems, virtual worlds and BIM. Ning is a pioneer of applying leading-edge information technologies in design and learning and has established an international collaborative design studio using Second Life.

He has also designed and implemented a wide variety of collaborative virtual environments and applied them in his teaching and research in numerous Australian and international tertiary design institutions including the University of Newcastle, University of Sydney, MIT and Columbia University. He has published extensively in the field of design computing and design education. He is Research Leader of the Collaboration Platform project in the Cooperative Research Centre for Construction Innovation (CRC-CI).

Dr. Leman Figen Gul is an associate professor at the Architecture Program at the International University of Sarajevo. Dr. Gul's work is featured with design studies and design education. Her research interests include investigating design cognition in virtual worlds, design teaching in virtual environments, human–computer interactions and computer-supported cooperative work. She received her BArch (1993) and her MUCon (1986) in the Urban Conservation Program at the Mimar Sinan University in Istanbul and MDes (2003) in Digital Media and PhD (2007) in Architecture at the University of Sydney. She was a lecturer and tutor at the University of Sydney, and a research fellow at the University of Newcastle (Australia) before joining the International University of Sarajevo in 2009.

Associate Professor Anthony Williams is currently the Head of School of Architecture and Built Environment at the University of Newcastle, Australia. He has conducted research into the design domain across two primary areas, Design Team Collaboration and Design Cognition, covering both design education and spatial abilities. Anthony has authored over 150 publications in the fields of design cognition, teaching methodologies, design education and assessment of design activities. He is currently involved in an ARC project on Attitudes and Behaviours relating to Environmentally Friendly Shopping Centres.

Dr. Walaiporn Nakapan graduated from the Faculty of Architecture, Chulalongkorn University in 1995. Then she obtained her Masters and PhD in Nancy, France, specialising in Computer-Aided Design and building product databases. Since joining the Faculty of Architecture, Rangsit University in 2002, she has been program director of the MSc Program in Computer-Aided Design and Master of Architecture Program in Computer-Aided Design.

Chapter 10

The Theatre of Performance Appraisal: Role-Play in Second Life

Shona Morse, Fiona Littleton, Hamish Macleod and Rory Ewins

10.1. Introduction

Performance appraisal is often seen as a source of stress in the workplace, both for appraisers and for those appraised (Tomaka, Blascovich, Kelsey, & Leitten, 1993). The prospect of having one's strengths and weaknesses scrutinized by managers can lead to anxiety among staff members, requiring considerable care on the part of management.

Performance appraisal has many critics and has been a controversial issue in educational and working environments (Fletcher, 2004, 2008; Armstrong & Baron, 2005; Mullins, 2005, 2007; Bratton & Gold, 2003, 2007; Torrington, Hall, & Taylor, 2002; Lucas, Lupton, & Mathieson, 2006; Bartlett, Ghoshal, & Beamish, 2008; Tournish, 2006). While alternative appraisal strategies do exist, such as focusing on process using total quality management (Lam & Schaubroeck, 1999), or multi-source or team assessments, the conventional 'person-to-person' model still predominates. With so much responsibility resting upon individual appraisers, appropriate training has long been considered necessary and valuable (Zedeck & Cascio, 1982). Role-play, in particular, has been an important component of such training (Carlton & Sloman, 1992).

Computer-assisted appraisal training has a similarly lengthy history (Davis & Mount, 1984), while role-play has been a feature of online gaming since the earliest text adventures of the 1970s. Most recently, online 3-D virtual worlds have created an opportunity to explore possibilities in extending the use of role-play in training beyond its current limits, allowing experiments with roles that would be difficult to enact in real life.

Higher Education in Virtual Worlds
Copyright © 2009 by Emerald Group Publishing Limited
All rights of reproduction in any form reserved
ISBN: 978-1-84950-609-0

This study investigates the potential of role-play within Second Life to substitute for and improve upon face-to-face role-play in performance appraisal training, building on a paper by Morse (2008). Because Second Life allows users to create avatars of any appearance, age, race and gender, it offers possibilities for role-play that do not exist in face-to-face training scenarios. Trainees can take on characters dramatically different from their real-life identities without giving any indication of those true identities, unlike in face-to-face role-playing where physical appearance cannot easily be changed (apart from one's dress).

This raises many questions about whether and how such 'identity play' affects role-play for appraisal training purposes. Before these can be explored, however, we need to know whether virtual appraisal training is feasible within the kind of time frames faced by appraisal trainers, what the practical and technical obstacles might be and something of the effectiveness of the experience from trainees' points of view.

Our study drew on the extensive use of Second Life in the University's MSc in E-learning (Bayne, 2008; Hemmi, Bayne, & Land, 2009) and involved students of the University of Edinburgh's MSc in the Management of Training and Development as participants. Most had prior professional experience of appraisal situations. After initial training in the use of Second Life, they were provided with standard avatar costumes — bodies and clothing — to wear during role-play scenarios held in an office-like environment in-world. Different scenarios gave each trainee experience of playing both appraiser and appraisee. Follow-up questionnaires were conducted after each session, and in-depth focus groups were held at the end of the study.

A range of useful lessons emerged from this preliminary work, which we envisage will lead to further studies exploring the effect on appraisal role-play of more wide-ranging identity changes such as gender swaps and other forms of 'identity tourism' (Nakamura, 2002), as well as to the refinement of methods of delivering such training to larger groups.

10.2.   Performance Appraisal Training Development Possibilities

Performance appraisal is widely used in business and education and over time has been much debated by psychologists, management and human resource theorists. A 1965 study comments that 'criticism has a negative effect on achievement of goals' and 'praise has little effect one way or the other' (Meyer, Kay, & French, 1965, p. 124). In a more recent example, appraisal has been comprehensively critiqued as flawed on almost every level (Tournish, 2006).

Criticisms focus variously on the use of performance appraisal by organizations as a form of motivation and control (linked to pay and rewards) with a focus on the individual, rarely the process; on the lack of skills of appraisers (a tendency to leniency or stringency, the halo/horns effect, a centralizing tendency to rate everyone in the middle and a lack of transparency or equity) (Feldman, 1981; Murphy & Margulies, 2004; Tournish, 2006; Muller-Camen, Croucher, & Leigh, 2008); on concerns about the effectiveness of training (Woehr & Huffcutt, 1994) and on people's innate resistance towards being negatively criticized (Feldman, 1981; Tournish, 2006).

Despite these concerns, use of performance appraisal and performance monitoring is growing (Stanton, 2000), and so, it would seem prudent to explore which type of appraisal training has the greatest positive impact. Until now, the focus of such training has been on information-giving (knowledge) and role-play (skill development and experience), the latter being one of the most effective training methods in the field (Carlton & Sloman, 1992). We hypothesized that by exploring different ways of engaging in role-play, this repertoire might be expanded. Consequently, to inform our study, we first focused on literature addressing role-play and identity exploration.

10.2.1. Role-Play

Role-play has a long history, with different sources giving diverse definitions. On a simple level, stemming from the earliest playacting, the concept is one of taking a 'role', a term thought to derive from the 'rolled up' scripts used by actors in ancient Greece (Blatner, 2002). Van Ments (1983, p. 20) proposed that the difference between acting and role-playing is that acting aims to create something for an audience, whereas role-players aim to 'feel, react and behave as closely as possible to the way someone placed in that situation would do' for the benefit of themselves rather than an audience. Role-playing has been put to multiple uses as a rehearsal or learning activity, including rehearsing for job roles. Examples from the early twentieth century are found in education and in clinical psychiatry (psychodrama), while later examples include working in flight simulators, training social workers and doctors, leadership training and, from the 1940s onward, organizational development (Blatner, 2002).

Blatner (2002) suggests that role-playing is a 'method for exploring issues involved in complex social situations', making connections to Piaget's modes of learning (assimilation and accommodation) and arguing that, unlike the 'rote' learning of assimilation, the skill development in role-play is a form of accommodation learning, which 'is almost impossible to fully forget'. The mix of thinking, emotion and action can make this type of learning very powerful. Role-play also promotes increased self-awareness, which is thought to enhance performance (Fletcher & Bailey, 2003). Speaking and assessing from different role perspectives may help us think about the basis of our own and others' views and prejudices, potentially revealing valuable insights.

If real-life role-play carries such benefits, what are some of the benefits of online role-play?

In real life, role-play 'involves immediate interpretation of, and reaction to, signals from others' (Bell, 2001, p. 68). Online text-based role-play allows more time for reflection and potentially the time to consult mentors or others during a scenario without the awareness of other participants, thus maintaining the integrity of the scene. This could even be true with voice communication, assuming the user controls when voice is transmitted.

Moving role-play from the real world to the virtual may offer advantages in connection with motivation and play. In their accounts of web-based role-play in educational settings, Linser, Naidu, and Ip (1999, p. 2) and Ip and Naidu (2001) refer to 'having fun' by 'playing with possibilities and alternative worlds' as a critical motivator for students engaged in role-play.

Online role-play potentially allows for greater suspension of disbelief during a scenario than in real-life equivalents. The physical presence of their counterparts, a constant reminder that they are not actually the people represented in their roles, could prompt players to slip out of role, which their representation as textual presences or 3-D avatars may prevent. This could be particularly helpful when the roles assigned are significantly different from the players themselves in age, race, gender or simply physical demeanour.

This could also bring cost benefits. Companies such as Just Roleplayers (2006) provide professionally trained actors for business role-play training to 'truthfully maintain characters, emotions, attitudes' in a 'consistent' and 'objective' way, making them 'more believable'. If trainees themselves can achieve better levels of believability, this expense could be unnecessary. Having more roles played by trainees could also significantly reduce training time by giving each a turn at role-play in fewer sessions overall, or allow for more attempts within the same time frame to reinforce its lessons.

Having considered the rehearsal aspect, we also considered the impact of 'otherness' and identity exploration.

10.2.2.   Identity Exploration

Prensky (2009) has commented on the plasticity of the brain, arguing that sustained interaction with technology may generate adaptations that 'restructure' the brain, with consequences for cognition. He also considers prolonged exposure to realistic simulation a potential trigger for development from which new moral and ethical choices may emerge. Key writers have alerted us that coming generations seem to think differently as a result of their gaming experiences (Turkle, 1996, 2005; Gee, 2007; Beck & Wade, 2004; Taylor, 2002; Hine, 2000); organizations may need new development strategies to take these new ways of thinking into account. One area that has emerged from such writers is identity exploration.

Identity exploration takes us beyond the physical notions of passport, fingerprint or iris. Exploring one's own identity and perhaps experimental identities, and thus being prompted to consider how others might react or think, is the essence of this enquiry. The ability to imagine the situation of another could be extended by *rehearsing to be* an 'other' personality.

Our underlying question therefore has been: could initial learning about performance appraisal in the virtual environment stimulate not only the exploration of a task scenario (which is already possible in real life) but also experimentation with ways of being that are less achievable in real life, such as being a different race, gender or age? Would this enhance effective learning, promote imagination and offer deeper insights into the world of the other party in the process?

Virtual worlds, including Second Life, offer opportunities to explore these different 'ways of being'. One can create a new physical representation, character and, to an extent, skills and attributes. The environment can change over time. Both text and voice can be used to exchange and interact. For participants, there is creativity and potential for experiment. What is the impact of creating such identities?

In an interesting study of high school students exploring 'possible selves' and what they learnt about 'identity, culture, stereotypes and prejudice in the first-hand experiential context of a virtual world', Lee and Hoadley (2007) found that by choosing to be of a different gender, students discovered that 'boys who played as girls observed more incidences of courtesy, flirting, and in some cases, sexism'. Also, they found discrimination based on appearance.

Lee and Hoadley argued that these discoveries enabled students 'to think beyond themselves in an experiential, tangible way' (*ibid.*) and that this had a radical effect on classroom discussion. Finally, the study led them to propose that

> *This identity adoption process trains students to solve problems from the point of view of the roles they are assuming, opening them up to new perspectives and challenging them to think in new ways (ibid.).*

This connects with Prensky's argument that human intelligence and digital simulation will enable the mind to go 'further and faster':

> *A person's ability to create, interpret, and evaluate the models underlying the simulations plays a large role in his or her ability to use them wisely.*
> (Prensky, 2009, p. 4)

Certain strategies and patterns of behaviour in performance appraisal training may contribute to poor experiences and results; when faced with new work responsibilities such as managing or appraising others, how one learns to undertake them can be significant in subsequent years. Good initial learning should promote good practice, but poor skill and understanding may require both unlearning and re-learning (Lewin, 1951; Becker, Hyland, & Acutt, 2006) — an expensive business for all concerned.

When organizations change how they operate, there is a pattern of behaviour modification where a planned change of the existing culture (unfreezing) by 'reducing those forces that maintain behaviour in its present form' (Lewin, cited in Mullins, 2007, p. 736) is followed by active development of new attitudes or behaviour and stabilizing the changes through new structures and policies (*ibid.*). Similarly, in learning/rehearsal for a role, some attitudes and perspectives can be challenged and unfrozen, amended through experience and 're-frozen' in a different form.

In learning how to appraise others, exploring and testing scenarios in a virtual setting where you can be both yourself and 'yourself as another' may encourage more reflective and therefore less reactive practice in the 'real' world. Enhancing empathic understanding (Blatner, 1988, pp. 146–148) and recognition of cultural and social perspectives should address some of the key failings currently besieging the field of performance appraisal training.

To gather some initial answers to these complex questions of identity, and to explore the feasibility of using online role-play in Second Life for performance appraisal training, we carefully designed and conducted the small-scale proof-of-concept study now described.

10.3. The Study

Participants were recruited into the study through the MSc in the Management of Training and Development, a programme that attracts an international mix of students. Potential participants were identified on the basis of having some employment experience and thus some possible direct experience of performance appraisal in the workplace and were approached individually after class. Voluntary agreement to participate was secured from 10 people who indicated some such experience, either as appraiser or as appraisee.

As a number of stages were planned for the study, all were asked to sign an agreement setting out the commitment expected of them and the reward being offered for their involvement (book tokens). The estimated time frame for their activities totalled 12–14 hours over a seven-week period. It was, of course, emphasized that they could withdraw from the study at any time. We also submitted this project to the university ethics committee.

All participants were asked to take part in three different role-play scenarios, taking the role of appraiser and appraisee on at least one occasion each. Participants were brought together for a preliminary briefing meeting before the first role-play session and were also asked to attend one of two group interview sessions at the end of the study. At the preliminary meeting, they completed a brief survey questionnaire about their recreational involvement with various game-, narrative- and performance-related activities. None were found to be unusual with respect to their technical or games-related experience.

The briefing meeting introduced participants to the Second Life system, explained what would be done in the role-play exercises and allowed them to raise any questions about the study. We indicated that the study was exploratory, and thus, we preferred not to discuss with them the specifics of our hypotheses. They were assured, however, that we would disclose these after the study.

As the study progressed, participants visited a university computer laboratory at scheduled times and were asked to sit at a particular computer. Movable room dividers screened them from one another visually, and two separate computer labs were used so that members of appraiser/appraisee pairs were isolated from each other. Because we were interested in the part played by the potential anonymity afforded by the medium of Second Life, they were expressly asked not to discuss their experiences with one another between sessions; although the participants knew one another, they were not told with whom they would be paired during the role-play and were asked not to take steps to identify the other participant. All were asked, however, in each end-of-session questionnaire, whether they thought they knew their partner on that day. The questionnaire also asked about their experience of the session, how engaged they felt with the exercise and how comfortable they felt with the medium of Second Life.

The information garnered from these questionnaires partially informed the questions posed in the group interview sessions, which will be discussed in more detail in Section 10.3.4. We encountered some fascinating issues (and differences) in regard to use of the technological, interpersonal issues and more.

10.3.1.   The Virtual Arena Context

The use of virtual worlds in higher education for research, teaching, collaboration and simulation has grown enormously in the recent years. The University of Edinburgh was one of the first in Britain to build its own island in Second Life. In early 2007, The School of Education co-founded the Virtual University of Edinburgh (Vue), an educational and research institute bringing together all those using virtual worlds for teaching, research and outreach. Through Vue, we have found Second Life to be an excellent environment for community formation among students, formal teaching and forging new partnerships and collaborations among colleagues within and beyond our university (Littleton & Bayne, 2008).

For this project, we used Holyrood Park (Picture 10.1), the home of the School of Education on Vue Island. This 16-acre parkland has three distinct tutorial spaces — a garden, a grove and a beach — and a café for socializing. A student described the space upon its launch as 'beautiful':

> *Much thought has been given to sound and shapes. The variety of trees and flowers is impressive. The soft lines and recreation of different textures and colours. The swings, the hammock, the wooden and hanging bridges, the porch. It is a real 3D work of art.*

Space on the ground is limited in Holyrood Park, and so, we constructed our role-play venues in the sky above it, ensuring that each was at least 25 m from the others to avoid chat overlap for the participants, that is, they would not be able to eavesdrop inadvertently on other pairs' conversations, which would have appeared in their chat transcripts were they within range. These constraints had some interesting consequences, as we will discuss.

The process constructed for the participants had various stages. The first briefing session gave participants some training in Second Life: they created an account and went through the standard process of creating an avatar. We asked participants to create avatars of their own gender, with names bearing no relation to their real ones. Once this was done, we showed them how to teleport to Holyrood Park, rather than

Picture 10.1: Holyrood Park

proceeding to the usual Second Life welcome areas, so that they could learn directly from our resident Second Life expert. They were taught how to move and control their avatar and how to modify its appearance and also how to save transcripts of their chat history. Their experience of chat itself at this stage was limited: we sought to limit interaction between their avatars during the briefing, particularly in comparison with our usual training sessions in Second Life, to preserve their anonymity.

In subsequent sessions, each participant logged in to Second Life and teleported to the main area of Holyrood Park. A folder was given to each avatar's inventory, containing the body, appearance and clothes for their role. Effectively, this was their costume for that day's scenario. Participants opened their inventories and dragged these entire folders onto their avatars to begin getting into role. This 'folder method' meant that participants did not have to understand the complexity that lay behind creating these costumes and transferring them to each participant. Our Second Life expert designed the costume avatars after deliberation by the team during the drafting of the scenarios.

Once participants were in costume, they divided into pairs (under instruction from a tutor avatar controlled by one of our team) and asked to sit in those pairs on different scripted park benches, which then ascended into the sky above Holyrood Park. This transportation from sunny parkland to a box-like 'arena' in the sky was, like putting on their 'costumes', part of the process of getting into role: this was their moment of walking on-stage (Picture 10.2).

Within the arena of the skyboxes were an outer waiting room and an inner office where each participant would take up their seats across a table: first the appraiser and then, once the appraiser invited him or her to enter the office, the appraisee. This signalled the beginning of their appraisal role-play proper (Picture 10.3).

As participants moved through each of these stages, the aim was to draw them into the fantasy context of the role-play and the role itself. The discontinuity between

Picture 10.2: Holyrood Park with temporary skyboxes

Picture 10.3: Inside view of skybox office

Holyrood Park and the skybox offices was such that they were transported even further from their real-life selves, through their original avatar as chosen and modified during the briefing, into the virtual manifestation of their role, all of which contributed to the sense of immersion. Second Life allowed us to create a theatrical experience without the need for a dedicated, physical theatre.

Although the participants were immersing themselves in their roles on-screen through their avatars in-world, their physical and intellectual personae remained anchored in the lab in front of the computer. While the fantastic aspects of the virtual world enhanced the sense of immersion, we were also employing the virtual world's ability to isolate the real, virtual and projected identity (Gee, 2007) in role-play. These aspects deserve some discussion.

10.3.2. Taking Role-Play Online while Keeping Learners in the Classroom

The argument for taking role-play online is that the fantasy environment that can be created there can contribute to the realism of the role being played. The virtual environment can both augment the narrative of the exercise by the addition of an appropriate backcloth and props and can remove the distraction of known faces and mundane surroundings. This argument is based on an anticipated increased likelihood that the participant will become immersed in the role-play and thus will benefit more from the exercise. While our observations indicated a high level of engagement on the part of the participants in the task in hand, we also observed an important element of *disengagement*, which we would like to discuss and which we intend to build upon in subsequent studies.

This was first drawn to our attention by casual observations of participants smiling, laughing or snorting to themselves about something happening on the screen. That is, the person engaged in the role-play was able to react, out of character, to social interaction in the role-play without that reaction interrupting and contaminating the ongoing narrative. At a simpler level, participants were able to break off from their online interaction to turn and seek advice from the tutor. This might have been a technical question about the interface but was more often to consult on some aspect of the ongoing role-play.

This dynamic suggests ways in which the role-play experience could be enhanced by tutor intervention and direction that would not be possible in role-play conducted face-to-face. The participant can be, at the same time, in role and in the classroom. Both identities — the player and the role being played — can simultaneously be active. This can be further understood by reference to Gee's analysis of the three identities present when video gaming (2007). First, there is the real person choosing to spend their time playing the game; what Gee calls the *real-world identity*. Then, there is the character played in the game that Gee refers to as the *virtual identity*. So far, we have the trainee participating in the educational role-play activity, and we have the role that he or she has been given to play. To these, however, Gee adds the notion of the *projective identity*. He intends the term to convey both the projection of the learner's real-world values, experience and motives into the character being played, and also the sense in which the character within the role-play is a 'work in progress' owned by the learner.

The projective identity, then, is something around which the student and the tutor can have a conversation, either at the end of the exercise or while the role-play takes place. The projective identity is externalized on the screen, in the form of what the virtual identity says and does, for the learner (the real-world identity) to reflect upon and the tutor to enquire about. The tutor can thus assist the learner in the conduct of an ongoing cognitive task analysis (Crandall, Klein, & Hoffman, 2006) of their agenda as manifest in their behaviour (or the behaviour of their virtual identity) within the role-play.

One future area for exploration and development will be to design approaches to online role-play that allows us to harness the potential of this projective identity.

10.3.3.   The Scenario Exercises

The three scenarios were essentially as they might have been in face-to-face role-play appraisal training. One, for example, involved the 40-year-old warden of a student hall appraising a 25-year-old assistant who had been in the job for six months and had occasionally overstepped his/her role, with a complaint being lodged on one occasion by a student's parents; the appraisee, meanwhile, felt that he/she had done reasonably well and was keen to take on more responsibility.

Participants kept to their own gender in these exploratory sessions, meaning that each scenario had male and female appraiser and appraisee costumes associated with it, all of them different — that is, 12 in total. As our participants came from a range of international backgrounds, we were careful not to make the costume avatars look too Northern European; they ended up somewhat Mediterranean or Middle Eastern in appearance.

Scenario sessions were held approximately a week apart. Once they were set up, we asked participants to spend 30 minutes on each scenario from the time their avatars entered the skybox offices. Full transcripts were carefully collected for each pair. One of the tutoring team also took screenshots by hovering outside the skyboxes and manipulating camera controls (so as not to intrude on the sessions themselves) and captured in-world video of certain sessions using third-party plug-in software. (The participants were aware of this at every stage.)

After the sessions, participants completed a questionnaire by giving ratings on a five-point Likert scale for statements about levels of comfort, engagement, learning, and success in playing the role. They were also asked open-ended questions about what they might have changed about their avatars, how this session went compared with the last and what could have been improved during the role-play.

The questionnaire results were generally modest, with few long-form answers, and would not stand up to substantive quantitative analysis, but some of the points raised were carried over to the final interview stage of the study.

10.3.4.   The Interviews

We held two concluding interview sessions, a group interview with more directed questions and a focus group with fewer, broader questions. Participants were asked to attend at least one; nine attended the group interview and five attended the focus group. The sessions were recorded on video and each lasted approximately an hour. The questions we asked drew upon our own experience of the scenario exercises and participants' answers to the questionnaires. These included:

Group Interview
- How did you feel about your avatar? Did any aspects of your manifestation in the world distract you or detract from your comfort in playing the role?
- Would you be curious about a more radical change in appearance — gender, race, disability or a significant age difference?
- Do you remember feeling apprehensive during the role-play? For example, about what your interlocutor might say next?
- Did you feel engaged in the role? How did you recognize this?
- Did you feel that your inexperience with the technology impeded your engagement with the role-play? Did this become less intrusive with time?

Focus Group
- How viable do you find Second Life role-play for inducting people into the business of participating in appraisal interviews?
- How might it differ from role-play conducted face-to-face? Would one or the other be more likely to lead to useful experiential learning?

10.4.   Findings

Not surprisingly, the opinions expressed in the two interview sessions were highly varied, sometimes contradictory between participants and in some cases self-contradictory.

10.4.1.   *Frustrations with Text Chat*

Because we were exploring the importance of anonymity in this situation, we had to steer away from voice-based interactions. Voice masking would also have been a complicating overlay, and sticking to text meant we were using less bandwidth than voice would require. However, the text-based conversation medium was unpopular with our participants, who found its speed limiting, and was a particular focus of complaint for our participants. Their awareness that voice channels were possible seemed to add to their frustration. Participants felt they were being overly clear about what they were trying to say, and therefore overly polite and less natural, as they did not want to miscommunicate. They regretted the absence of the voice tones that would have indicated that their counterparts had finishing speaking.

Some participants observed that being compelled to formulate one's conversational response and then type it was an additional cognitive load, which interfered with the flow of conversation. Having to type rather than speak was an added burden, even more so if one was working in a second language, which was true for some of our participants.

It is often argued, though, in relation to text-based communication in other settings, that delays in formulating and sending one's messages allow for a degree of monitoring and self-censorship. Slowing down the conversation helps one monitor one's actions and words. This has clear value in a performance appraisal setting.

A flip side of this was the 'stepping on toes' effect familiar to anyone using synchronous chat: typing over each other, where replies to previous questions effectively play hopscotch, is something with which people seem to become comfortable once they have used these technologies for a while. As our surveys showed, however, our participants were not heavy users of online communication and so reacted to such phenomena as annoying novelties.

One drawback of slowing the pace to improve communication is that it reduces the amount that can be covered in the time available. Participants reported cases where others would respond swiftly if upset or angry and suspected that some would have accepted a harsh comment just to finish on time.

10.4.2. The Degraded Nature of Communication in Second Life

Many participants felt that the communication opportunity was not rich enough to encourage engagement with their manifest representation in-world in the way that we had wished and speculated. However, their observations suggested that more complicated issues were involved than some of their rhetoric suggested: for example, issues of politeness and feelings of embarrassment. This pattern would be very familiar to anyone used to using synchronous chat, and in that respect, Second Life should be no more confusing than any other synchronous chat medium. Our previous experiences of teaching in Second Life show that students do adapt to the technology, but what takes longer is adapting to the technique. Blatner (2002) points out that there is a

> common tendency to assume that interpersonal skills are easier than technical skills – though in fact they are even more difficult – and so people tend to think they can engage in directing role playing before they've really achieved a level of bare competence (much less mastery).

Two issues arose when considering how to augment the social and interactive nature of the experience:

- facial expressions — tone of voice, lack of reaction;
- the greater impact of their partner's avatar's appearance — participants were not so conscious of their own.

Participants pointed out the 'lack of cues when you only have words' — during the role-play, they got little useful visual feedback from their own avatar or their partner's. Unlike in a fully embodied conversation, the behaviour of their avatars provided no clues about how participants were feeling; indeed, it could sometimes be unhelpful, such as when avatars adopted the defensive-looking default posture of crossed arms. While we had not aimed to do so in this preliminary study, the response of participants suggests that facilitating facial gestures, such that the posture and expression of avatars could be in keeping with the content and tone of the conversation, would be valued. Such gestures are easily implemented and could readily be incorporated into further stages of the research.

Working against any such developments would be the complaint from some participants that they were too focused on the chat box during the role-play and not really taking in the office or their counterpart. This could be addressed by reinforcing ways to limit the visual impact of the chat history on the screen overall during induction.

10.4.3. Engagement in the Role

Second Life was not a neutral space in which to conduct a research study. Some participants said they felt they were involved in a game rather than in a research activity. Some participants had days where they felt they were 'in role' while on others they were playing along. While this may have afforded them the unconscious learning benefits of play noted earlier, it might also have worked against their engagement with the activity.

We did find signs of such engagement, however. While some participants said they did not feel emotionally connected to their avatars, either in or out of role, other comments were inconsistent with this. One participant recalled feelings of annoyance and embarrassment that a particular 'costume' avatar was wearing flip-flops, as she would never attend a business meeting in such casual attire (our designer had assumed that nobody would be looking at their feet!). Others expressed embarrassment at their avatars inadvertently standing on the office table or walking through walls in an unbusinesslike way. Another avatar mistakenly took the appraiser's chair when the appraiser politely stood up as the appraisee entered the office. Participants noted the offence this might cause if it happened in real life. All of this suggests a degree of identification with their roles.

Participants suggested that the lack of connection they felt with their scenario avatars might have been different had they created their own avatars or used the ones created during induction — some noted that their original avatars felt relatively unused and hence wasted. We would note that these original avatars did actually play an important part by providing a constant baseline appearance with which participants could identity from week to week, upon which each week's 'costume' was placed — an important part of getting into role. Future work could perhaps focus on participants making their own avatars, but with scenario roles in mind. Costumes might also be restricted to clothes alone, rather than clothes and bodies, although this would undermine the potential for roles of a different age, race or gender.

At least one participant spoke directly to the themes of donning costumes and setting the scene. She noted the moment when avatars sat in pairs on each bench in Holyrood Park and were transported up to the office as being particularly effective for getting into role.

Some, however, said that the 'emotional reality' created by tense, difficult engagement was not really present in their role-playing. (This contradicted the experience of at least one team member, who sat in for an absent student during one session and felt that tension in-role surprisingly strongly.) This may have been, they speculated, because there is more focus on competition and power in real life.

One participant noted feeling more serious in the appraiser role but less serious as appraisee. There is certainly scope for further exploration of why this may be. Is the sense of emotional risk greater as appraiser than appraisee because the threat of dismissal and the reward of pay rises feel insufficiently 'real' in Second Life? Might a reward in Second Life's Linden dollars be a possible replacement?

One factor that had a marked impact on engagement was when participants received their one-page scenarios. In the first role-play, these were handed out at the beginning of the session. For subsequent sessions, they were circulated by email the day before, giving participants a chance to imagine possible strategies and responses. Participants reported feeling more focused on the scenario and the role-play when this was done. Of course, this factor would presumably apply in face-to-face role-play as much as in Second Life, but it does indicate that Second Life role-play can be affected by such factors in similar ways to face-to-face role-play, suggesting that ours was indeed an effective role-play environment.

Certain skills were notable in determining how fully participants engaged with the role-play: previous experience of role-playing, computer literacy and good command of the language. These should not be surprising but do present challenges for those seeking to use this environment with trainees who have little or no such experience. Participants agreed on the usefulness of online mentoring to overcome some of these gaps. All felt that their technical skills in this environment improved over the course of the study. The main area with room for improvement seemed to be the conduct of the role-play itself: they suggested that it would be useful to pair off initially to develop and practice such conventions as signing-off in text chats and simply for opportunities to sit and chat. This certainly sounds as if it would be helpful in future work.

10.4.4. Anonymity and Radical Identity Changes

Only one participant stated directly that anonymity was powerful in these sessions, but other comments suggested we were right to separate them from the social connections they had formed in class: a few noted that sometimes they could deduce who the other avatar was and that this undermined the authenticity of the role-play.

However, maintaining anonymity had its drawbacks. Participants felt that our seemingly arbitrary approach of isolating them in the induction before their first appraisal meeting meant they lost valuable opportunities for communication that would have better oriented them to the environment and to communicating within Second Life. As tutors during initial training, we also found this constraint awkward. We would now seek to incorporate an interactive stage into future inductions but would need to allow for the increased time it would take to orient a new participant to the system before role-play could take place.

One motivation for preserving anonymity was to preserve the potential for identity-play. But when asked about changing their avatar's appearance in radical ways, participants appeared not to have considered the possibilities. It had not occurred to them that they could role-play in a different gender, for example, to test how that might affect them. Some questioned whether it would make a difference, while others thought the changes might be interesting — but all responses were, in the end, speculative. It will take further, more focused studies to uncover this deeper potential for Second Life role-play in appraisal training.

10.4.5. *Learning from the Role-Play*

To our surprise, at least one participant claimed to have learned nothing from the role-play exercises — although he made this claim relatively early in the first interview session and resiled from it afterwards as the discussion deepened.

Part of the problem seems to have been that many participants would have liked a better understanding of the objectives of the study. A handout for the briefing explained the objectives thus:

> *Can appraisal be done in a computer-based environment? Can you learn, can you be prepared in a virtual or computer based environment? Could early appraisal training be started online? Our hypothesis is that there may be some benefit in using this medium for early training in performance appraisal skills.*

To explain our motives further at the outset, we felt, would have risked skewing the results. Yet, in the absence of explanation, participants constructed their own explanations of what we were looking for. As the relative predominance of the various findings above indicates, these largely revolved around the technical limitations of Second Life as a communications environment, rather than on its potential as a role-play training environment. In future studies, we will have to seek ways to clarify the focus of our studies to participants without contaminating the results.

When learning issues were discussed more directly in the interviews, it was clear that the scenarios themselves — looking beyond the virtual and role-play trappings — had left an impression. In certain cases, participants felt, they had learned what *not* to do during an appraisal, which from a training point of view is certainly useful.

10.5. Conclusions

Our study was not simply a case of technology for technology's sake. It was far from labour-saving, requiring training students in the use of the software and considerable development time. Conducting traditional face-to-face role-play training would have been quicker and simpler. However, we felt that a virtual approach to role-play could add value to performance appraisal training and wanted to explore that potential. This value was confirmed, directly and indirectly, by what our participants said in their final interviews. Our approach was not merely 'more of the same' repackaged in a post-modern form.

We wanted to generate the complexity and authenticity of a real experience while offering the kind of safe learning environment described by Ip and Naidu (2001) in relation to web-based role-play. Trying to understand how others think and feel can be to the common good. However, it should be remembered there is also scope for manipulation and for learning the best ways to exploit people to meet selfish ends. There may be issues of privacy to consider. Therefore, exercises such as ours need careful planning and evaluation. It is critical to ensure that boundaries are established and vulnerable staff or students are not treated inappropriately in the online environment.

There is still more that could and may well be reported from this preliminary study: for example, more detailed accounts of how the arena and costumes were constructed and of the induction process. In the future development of the project, we plan to provide participants with an accessible way of selecting elements of their appearance without having to know a great deal about the technologies of Second Life. Already there are venues in Second Life where users can choose from a selection of general morphological characteristics (appearance, race and gender), physiognomy and clothes, which they literally drag off the peg and onto their avatars. We suspect that working on one's own appearance for a specific scenario and role using easily manipulated clothes and morphology would provide trainees with even greater theatrical immersion in a role.

The project could head in various directions, but the most intriguing possibility is a thorough investigation of the impact of identity swapping in Second Life on role-play training. It has been clear for some time that disturbing effects can be at play when Second Life avatars take on drastically different appearances (Au, 2006). Seeing how others' reactions change towards an avatar that changes race, age or gender could be a powerful source of insight and learning for role-play trainees. Given the international mix of our student trainees, we might also explore whether and how people from different cultures would react differently to these simulations.

In light of the demographic changes and aging populations, we see in some countries, many people may have to work longer in future than today, and it may become more common to have three generations in one company. The relative levels of digital experience among employees will alter over time, but eventually all employees are likely to be part of the digital revolution. Second Life and its successors may one day be used not only for appraisal training but during performance appraisal itself, by national and international companies seeking cost-effective ways to bridge large distances. The lessons we learn through role-play training in Second Life today could have even greater value tomorrow.

Acknowledgement

The authors acknowledge the invaluable contribution of Marshall Dozier of Information Services at the University of Edinburgh to the conceptualization of the Second Life environment constructed for this study.

References

Armstrong, M., & Baron, A. (2005). *Managing performance: Performance management in action.* London: Chartered Institute of Personnel & Development.

Au, W. J. (2006). The skin you're in. *New World News* blog post, 23 February. Accessed July 3, 2009, from http://nwn.blogs.com/nwn/2006/02/the_skin_youre_.html

Bartlett, C., Ghoshal, S., & Beamish, P. (2008). *Transnational management: Text, cases, and readings in cross-border management* (5th ed.). New York: McGraw-Hill International.

Bayne, S. (2008). Uncanny spaces for higher education: Teaching and learning in virtual worlds. *ALT-J Research in Learning Technology, 16*(3), 197–205.

Beck, J., & Wade, M. (2004). *Got game: How the gamer generation is reshaping business forever.* Boston: Harvard Business School Press.

Becker, K., Hyland, P., & Acutt, B. (2006). Considering unlearning in HRD practices: An Australian study. *Journal of European Industrial Training, 30*(8), 608–621.

Bell, M. (2001). A case study of an online role play for academic staff. Paper presented at the 18th annual conference of ASCILITE, Melbourne, Australia, 9–12 December. Accessed July 3, 2009, from http://www.ascilite.org.au/conferences/melbourne01/pdf/papers/bellm.pdf

Blatner, A. (2002). *Role playing in education.* Accessed July 3, 2009, from http://www.blatner.com/adam/pdntbk/rlplayedu.htm

Blatner, A., & Blatner, A. (1988). *The art of play: An adult's guide to reclaiming imagination and spontaneity.* New York: Human Sciences Press Inc.

Bratton, J., & Gold, J. (2003). *Human resource management: Theory and practice* (3rd ed.). Hampshire: Palgrave Macmillan.

Bratton, J., & Gold, J. (2007). *Human resource management: Theory and practice* (4th ed.). Hampshire: Palgrave Macmillan.

Carlton, I., & Sloman, M. (1992). Performance appraisal in practice. *Human Resource Management Journal, 2*(3), 80–94.

Crandall, B., Klein, G., & Hoffman, R. (2006). *Working minds: A practitioner's guide to cognitive task analysis.* Cambridge, MA: MIT Press.

Davis, B. L., & Mount, M. K. (1984). Effectiveness of performance appraisal training using computer assisted instruction and behavior modelling. *Personnel Psychology, 37*(3), 439–452.

Feldman, J. M. (1981). Beyond attribution theory: Cognitive processes in performance appraisal. *Journal of Applied Psychology, 66*(2), 127–148.

Fletcher, C. (2004). *Appraisal and feedback: Making performance review work* (3rd ed.). London: CIPD.

Fletcher, C. (2008). *Appraisal, feedback and development: Making performance review work* (4th ed.). Abingdon: Routledge.

Fletcher, C., & Bailey, C. (2003). Assessing self-awareness: Some issues and methods. *Journal of Managerial Psychology, 18*(5), 395–404.

Gee, J. P. (2007). *What video games have to teach us about learning and literacy* (2nd ed.). New York: Palgrave Macmillan.

Hemmi, A., Bayne, S., & Land, R. (2009). The appropriation and repurposing of social technologies in higher education. *Journal of Computer Assisted Learning, 25*(1), 19–30.

Hine, C. M. (2000). *Virtual ethnography*. London: Sage.

Ip, A., & Naidu, S. (2001). Experienced-based pedagogical designs for eLearning. *Educational Technology, 51*(5), 53–55. Accessed July 3, 2009, from http://users.tpg.com.au/adslfrcf/lo/LearningExperience.pdf

Just Roleplayers. (2006). Why *use an actor-roleplayer rather than an existing staff member?* Accessed July 3, 2009, from http://justroleplayers.com/page3.html

Lam, S. S. K., & Schaubroeck, J. (1999). Total quality management and performance appraisal: An experimental study of process versus results and group versus individual approaches. *Journal of Organizational Behavior, 20*(4), 445–457.

Lee, J. J., & Hoadley, C. M. (2007). Leveraging identity to make learning fun: Possible selves and experiential learning in massively multiplayer online games (MMOGS). *Innovate, 3*(6)Accessed July 3, 2009, from http://innovateonline.info/?view = article&id = 348

Lewin, K. (1951). In: D. Cartwright (Ed.), *Field theory in social science; selected theoretical papers*. New York: Harper & Row.

Linser, R., Naidu, S., & Ip, A. (1999). Pedagogical foundations of web-based simulations in political science. Paper presented at the 16th annual conference of ASCILITE, University of Wollongong, NSW, Australia. Accessed July 3, 2009, from http://www.ascilite.org.au/conferences/brisbane99/papers/linsernaidum.pdf

Littleton, F., & Bayne, S. (2008). Virtual worlds in education. *Escalate News* (10), 26–28.

Lucas, R., Lupton, B., & Mathieson, H. (2006). *Human resource management in an international context*. London: CIPD.

Meyer, H. H., Kay, E., & French, J. R. P., Jr. (1965). Split roles in performance appraisal. *Harvard Business Review, 43*, 123–129.

Morse, S. (2008). Using virtual worlds for development of appraisal skills: Can the virtual worlds. Context offer anything new to teaching or business? Paper presented at the 8th international conference on HRD research and practice across Europe, Lille, France, 21–23, May, 2008.

Muller-Camen, M., Croucher, R., & Leigh, S. (2008). *Human resource management: A case study approach*. London: CIPD.

Mullins, L. (2005). *Management and organisational behaviour* (7th ed.). Harlow: Pearson Education.

Mullins, L. (2007). *Management and organisational behaviour* (8th ed.). Harlow: Pearson Education.

Murphy, T. H., & Margulies, J. (2004). Performance appraisals. Paper presented at mid-winter meeting, ABA Labor and Employment Law Section, Equal Employment Opportunities Committee, 24–27, March, 2004.

Nakamura, L. (2002). *Cybertypes: Race, ethnicity, and identity on the internet*. Abingdon: Routledge.

Prensky, M. (2009). H. sapiens digital: From digital immigrants and digital natives to digital wisdom. *Innovate, 5*(3)Accessed July 3, 2009, from http://innovateonline.info/index.php?view = article&id = 705

Stanton, J. M. (2000). Reactions to employee performance monitoring: Framework, review, and research directions. *Human Performance, 13*(1), 85–113.

Taylor, L. (2002). *Video games: Perspective, point-of-view, and immersion.* Masters Thesis, University of Florida. Accessed July 3, 2009, from http://purl.fcla.edu/fcla/etd/UFE1000166

Tomaka, J., Blascovich, J., Kelsey, R. M., & Leitten, C. L. (1993). Subjective, physiological, and behavioural effects of threat and challenge appraisal. *Journal of Personality and Social Psychology, 65*(2), 248–260.

Torrington, D., Hall, L., & Taylor, S. (2002). *Human resource management* (5th ed.). Harlow: Prentice Hall.

Tournish, D. (2006). The appraisal interview re-appraised. In: O. Hargie (Ed.), *The handbook of communication skills* (3rd ed., pp. 505–530). London: Routledge.

Turkle, S. (1996). *Life on the screen.* London: Weidenfeld and Nicolson.

Turkle, S. (2005). *The second self: Computers and the human spirit* (2nd ed.). New York: MIT Press.

Van Ments, M. (1983). *The effective use of role-play: A handbook for teachers and trainers.* London: Kogan Page.

Woehr, D. J., & Huffcutt, A. I. (1994). Rater training for performance appraisal: A quantitative review. *Journal of Occupational and Organizational Psychology, 67,* 189–205.

Zedeck, S., & Cascio, W. F. (1982). Performance appraisal decisions as a function of rater training and purpose of the appraisal. *Journal of Applied Psychology, 7*(6), 752–758.

Author Biographies

Shona Morse has been a lecturer on the MSc in the Management of Training and Development in the School of Education, University of Edinburgh, since 2002. Her research interests include human resource development, challenges in teaching international students, globalization and the use of virtual worlds in the training and development arena. In an earlier career, she had various roles in social work, eventually becoming involved in training social workers completing their professional qualifications. This led to a wider training and development role within a large public authority.

Fiona Littleton is the Second Life Support Officer for the MSc in E-learning programme at the University of Edinburgh and also tutor on the programme. She is the Second Life educational development adviser to various schools in the University of Edinburgh, was integral in the establishment of Vue, the university's island in Second Life, and has published various papers on her work in the area. Her research interests include virtual worlds in education, videogame-based learning and student learning.

Hamish Macleod is a senior lecturer within the Department of Higher and Community Education at the University of Edinburgh and acting Programme Director of its MSc in E-learning. His research and teaching interests are in the psychology of computer use, particularly the applications of information technology in teaching and learning. Part of his activities over recent years has been in support of the University's IT Literacy Programme. He also taught for many years in the University's Department of Psychology.

Rory Ewins is lecturer in E-learning and Managing Information at the University of Edinburgh. He has worked in universities in Australia, New Zealand and the United Kingdom. Previously, he was Research Fellow in ICT Policy and Strategy at the Scottish Centre for Research into On-line Learning and Assessment, Advisor on IT Policy to the Australian Vice Chancellor's Committee and support officer for the Australian government's Higher Education IT Consultative Forum. He has been teaching in Second Life since 2006 as part of the University of Edinburgh's MSc in E-learning team.

Chapter 11

Using Second Life at the Open University: How the Virtual World Can Facilitate Learning for Staff and Students

Steph Broadribb, Anna Peachey, Chris Carter and Francine Westrap

11.1. Introduction

In November 2008, the inaugural Research and Learning in Virtual Environments conference[1] was considered a success by many measures, but perhaps most strikingly in that it served to illustrate the groundswell of Higher Education (HE) institutions that are turning their attentions to the vast learning potential of virtual world environments. Whether academic or predominantly practitioner-based, delegates including this chapter's authors (who, incidentally, embrace aspects of both roles) were left inspired by numerous success stories where the use of virtual worlds had created a meaningful, positive learning experience for both students and staff within HE institutions (Picture 11.1).

Whilst ReLIVE is by no means the only conference addressing learning in virtual environments,[2] its host in 2008 — The Open University (OU), based in Milton Keynes, United Kingdom — was perhaps somewhat fitting. As an established provider of distance education, the OU brand is recognized on a worldwide scale, signifying openness 'to people, places, methods and ideas' (The Open University Mission online, 2008). Embracing the learning potential of emerging technologies, such as virtual environments, therefore seems a logical strategy for the institution.

---

1. See www.open.ac.uk/relive08
2. For example, see www.vs-games.org.uk, www.vwbpe.org, www.rezed.org

Higher Education in Virtual Worlds
Copyright © 2009 by Emerald Group Publishing Limited
All rights of reproduction in any form reserved
ISBN: 978-1-84950-609-0

Picture 11.1: Reception area

The current global economic climate, combined with an increasing focus on the environmental impact of travel, means that consideration of alternative methods for course delivery has become a priority.

The OU seeks to be a world leader in distance education, and to maintain this position, it is crucial that staff stay current with developing technologies. With rapid growth in the public profile of virtual environments, it seems appropriate that the technology is explored not only with the University's customers, the students, but also within staff development activity. We anticipate that this will be the case for many fellow HE institutions, as we collectively evaluate how Web 2.0 might address our organizational needs. With this in mind, in this chapter, we present a case study of how one UK-based HE institution has used the open virtual world of Second Life with both its students and its staff. Whilst the OU was an early adopter in its use of virtual environments in this context, it is our hope that the subsequent discussion of 'lessons learned' in both strands of research will be of use to all readers, regardless of direct experience in this area.

The chapter opens with a description of the OU's first steps in using Second Life, followed by an account of how this virtual environment has been used with particular cohorts of students, and how a thriving in-world learning community has developed as a result. Following from its use with OU students, we summarize the theoretical and practical implications of an exploratory project using Second Life as a vehicle for skills practice-based staff development. Using a controlled experimental design, in this context, we sought to answer the following question: can in-world virtual role play provide us with a viable alternative for providing staff with valuable skills practice? The positive results from the research to date, set against a background of institutional support, have motivated a drive to extend the research further and ultimately provide a case for Second Life to become a natural component of the learning toolkit for both staff and students at the OU. The chapter closes with a discussion of some of the waypoints for achieving this ambition, including a number of practical implications for HE institutions to consider in using virtual environments.

11.2. Using Second Life with Students

The 2008 Virtual World Snapshot report, commissioned by Eduserv, found that most educators in the United Kingdom who are already working in virtual worlds now believe that virtual worlds are moving towards becoming mainstream (Kirriemuir, 2008). As touched upon previously, the OU has taken a lead in virtual world presence and was in fact one of the very first UK educators to work in-world. In June 2006, the University purchased its first 'island' in Second Life. Cetlment Island was a pilot project for a fellowship through COLMSCT — The Centre for Open Learning in Maths, Science, Computing and Technology. COLMSCT is one of the Centres for Excellence in Teaching and Learning (CETLs) created in 2005 by the Higher Education Funding Council for England (HEFCE), and Second Life was felt to represent an appropriate platform for achieving many of the objectives that COLMSCT set out for the service it provides to home students.[3]

A second OU island, SchomeBase, was established in December 2006 and was managed as a main grid presence for the Schome project: a new form of educational system focusing on meeting the needs of society and individuals in the 21st century, whilst supporting life-long learning.[4] Both islands were experimental spaces where any user could create or rez[5] objects and contribute to the evolution of the island. Students were welcome to visit, and two formal tutorial groups for a 30 credit level one technology course were run on Cetlment Island. However, this Second Life presence was deliberately not promoted at a general level within the university, and subsequently, there was little regular activity or casual social interaction on either island.

Evidence of participation and retention rates from a range of pilot studies in 2006/2007 was encouraging (Bennett & Peachey, 2007), and the CETL was keen for research to build on this work with future cohorts of students. As a result, Open Life Island was delivered in March 2008 and was sited next to SchomeBase, with a development plan to landscape the two islands as complementary spaces. Whilst effectively superseded by Open Life, a key lesson that came from the extended exploratory learning on Cetlment Island was the importance of providing an attractive and engaging environment in which students could interact. It soon became apparent that re-creating real-world buildings were generally unnecessary and that most social connection actually occurred in open spaces. With minimal indication of future uptake for the islands, it was decided to create spaces that were simply as attractive, engaging and flexible as possible within the context of the environment.

An outline design for Open Life and Schomebase subsequently evolved from discussions with fellow stakeholders providing education in virtual worlds. This informal survey of approximately fifty Second Life users, including academics,

---

3. See http://www.open.ac.uk/colmsct/about/
4. See www.schome.ac.uk/wiki/Main_Page
5. A Second Life word for taking an item out of inventory and making it appear as 'real'

students and others in student support services, informed the creation of a larger island that made good use of height and depth and that displayed an abundance of greenery and seating areas using real-world metaphors. This enabled people to feel grounded and 'safe' within the environment, whilst the areas were decorated with unexpected treats and surprises designed to encourage people to return and explore further.

Whilst the growth of a more permanent in-world community on Open Life Island was an exciting development, there was a downside to the significantly increased level of social activity that was generated. Tutors were beginning to use the public spaces for formal tutorial and teaching sessions with their students and sometimes found themselves with an inquisitive audience: bystanders who were on the island to socialize rather than study. The tutors involved were generous enough to include and welcome the visitors, but this was clearly not a scalable solution for the long term. After some discussion with the Schome project, the areas that users typically used for socializing were relocated to SchomeBase Island, and the natural division between spaces for formal and informal learning was ratified.

We would recommend and welcome readers to visit The OU in Second Life, though it should be noted that SchomeBase has since been replaced by Open Life Ocean and Open Life Village, as a new, dedicated social community island. This is a thriving development, driven in large part by an egalitarian mix of staff and students who are in-world not for any formal teaching or learning commitments but because they derive value from being active members of a regular community. Recognizing that for many this virtual community provides a 'third place' (Oldenburg, 1991) — a regular social opportunity that is neither at home nor at work — facilitation has sought to provide support for activity that is community driven, rather than to impose activity (Peachey, 2008). To date, events on the islands have included art exhibitions, visiting speakers, collaborative builds, discussion groups, themed parties and even an in-world Christmas pantomime.

Students on a small number of OU courses continue to benefit from tutorial support in Second Life. In 2007/2008, tutorial groups from a technology course began to use the island formally along with a number of smaller, individual tutor groups from various other courses. The same time period also saw support extend from regular tutor groups to events open to the national cohort (an audience of approximately 1000 students). Throughout 2009, some courses will provide dedicated in-world resources to illustrate key concepts from the two-dimensional web-based material, with learning points developed further through student participation in in-world discussion groups.

Furthermore, an exploration into the potential of the environment for a virtual residential school has been initiated and the University is significantly increasing its investment into virtual world research, with long-term prospects for the substantial mainstreaming of virtual world support into faculty-based courses.

It is the experience of the OU in Second Life to date that approaches of both social and cognitive constructivism can be found in the emerging pedagogies. In social constructivism, the focus emphasizes interaction with people and co-construction of knowledge (Vygotsky, 1978), whereas in cognitive constructivism, the focus is on interaction with content and individual construction of knowledge (Felix, 2005). The OU social community readily demonstrates both: individuals in the community work together, and it is this collaboration, both within and external to the environment (e.g., in FirstClass forums, Facebook instant messaging), that enables individual reflection and learning. For other groups, such as the users of the nOUBie Building on Open Life Island — an area developed by the community to provide a welcome centre for newcomers — collaboration is not inherent to their learning experience as they interact primarily with content rather than people to construct their understanding.

Consideration of how the institution's use of virtual environments with students has developed serves to illuminate a number of key points of interest surrounding both the design of such environments and the types of activity that it can successfully support. Indeed, the University's experience of using Second Life with students to date appears to indicate that this type of environment *can* support the learning experience for individuals, whether through providing virtual opportunities to discover content directly or through the formation of online collaborative working and social groups. It was with this in mind that that we turned our attention to a different challenge: how Second Life could be used in staff development.

11.3. Using Second Life in Staff Development

Prior to addressing the issue of 'how' Second Life could be used within staff development, it is perhaps important to firstly address 'why?' As momentum continued to gather in the University's use of virtual environments with its students, it became apparent that there was a potential disconnection between staff and student developmental experiences. The use of virtual environments to support staff–student interactions was increasing but had not yet been considered as a tool for use in staff development. Given the strategic goals of the University, the potential of using virtual environments for this purpose seemed to present a significant opportunity for supporting aspects of developmental activity within the institution.

To address this, it seemed appropriate to incorporate a trial of a Second Life–based activity within a staff development intervention currently provided by the Human Resources Development team. The identified outcomes of doing so were to support University staff to gain exposure, knowledge and confidence in using this emerging technology. In addition to providing an enhanced awareness of virtual environments, and the opportunities they present for engaging in learning activities, it was felt to be important that the Second Life–based activity would add real, tangible value as part of the developmental intervention in which it was embedded. Furthermore, it was deemed crucial that the process could be evaluated as having made a direct contribution to the learning outcomes. The challenge, therefore, became to identify an area of professional development that would provide a suitable vehicle to deliver on both these objectives.

Evaluative feedback from the participants of previous staff development sessions indicated that when using traditional role-play activities as a form of skills practice, relatively high levels of discomfort and disengagement with the task were reported. Over time, this had led to staff development activities primarily focused on the embedding of new skills, often provided solely through group discussion. This issue, however, does not appear unique to the OU's learning and development practitioners. Swink (1993) presents a compelling anecdote illustrating the dislike that many employees share for role-play activity, mainly, he argues, 'because they are afraid of making mistakes in front of their peers' (p. 91). This perspective is further supported by findings linked to public self-consciousness (e.g., Fenigstein, Scheier, & Buss, 1975), fear of negative evaluation (e.g., Watson & Friend, 1969) and issues regarding self-presentation (e.g., Goffman, 1959)

Potential antecedents for the reported negative affect towards role play may run deeper than impression management or self-confidence, however. Jackson and Lawty-Jones (1996) found strong positive statistical relationships between scores of extraversion in individuals and their preference for 'active learning'. This finding was replicated by Bakx, van der Sanden, and Vermetten (2002), who reported that the extraverted students in their study preferred role-play activities as a form of learning significantly more so than the introverts. It is perhaps unsurprising then that individuals of a more introverted personality type, perhaps with a greater preference for a more reflective rather than activist learning style (e.g., Furnham, 1992), may be less comfortable with the social form of learning that role play embodies.

From an organizational perspective of 'Best Practice', we had been seeking an alternative to real-life role play that could still offer our staff the opportunity of a 'learning through doing' experience. From our initial scoping exercise, it appeared that Second Life could offer the University such an alternative, or as Broadribb and Carter (2009) described it, 'virtual affordances [that address] real needs'. In particular, the virtual environment presents the participant with the opportunity to role-play a situation through an alternative identity: the individual's three-dimensional virtual character, or 'avatar'. We hypothesized that role playing in Second Life would provide a 'safer' environment in which the participant could express themselves, as there would be a greater delineation in the attribution of actions to the individual compared to traditional 'real-world' role play. Furthermore, by designing an activity that encouraged collaborative group control of a single avatar, discomfort may be further reduced as actions would be attributed to a small collective rather than a single individual.

In selecting a developmental workshop as a vehicle for introducing virtual environments to staff, it was decided that a session focusing on feedback skills would be most appropriate. This was primarily due to its focus on interpersonal skills development. In 1983, Bailey and Butcher emphasized that effective interpersonal skills training should focus on developing perceptual, cognitive and behavioural skills components together.

We felt that Second Life provided a platform for just that although a conscious decision was taken to avoid the transition into an exclusively virtual session. Indeed, adopting a blended design would be crucial in contributing to one of the most salient findings of the research to date. From this starting point, we set out to explore whether virtual role-play activity could provide a viable alternative to its traditional, real-life counterpart. Furthermore, answers were sought with regard to whether Second Life could provide a comfortable 'learning through doing' experience for colleagues of varying professional backgrounds and levels of experience in using virtual environments.

11.4. From Theory to Practice

Our first steps were to conduct a pilot session, based primarily on the format of the existing half-day feedback skills workshop offered by the Human Resources Development department. Originally delivered in a traditional, exclusively 'real-world' format, the workshop was re-structured to incorporate an interactive blended learning design, focused specifically on developing the attendees' skills in providing and receiving feedback. The primary purpose of the pilot was to assess the impact of the Second Life virtual role-play activity on the attendees' perceived levels of confidence to provide (and receive) feedback effectively. A secondary objective was to compare the learning outcomes of participants against those reported by participants engaging in more traditional forms of skills practice. As with every workshop conducted to date, attendees of the pilot session represented a variety of ages, pay grades and job roles throughout the organization, although most participants were female.

The lead facilitator began by introducing concepts and models relevant to both giving and receiving positive and critical feedback in an effective way. Following this predominantly didactic format, twenty-two participants split into three groups to experience one of three forms of skills practice: script writing, traditional 'real-life' role play or virtual role play using Second Life. Each group worked with the same case study, featuring a bespoke scenario carefully constructed to be relevant to the institution. For this session, a group of eight participants were assigned to the Second Life virtual role-play condition, and then split further into two groups of four. Each group had the support of a facilitator experienced in the use of Second Life and a laptop connected to the platform. The virtual role-play activity took the form of a discussion between two avatars, based on the case study provided. Each group collectively used their avatar to provide feedback to a corresponding avatar, controlled by a learning and development professional seated in a separate room.

Towards the opening of this chapter, we described the in-world relocation of one of the communal areas on Open Life Island. This left a vacated space on the island, creating an opportunity for virtual offices to be created specifically for the purpose of the planned workshop. Identified as an opportunity to investigate the immersive aspects of the environment, this was felt to be an appropriate way in which to fill the empty space. The construction of a relatively high fidelity representation of a real-world office environment was justified to allow participants to identify appropriate locations within a formal workspace for providing feedback to others. As Picture 11.2 illustrates, the virtual office environments provided multiple areas for participants to conduct their feedback practice, from open-plan and meeting room spaces to a staff

Picture 11.2: The office spaces

room with coffee facilities. Whilst any Second Life user may explore these environments when not in active use, an invitation-only group was created for restricted access to the virtual offices for the duration of the workshop. This ensured a secure and private space for the participants (Picture 11.2).

At the outset of the skills practice session, participants were assigned a pre-constructed avatar. They were then provided with a tour of the virtual office environment and an overview of basic avatar movement and text-speech. Participants were given thirty minutes in which to agree their group approach to the case study, before engaging in a twenty-minute virtual role play in which participants took turns in 'driving' their group avatar. Interaction took place within Second Life through movement around the virtual office and text-based conversation with a corresponding avatar.

Simultaneously, in the real world, the group discussed what their text-based responses might be, with the 'driver' of the group's avatar typing them in. At the end of the virtual role-play activity, the two groups re-united for a discussion with the facilitators on their experience of the skills practice, before regrouping into the larger cohort for a final review of their learning. We now turn our attention to how we evaluated our first steps in using Second Life for staff development.

11.5. Evaluation and Development

Feedback from attendees of the pilot session pointed to a number of learning points that we utilized to make improvements in the next workshop. Specifically, we amended our session design to extend the length of virtual role play time to forty minutes and extended the group debriefing session. Additionally, we provided attendees with a printed text-speech transcription of their virtual role-play activity. This was designed as a self-analysis prompt for the groups to reflect on their performance during the virtual role-play activity. The resulting workshop, incorporating the revised intervention design, was conducted with fourteen participants in total.

In evaluating the aforementioned workshops, we were keen to progress from traditional 'happy sheets' and move towards a more rigorous approach. However, firstly, key learning objectives at both the organizational and the individual levels needed to be outlined. At an organizational level, the learning objectives were to:

a) increase staff confidence in handling difficult interpersonal situations at work and
b) increase staff awareness and interest in using emerging technologies (specifically Second Life).

At the learner level, this was translated into measurable outcomes of:
a) increased confidence in providing and receiving both positive and negative feedbacks in interactions with colleagues and
b) a positive experience of using new technology in a developmental setting.

To achieve this, online surveys were delivered at two time points: shortly before the workshop as part of the participants' pre-work and then a fortnight after the event. This approach enabled a direct comparison to be made and indicated whether the individual and organizational objectives had been met. Using a combination of self-rating Likert scales and comment boxes, the online survey administered for both the pilot and the first 'proper' workshop contained 11 items in total. Items were included in both pre- and post-session surveys that addressed self-perceived ability to meet the pre-defined course objectives, level of confidence in providing and receiving feedback effectively and level of comfort in participating in role-play activities. Control items addressing levels of computer keyboard skills, typing confidence and previous experience using Second Life were included within the pre-workshop survey to ensure that data was not skewed by extraneous variables. Finally, levels of satisfaction and engagement with the skills practice activity were measured in the post-workshop survey.

Analysis of the data from both workshops revealed some interesting findings. In the pilot session, paired sample t-test analysis revealed statistically significant increases between pre- and post-workshop surveys in the participants' self-ratings of ability to meet the pre-defined course objectives, in level of confidence in providing and receiving feedback effectively and in the level of comfort participating in role-play activities. Furthermore, all participants reported feeling satisfied and engaged by the skills practice activities, with 100 percent reporting that they felt both the course and their own personal objectives had been met. Combined with the content analysis of the qualitative data, which indicated that Second Life was felt to have enabled 'putting theory into practice', to have 'reflected real life' through its synchronous form of communication and was 'a refreshing change from a variety of other courses', it seemed that the use of Second Life as an alternative medium for role-play activity had been a success. As one attendee commented as follows:

> *[My key learning points were from] the excellent Second Life role play exercise, which was my first experience of this concept. I most definitely feel more confident in giving and receiving feedback in both my personal and professional life. I found the Second Life training very motivational.*

Whilst the findings from the quantitative analysis show glimpses of promise by illustrating statistically significant increases in self-ratings following the workshop, the ability to make any definitive conclusions on the comparative worth of the different skills practice activities is limited by the sample size. Despite this, however, the qualitative data and anecdotal feedback following the pilot workshop illustrated an overwhelmingly positive reaction to the introduction of the virtual environment as a development activity. For instance, another attendee noted as follows:

> *The most useful parts [of the workshop] were the role play – putting the theory into practice. Using Second Life was very interesting; much more fun than I'd anticipated. As a result of the course I will be more open to*

initiating feedback discussions [...] using Second Life was quite memorable.

With the above in mind, the workshop directly following the pilot set out to explore how a larger group of attendees found the virtual skills practice experience, measured using the same pre- and post-session surveys. Although pre- and post-data sets were available for only eleven participants, results were again extremely positive, indicating that participants felt the use of Second Life to have been a success. Paired sample *t*-tests again indicated statistically significant increases in the attendees' self-perceived ratings of ability to satisfy the pre-defined course objectives, in the level of comfort in using role play and in the level of confidence to provide positive and constructive feedback to others.

Presented with a steadily expanding set of data that suggested a number of positive outcomes of using Second Life for staff development, it became clear that a period of reflection was required. A number of observations made by the facilitators were felt to be of importance here. Discussions in the facilitator debrief following both workshops indicated that participants appeared to be practicing the techniques for giving effective feedback not only during the in-world virtual role-play activity but throughout the group's interaction with each other in the real world. This manifested in the form of peer debate and peer-to-peer feedback on ideas for taking the in-world conversation forward. As one respondent noted in her feedback:

Working in a group collectively on the preparation was useful as it gave different perspectives and [the] time to discuss them ....

The first of two key learning points emerged: collaboratively controlling the Second Life avatar within the virtual role play seemed to offer more developmental benefits than were initially anticipated. Initial concerns about whether participants within the small role-play groups would be able to engage with the activity when for periods of time they might not even be in direct control of the avatar were rapidly allayed through observation and the data collected. Not only did participants typically report high levels of engagement with the activity in the post-session surveys (100 percent reasonably-to-very engaged in the pilot, 75 percent in the following workshop) but were frequently observed as discussing best ways to proceed with activity. Groups appeared to move in and out of the role play with relative ease, whilst discussing in the real world how their next response related back to the theoretical grounding provided at the outset of the workshop. As well as helping the skills practice activity to become a more comfortable experience, sharing a support network of fellow group members may also have provided the appropriate scaffolding required for individuals to move effectively through their own proximal zones of development (Vygotsky, 1978).

In using a virtual role-play scenario within a real-world setting, there appears to be potential for two strands of learning: what could be termed as 'direct' learning, through the virtual role-play scenario to practice feedback technique and skills, and 'indirect' learning, achieved through more informal debate and constructive challenge with peers in the real-world groups. This leads onto our second key learning point. The decision to opt for a blended design in the workshop was not only necessary given the traditional on-site nature of developmental activities within the organization but also crucial in enabling participants to experience how technologies such as Second Life can facilitate the development of skills that do not simply have to be left behind in the virtual world once they have logged off.

The opportunity to instantaneously print out transcripts of the in-world role play dialogues and analyze them within a facilitated discussion following the activity is just one small but salient illustration of how such a technology can enable learning from within the real world to the virtual world and back again. Whilst it is not inconceivable that the same effect could be achieved with exclusively virtual content, this is perhaps an area of investigation for the future rather than a solution for the present. The OU has strong links with the Sloodle project (www.sloodle.org) and it is anticipated that developments within the University virtual world provision will incorporate this sort of mashup learning management solution. Thus, we would argue that learning through a blended design adds a level of richness that is perhaps harder to achieve when offering a purely real-world or virtual-world experience.

11.6. The 3 Rs: Rigour, Relevance and Re-iteration

As previously mentioned, Second Life does appear to have contributed to the positive experiences of OU staff as part of their in-house developmental activity. Evaluation of participant feedback has indicated that both increased confidence and high levels of engagement have been reported. Participants were given the opportunity to construct meaning through purposeful collaboration, drawing on a socio-constructivist approach that appears to suit virtual environments such as Second Life. Specifically, individuals applied their own perspective to the skills practice as well as the collective view of their working group, demonstrating aspects of a pragmatic or emergent constructivist approach (Cobb, 1995; Gredler, 1997).

Recalling the introduction to this chapter, our original rationale for utilizing a virtual environment as an alternative form of skills practice was based on the hypothesis that participants might feel more comfortable and confident role playing through the medium of a collaboratively controlled virtual identity in Second Life, rather than through their own physicality within the real world. Though the evaluation studies conducted to date have been necessarily small in scale — a criticism that is countered through both the expanding body of data that continues to be collected and the use of a well-established developmental workshop as a vehicle for the research design — the overwhelmingly positive feedback from those having attended the workshops suggests to us that Second Life has every chance of becoming a natural component in the OU developmental practitioner's toolkit. Perhaps, the same can be achieved in fellow HE institutions too.

However, with every statement proclaiming the omnipotence of a novel technology come the inevitable caveats. Indeed, there will be those who argue that equivalent success, perhaps in terms of positive developmental outcomes or increased levels of confidence, can be achieved through blended workshop designs utilizing any number of alternative forms of technology. Relevant examples might include high definition video capture, Personal Digital Assistants (PDAs) or web-based social networking sites. In developing interview skills, for instance, it might be the case that video is a more appropriate medium for practicing, recording and reviewing such skills than Second Life. The latter has yet to fully develop the capability to realistically mimic the subtlety and complexity of human body language or spoken intonation. Virtual worlds such as Second Life appear to have a great deal to offer in some areas of skills development, but they should not be seen as a one-size-fits-all solution to every developmental need.

Moving forward within the OU, we seek to capitalize on the positive affordances of working in virtual worlds through a cycle of rigorous planning, execution and evaluation. To extend the toolkit analogy, simply because an interesting and shiny new tool appears to have been effective in one task does not mean that it should become the work-person's tool of choice for all subsequent tasks, regardless of context. We feel that this is a crucial point that practitioners looking towards new technologies need to consider when designing their methodologies. Indeed, we continue to ask the same question of our own work as we plan the next phase of our research using Second Life in staff development.

Despite the numerous, diverse courses that the OU's Human Resources Development team run throughout the year, the focus on feedback skills still appears to be the most relevant for incorporating the use of Second Life. A key reason for this is the relationship between the interpersonal basis of providing feedback and the opportunities that Second Life offers for peer-to-peer interaction. However, with our third (and most recent) iteration of the workshop design, a number of criticisms have been addressed. Most notably, the workshop has embraced a 360-degree feedback approach for its evaluation. Eighteen participants were asked to nominate three colleagues each — typically a manager, a peer and a subordinate — to accompany them in completing a version of the online survey used in previous workshops, but that now focused on context-specific behavioural outcomes in addition to ratings of confidence and satisfaction. Whilst a detailed analysis of the results has yet to be conducted, it is hoped that this multi-source approach will present a more robust indication of each participant's feedback skills development, thus leading to a workshop that fully embraces the organization's commitment to 'Best Practice'.

11.7. Reflections and Lessons to be Learned

As with any developmental tool, the effective use of virtual environments within a blended workshop design is explicitly linked with a clearly defined purpose for that virtual activity. However, we have realized that it is not simply a case of taking a traditional activity and adjusting it to a virtual world environment. We believe it is important that we do not merely recreate identical activities in a virtual world from those we have previously conducted in the real world. Whilst the evaluation data from the three workshops run thus far appear to demonstrate similar levels of achievement of the pre-defined learning objectives, the pilot workshop appeared to motivate and maintain a particularly high level of engagement and energy within the session. The second and third workshops, on the contrary, were felt by the sessions' facilitators to lack much of the energy and excitement of the pilot.

Following a period of reflection, it is our belief that that this difference was largely due to the more flexible, experimental nature of the first workshop. Quite simply, it engendered a high energy and fun atmosphere. Conversely, the second workshop was far more tightly structured in terms of time and activities, resulting in what we feel to have been less flexibility to 'enjoy' the virtual world itself. This appears to correspond with the views of Castronova (2005, 2006), who urges educators and business people to consider the design of learning activities from the perspective of game theory. Castronova maintains that a virtual environment alone will not effectively harness the energy of virtuality, but that it is the environment combined with the design of the activity that will engage or detract from the learning experience.

As Addison and O'Hare (2008) suggest, technology can offer an opportunity for enhanced social interaction as a pathway to constructing meaning and knowledge. It is this opportunity for shared thinking and sensemaking that we wish to capitalize on within our blended learning design. Hollins and Robbins (2008) draw parallels between virtual world environments, such as Second Life, and massive multiplayer online role-playing games such as World of Warcraft. Whilst they conclude that they are not identical counterparts, it is suggested that both provide a 'playful' immersive experience. We would concur that this element of 'playfulness' is an important ingredient in successfully engaging participants in the blended learning experience. This has led us to consider how we might redress the balance of structure and playfulness to create a more consistent, high energy learning intervention.

Another key element of online games is the use of quests to initiate users into the environment of the game and to support them in developing basic user skills. As observed by Jeffery (2008), this serves to entertain as well as educate users. Consequently, we revised our latest workshop design to incorporate a series of stepped quests, or goals, for participants to engage in along the learning pathway. This included providing goals within the real world, such as identifying strengths or weaknesses of various approaches to giving feedback, as well as group activities in the virtual world, which begin with an orientation 'treasure hunt' and ultimately progressed to the role-play activity. Through successful achievement of each quest or activity, the participants progress to a more challenging one. We anticipate that this will enable us to build upon our fledgling notion of 'direct' and 'indirect' strands of learning that was discussed previously. Ultimately, however, we hope that by providing a structured but fun approach to using Second Life, it will invigorate and utilize the sense of energy in users that a virtual world environment can readily inspire.

However, the irony of embracing the many positive learning-based elements of engaging in games is that for some, virtual environments will always represent a frivolous waste of time: a pursuit unfit to grace the arena of traditional, 'serious' learning. Whilst we readily encourage readers to consider the ways in which virtual environments might add value to developmental activity within their institution, we would also sound a warning to expect a degree of resistance. For every new adopter eager to try out innovative alternatives, there will be the staunch traditionalist: wary and highly sceptical of the change. There are likely to be further challenges found in the technical support of different institutions in permitting software such as Second Life onto its network. Indeed, one of the greatest technological obstacles we faced was enabling the computers required for our development sessions to bypass the University's highly secured firewall.

Fortunately, our initial sessions required only six terminals, so issues relating to bandwidth were not problematic. Some investment in hardware was required to ensure participants could receive the full benefit of Second Life. This was a crucial decision, as if we had used graphically incapable machines the quality of the virtual world environment would likely have detracted from the learning experience. What has been particularly interesting is that the positive change in institutional attitude to supporting Second Life has been dramatic in the time period following our pilot workshop, and we were fortunate to have received support from a high level within the organization; a luxury that may not be so apparent in fellow institutions.

Practitioners looking to utilize Second Life (or similar virtual world environments) as part of their development toolkit need to be mindful of how they introduce this into their institution or organization. With virtual worlds still relatively in their infancy compared to more traditional methods of delivering learning and development, engaging key stakeholders and enhancing their understanding of the technology will be essential. Confused perceptions of the purpose of virtual worlds and their ability to provide an appropriate learning environment will need to be acknowledged and addressed. We have found that providing an immersive session within which these key stakeholders can experience the learning activity for themselves is especially beneficial and would advise other practitioners to consider a similar approach.

The community of virtual world users is growing daily and provides a global resource from which to draw and exchange knowledge. Virtual worlds are a fascinating and evolving tool and their future depends very much on the use to which we put them. We look forward to our continuing participation in that evolution.

References

Addison, A., & O'Hare, L. (2008). *How can massive multi-user virtual environments and virtual role play enhance traditional teaching practice?* Researching learning in virtual environments 2008. Retrieved July 3, 2009, from http://www.open.ac.uk/relive08

Bakx, A. W. E. A., van der Sanden, J. M. M., & Vermetten, Y. J. M. (2002). Personality and individual learning theories: A cross-sectional study in the context of social-communicative training. *Personality and Individual Differences, 32*, 1229–1245.

Bennett, B., & Peachey, A. (2007). Mashing the MUVE: A mashup model for collaborative learning in multi-user virtual environments. In: *International computer aided learning.* Austria: International Association of Online Engineering.

Broadribb, S., & Carter, C. (2009). Using Second Life in human resource development. *British Journal of Educational Technology*, *40*(3), 547–550.

Castronova, E. (2005). *Synthetic worlds: The business and culture of online games*. Chicago: University Press.

Castronova, E. (2006). On the research value of large games: Natural experiments in Norrath and Camelot. *Games and Culture*, *1*(2), 163–186.

Cobb, P. (1995). Continuing the conversation: A response to Smith. *Educational Researcher*, *24*(6), 25–27.

Felix, U. (2005). E-learning pedagogy in the third millennium: The need for combining social and cognitive constructivist approaches. *ReCALL*, *17*(1), 85–100.

Fenigstein, A., Scheier, M. F., & Buss, A. (1975). Public and private self-consciousness: Assessment and theory. *Journal of Consulting and Clinical Psychology*, *43*, 522–527.

Furnham, A. (1992). Personality and learning style: A study of three instruments. *Personality and Individual Differences*, *13*, 429–438.

Goffman, E. (1959). *The presentation of self in everyday life*. London: Allen Lane.

Gredler, M. E. (1997). *Learning and instruction: Theory into practice* (3rd ed.). Upper Saddle River, NJ: Prentice-Hall.

Hollins, P., & Robbins, S. (2008). *The educational affordances of multi user virtual environments (MUVE)*. Researching learning in virtual environments 2008. Accessed July 3, 2009, from http://www.open.ac.uk/relive08

Jackson, C. J., & Lawty-Jones, M. (1996). Overlap between personality and learning style. *Personality and Individual Differences*, *20*, 293–300.

Jeffery, C. (2008). *Using non-player characters as tutors in virtual environments*. Researching Learning in Virtual Environments 2008. Accessed July 3, 2009, from http://www.open.ac.uk/relive08

Kirriemuir, J. (2008). *The autumn 2008 snapshot of UK higher and further education developments in Second Life*. Accessed July 3, 2009, from http://www.scribd.com/doc/7063696/The-Autumn-2008-Snapshot-of-UK-Higher-and-Further-Education-Developments-in-Second-Life

Oldenburg, R. (1991). *The great good place*. New York: Marlowe & Company.

Peachey, A. (2008). *First reflections, Second Life, third space: Community building in virtual worlds*. Researching learning in virtual environments 2008. Accessed July 3, 2009, from http://www.open.ac.uk/relive08

Swink, D. F. (1993). Role play your way to learning. *Training and Development*, *47*(5), 91–97.

Vygotsky, L. S. (1978). *Mind in society: The development of higher psychological processes*. Cambridge, MA: Harvard University Press.

Watson, D., & Friend, R. (1969). Measurement of social-evaluative anxiety. *Journal of Consulting and Clinical Psychology*, *33*, 448–457.

Author Biographies

Steph Broadribb (Second Life: *Lorelli Loire*) is assistant director of HR Development for the Open University, leading strategic organizational and staff development initiatives across the Institution. She is a member of the Chartered Institute of Personnel and Development (CIPD) with an MSc in Human Resource Leadership from Manchester Business School, University of Manchester. Steph is particularly interested in exploring the impact and value of virtual learning experiences for workforce development, with a particular focus on the virtual learning cycle and learning styles methodologies. She is founder and co-author of the Staff Development in Second Life research project, detailed in this chapter, that has been shortlisted for the Serious Games Solution of the Year Award at the World of Learning 2008 Awards and featured in People Management (October, 2008). She co-presented research findings at the ReLIVE08 Conference in November, 2008, and at the American Academy of Management in Summer, 2009, and is co-author of an article for the British Journal of Educational Technology.

Anna Peachey (Second Life*: Elsa Dickins*) is the coordinator of Virtual World Activity for the Open University and a teaching fellow within the Centre for Open Learning in Math's, Computing and Technology, a Centre of Excellence in Teaching and Learning (CETL) based at Open, where she is researching learning communities in virtual worlds. Anna has been working with adults and teens in virtual worlds since 2006 and has published several papers on her activities as well as a chapter on identity for a forthcoming book on controversial issues in education in virtual worlds. She has been an invited speaker at a number of events and is the Academic and Organising Chair of Researching Learning in Virtual Environments, an international conference on research methods in education in virtual worlds. Anna was recently a finalist in the Times Higher Education Award for Outstanding Innovation in ICT for her work with the Open University in Second Life.

Chris Carter (Second Life*: Lavender Skytower*) works as a project officer within Human Resources Development. Having achieved an MSc in Occupational Psychology at the Institute of Work, Health and Organisations, University of Nottingham, he leads project-based evaluative studies throughout The Open University. Chris is particularly interested in exploring how research can be conducted in Second Life through the use of rigorous social sciences–based methodological design, and whether skills developed in the virtual world can readily be transferred to practice in the real world. Chris co-presented research findings at the Re:LIVE Conference held in November, 2008, and at the American Academy of Management in Summer, 2009. He is also co-author of the Staff Development in Second Life research project, detailed in this chapter, that has been shortlisted for the Serious Games Solution of the Year Award at the World of Learning 2008 Awards and featured in People Management (October, 2008) and co-author of an article for the British Journal of Educational Technology.

Francine Westrap (Second Life*: Frankie Laminsk*) is a learning and development specialist working with the Open University. She has an MSc in Occupational Psychology from the University of Hertfordshire and is interested in the design and delivery of virtual learning experiences and how staff engage with the learning experience. She is co-author of the Staff Development in Second Life research project, detailed in this chapter, that has been shortlisted for the Serious Games Solution of the Year Award at the World of Learning 2008 Awards, featured in People Management (October, 2008) and presented at ReLIVE08 Conference (November, 2008).

Chapter 12

Aging, Lifelong Learning, and the Virtual World of Second Life

Leslie Jarmon, Tomoko Watanabe Traphagan,
John W. Traphagan and Lynn Jones Eaton

12.1. Introduction

In the process of discussing the experiences of members of the Second Life (SL) class that will be the focus of this chapter, the authors learned about "Fred" (pseudonym), a former engineer, who had been injured in a car accident that severed his spine several years earlier. His injuries kept him homebound for nearly ten years – a situation that changed when he discovered the online virtual world of SL. Now, although he continues to be physically limited to his home, he no longer thinks of himself as "homebound." He not only serves as a fulltime tour guide for NASA's CoLab virtual community in SL, but he has also started to dance – virtually. He has been able to reconnect with the world, serve thousands of people from all over the planet, and participate in an active social life. He refers to the virtual world as truly his "second life."

Fred's case provides an example of the power of emerging virtual technologies for enhancing the lifestyles of older adults, who may fear or experience loss of social connectedness due to physical frailness despite having accumulated a lifetime of experience, and who desire to continue to contribute to society. In this chapter, our aim is to begin developing an understanding of the potential for SL to provide an additional living space for establishing and expanding social settings for older adults. We argue that engagement with virtual worlds in a course setting: (1) contributes to the facilitation of life-long learning that extends beyond the confines of the classroom, (2) has the potential to generate feelings of co-presence and connection among participants in and outside of virtual worlds, and (3) provides a context for considering how new technologies have the potential to enrich the lives of older adults.

Higher Education in Virtual Worlds
Copyright © 2009 by Emerald Group Publishing Limited
All rights of reproduction in any form reserved
ISBN: 978-1-84950-609-0

Aging and the rapid diffusion of technology into daily life are two of the most significant global trends facing industrial and post-industrial societies (Morgan, 2005). As indicated in the Year 2000 U.S. Census, there were 35 million people aged 65 or older in the United States. By 2030, it is estimated that there will be about 70 million older adults in the United States alone (Chadwick-Dias, McNulty, & Tullis, 2003). The confluence of these two trends, that is, the increased use of technology by older adults, is also a developing phenomenon in many industrial societies, including the United States. Recent studies have found that older adults' access to the Internet is increasing dramatically in the United States (Fox, 2004), although these adults may take more time to adjust to and to adopt new computer-based technologies than their younger counterparts (Morgan, 2005). The impact of computer-based technologies for older adults can be substantial and can enrich their lives with easier access to information, entertainment, and engagement with society (Bollier, 1989; Charness & Schaie, 2003; Kanayama, 2000).

Although we have just begun to understand the impact of prevalent computer-based technologies such as the Internet and email on the life of older adults, our understanding has not been extended to newer technologies, such as virtual worlds. In this chapter, we examine how SL may be perceived and understood by older adults, and we believe the study is the first that addresses older adults' learning and perception of virtual worlds in a classroom setting. With its significant potential to enhance users' social connectedness and access to information, the impact of older adults' learning about virtual worlds must be carefully examined. We address the following four research questions:

(1) How well did participants learn the key concepts of SL, and which concepts did they learn?
(2) What content and activity aspects of the course were perceived as being most effective for learning the key course concepts?
(3) Will participants use SL or other related technologies? If so, why?
(4) What impacts do participants perceive these technologies might have on their lives?

With the last research question, we will examine themes more broadly related to the lives of older adults as they relate to (1) the new generation of social networks in virtual worlds, (2) the experience of embodied connectivity and co-presence within a socio-technical system such as SL, and (3) lifelong learning and new technology.

12.2. Description of the Class and Types of Participation

During the mid-20th century, educational philosophy began to focus on Lifelong Learning for older adults. Programs were established to help enrich the lives of these adults through a wide variety of courses, travel adventures, and community service options. Lifelong Learning programs have since been initiated on a global scale. The Osher Lifelong Learning Institute (OLLI) was developed in 2001 to provide a distinctive array of non-credit courses and activities specifically developed for seasoned adults aged 50 or older who are interested in learning for the joy of learning. With few time constraints, many people in later life are able to devote time to learning in a way not previously experienced (Russell, 2008).

Our study was conducted during a six-session introductory course on SL offered to older adults participating in the OLLI program at a large south-western research university. There were no grades or credits assigned for this course, and it was purely voluntary in every aspect. This seminar presented a wide-ranging introduction to the 3D virtual world of SL, and the specific learning objectives were designed to facilitate the students' understanding of:

- What is the virtual world of SL
- The historical context of this virtual world environment
- How it is being used as of Year 5
- Integration of "real life" and "virtual life"
- Negotiating SL's uses
- Future trends including medical, educational, social/cultural, economic, and governmental/non-governmental

Fifty-two participants registered for the course, and they were mainly retired professionals, including former university faculty members and business executives. The class met for six consecutive Thursdays from 1:30 pm to 3:00 pm. Each week, the class began with a question regarding outside observations or takeaways from the prior class. The instructor then immediately logged into SL and the major portion of the rest of the class was spent visiting with experts in SL who shared their perspectives and virtual activities regarding the key topics of business, education, science, medical and health, government, culture, non-profit activity, and future trends.

The older adults involved in the study participated in SL at different levels. It is important to note these distinctions in advance because a person's SL participation level impacts on their perception and understanding of SL. At one end of the spectrum, and speaking generally, some people may have only read or heard about SL but never actually logged in to the online platform. Second, and in the case for our informants, the course participants were shown the activities of the instructor and her avatar in SL mediated through the instructor's laptop projecting onto a large screen in the classroom. Although they were able to watch and hear the interactions with others in SL through the instructor's avatar and were able to participate in question and answer sessions with the guest speakers, these students had no agency themselves; however, they may have experienced some degree of co-presence or participation in the virtual world. Finally, a number of the participants logged into the SL program on their own, outside of class and experienced participation with a fuller sense of personal agency. Depending on the number and frequency of their visits to SL, the probability increased that they experienced a sense of fuller participation, agency, and co-presence with others. This discrepancy of degrees of participation in SL influenced how informants responded to questions and impacted the research findings accordingly.

12.3. Review of the Literature

12.3.1. *Aging, Activity, and Technology*

Population aging brings with it various problems connected to an extended period of life following retirement. Fundamentally, post-retirement brings risks associated with the potential for an increasingly sedentary life-style, which in turn tends to produce greater potential for cognitive and functional decline. There is a broad literature on activity in old age – one that is too extensive to fully address in this chapter – that links activity and social connectedness to increased quality of life and better health for older adults.

For our purposes in this chapter, the most important thread of research focuses specifically on mental health and aging and relates to the maintenance or creation of social networks among the elderly. Petigrew and Roberts (2008) argue that both social and solitary pastimes have the potential to ameliorate feelings of isolation and alienation among older adults. Research has found that to avoid loneliness, it is important for many older adults to stay connected to friends and loved ones who provide social support and help them to sustain feelings of a quality life (Nycyk & Redsell, 2006; Minardi & Blanchard, 2004). Behaviors such as using friends and family as emotional resources and participating in gatherings with others for activities such as eating or drinking to maintain social connections can significantly reduce negative feelings among older adults. Cross-cultural research has shown the importance of social connection for maintaining subjective perceptions of physical and mental well-being and health. Traphagan (2000), for example, has argued that older Japanese often associate participation in group activities involving use of mental and physical skill with delay or prevention of senile dementia. However, many older adults no longer have their nuclear family nearby or resist moving away from friends to be near their adult children. In many cases, relocation is not an option for physical, financial or emotional reasons (Seals, Clanton, Agarwal, Doswell, & Thomas, 2008).

Lawhon, Ennis, and Lawhon (1996) reported that computer access and usage could enhance the lives of older adults and play a major role in their education, entertainment, socialization, and daily functioning. Keeping mentally active is critical to maintaining healthy cognitive functioning in the later years (Adler, 2002), and successful aging requires the maintenance and enhancement of these mental functions (Rowe & Kahn, 1998). As a major tool for communication and information services, the Internet has now become an important resource for the enhancement of mental functioning, and lack of access to the Internet can become a major disadvantage for many (Latimer, 2001). In a report on Internet usage, Fox (2004) observed that once they become familiar with the benefits of computer usage, older adults may feel enthusiasm equal to that of younger users (see also Czaja & Sharit, 1998; Shapira, Barak, & Gal, 2007; White et al., 2002). Rosenthal (2008) found that with time and opportunity available, many older learners would explore technological possibilities in a supportive, non-threatening environment as yet another way to remain connected to the world. Relationships are important sources of motivation for older adults (Rosenthal, 2008), and receiving encouragement from others in a classroom environment can augment their own willingness to learn.

To date, there has been limited research on elders and the use of recent technological innovations such as the Internet in terms of creating networks for social interaction. Much of the research that has been conducted focuses on the influence of computer use on cognitive or motor abilities or on the attitudes of older adults toward using computers (Xie, 2007, pp. 33–34), and little work has focused on older adults and perceptions of well-being in relation to Internet or other computer usage (White et al., 1999). Xie (2007) has conducted research on Internet-based learning programs among older Chinese; her findings indicate that her subjects find positive associations between Internet learning and well-being.

While there is limited research on perceptions of well-being and Internet usage among older adults, there is even less that considers the influence of Internet practices on creating feelings of communal connection among older adults. Gorini, Gaggioli, Vigna, and Riva (2008) have initiated important research examining virtual worlds and eHealth, specifically in SL; however, studies that tie empirical data to theoretical discussions of Internet in relation to community structure and formation are rare. In this chapter, part of our concern is to provide a link between the theoretical and the empirical sides of the research and the use of Internet-based resources, specifically the virtual world of SL, with older adults.

12.4. Co-presence and Embodiment in SL

Three critical elements for engagement in learning in the digital age are interactivity, connectivity, and access (Dresang & McClelland, 1999), and these are three key elements of SL. Research suggests that such a learning environment enhances student engagement through a sense of shared experiences, offers opportunities for collaboration, and provides access to the virtual environment and user-created content (FitzGerald, 2007; see also Nardi, 2005). Users of SL are represented through their avatars, and research on pedagogical agents suggests that the presence of avatars enhances engagement and learning beyond computer-mediated communication without such agents (Atkinson, Mayer, & Merrill, 2005; Moreno, Mayer, Spires, & Lester, 2001).

Research on shared virtual environments (SVEs) and on collaborative virtual environments (CVEs) is particularly relevant to our concerns because this research examines participants' sense of presence, co-presence, and place-presence. 3D virtual worlds such as SL provide synchronous collaboration environments and, compared to 2D text-based online learning settings, create an enhanced sense of place with the visual projection of oneself and other individuals. In SL, the participants themselves, as users, can become the creators of content, that is, of the artifacts to mediate their own interaction and learning (Ondrejka, 2005). Furthermore, collaboration can occur because SL virtual technology provides conditions for an experiential, embodied, and social reality, and this social reality provides a virtual "new space" wherein existing communication practices and social networking tools are converging (Jarmon, 2009).

In understanding embodiment in SL, it is helpful to think of two co-evolving systems, one social and the other technical. The social system includes the users, the entire SL community of residents, and their extensions in real life. The technical system includes the SL software, the individual computer and Internet connection of each user, and the vast expanse of virtual simulations that comprise the SL metaverse (a combination of the real world with the virtual world). For example, recall the case of the homebound engineer, Fred, who works from his home computer as a NASA guide for thousands of people visiting SL. The social system in this case includes his and other users' self-representations (avatars) who co-exist in SL and create social communities of people who share their interests in aerospace technology, where the technical system is the computer and the software that provides the SL social environments. All of these elements together constitute what might be called a complex situated learning environment (Lave & Wenger, 1991).

However, it is the experience of embodied social connection with others and the immediacy of social co-presence that users repeatedly reference. A 2009 study (Jarmon, Traphagan, Mayrath, & Trivedi, 2009) found that some students reported that the three-dimensionality of the SL environment facilitated the sense of personal presence and tangible experiences that enhanced learning. This extended sense of co-presence in a virtual world may have real life implications for older adults. Health researchers Gorini et al. (2008) have studied online technology and health issues and they suggest that:

> compared with conventional telehealth applications such as emails, chat, and videoconferences, the interaction between real and 3-D virtual worlds may convey greater feelings of presence, facilitate the clinical communication process, positively influence group processes and cohesiveness in group-based therapies, and foster higher levels of interpersonal trust between therapists and patients. (p. 2)

A user's ability to view or observe his/her own avatar while engaged in interaction adds an additional perspective to research on virtual co-presence and embodiment. Recent research in neuroscience and psychology has suggested that a network of mirror neurons in the human brain constitutes an experiential "simulation" and provides the basis for empathic understanding of one another in interpersonal relationships and in collaboration (Gallese, Eagle & Migone, 2007; Freedberg & Gallese, 2007; Gallese & Lakoff, 2005). Gallese et al. (2007) write:

> The neural circuits activated in a person carrying out actions, expressing emotions, and experiencing sensations are activated also, automatically via a mirror neuron system, in the observer of those actions, emotions, and sensations. It is proposed that this finding of shared activation suggests a functional mechanism of "embodied simulation" that consists of the automatic, unconscious, and noninferential simulation in the

observer of actions, emotions, and sensations carried out and experienced
by the observed. (p.131; see also Iacoboni, 2008)

This research may have critical implications for some special needs populations as
well as for older adults. For example, stroke victims visiting the protected virtual
area in SL for people with disabilities called SL Dreams have reported that the
experience of seeing themselves walking aided in their recovery (Stein, 2007).

12.5. Research Methods

Data were collected from the 34 of 52 course participants who volunteered to
participate in the study by responding to three surveys and/or joining in a voluntary
focus group. Paper surveys were conducted twice, at the beginning and at the end of
the six-session course, whereas a third survey was conducted online one month after
the course was completed. Survey 1 questions addressed participants' prior
knowledge and experiences of virtual worlds in general and of SL and related
technologies such as computer games (related to research question RQ1). Survey 2
questions addressed what participants learned (RQ1), effectiveness of class content
and activities (RQ2), whether or not participants would use SL (RQ3), and
perceptions of future impacts of SL on their lives (RQ4). Survey 3 questions
addressed whether or not participants would use SL (RQ3), and perceptions of future
impacts of SL on their lives (RQ4). All three surveys contained both closed-ended
(Likert-scale) items and open-ended items. The response rates were 94%, 56%, and
44% for Surveys 1, 2, and 3 respectively. The survey results from the closed-ended
items were summarized as descriptive statistics. The results from the open-ended
items were qualitatively analyzed for recurring themes.

A semi-structured focus group session was conducted with five volunteer
participants and three facilitators (researchers) for 1.5 hours about two weeks after
the course, addressing participants' insights and perceptions about SL. In particular,
the focus group provided an opportunity for participants to articulate how they
might consider using SL (RQ3). The focus group session was audio recorded and
transcribed, and the transcript was analyzed qualitatively for recurring themes. All
data from the four sources mentioned above were triangulated to yield an in-depth
understanding of the participants' perceptions as they related to the four research
questions.

12.6. Results

(1) How well did participants learn the key concepts of SL, and which concepts did
they learn?

Although the participants were enrolled in a course on SL, their familiarity with
virtual worlds or SL was limited at the beginning of the course (Survey 1). Only 28%

of the participants reported that they had heard about virtual worlds to some extent, whereas a majority reported little (44%) or no familiarity (22%). Also, 74% of participants had never heard about SL, 81% of them had never seen others using virtual worlds including SL, and 94% of them (all but two participants) had never used virtual worlds themselves.

The very few participants who had heard of SL before the course had heard about avatars (2)[1] or a community created by avatars (1), or business applications (1) of SL. This information was learned from the people who organized the OLLI course (3), the media (2), or from acquaintances (1). A few participants knew similar information about other virtual worlds that they were interactive social contexts accessed via computers (2) with avatars (2). One participant, for example, reported:

> *I consider Webkinz to be somewhat like a virtual world that my grandchildren live in. They buy things for their pets, etc, in that world. I also know there are many social network type virtual worlds that even have their own system of law.*

Again, before the course, their information came from the media such as magazines and newspaper (4) or TV (1), as well as from relatives (1). Reflecting their unfamiliarity with virtual worlds, a majority (71%) of participants were neutral about virtual worlds, whereas others split between liking (14%) and not liking them (14%).

However, the participants' knowledge of key concepts of SL dramatically increased in all aspects in Survey 2 conducted at the end of the course, and Survey 1 and 2 results are contrasted in Figure 12.1. At the beginning of the course, less than 10% of participants agreed that they were already knowledgeable about the six course concepts about SL. However, by the end of the course, more than 90% of them agreed that they understood what SL was, how it was used in its fifth year of operation, the integration of "real life" and "virtual life," and SL's future trends. Seventy-one percent of them agreed that they understood the historical context of SL. However, how to negotiate some of SL's uses appeared to be a more difficult concept to grasp; less than a half (47%) agreed that they understood it, and the rest reported "neutral" on this concept.

Specific learning about SL that respondents reported include its educational uses (10), medical uses (including training) (5), business uses (5), social connections (4), and the potential for handicapped people to do what they may not be able to do in their real lives (e.g., dancing for people confined to wheelchairs) (3). By the end of the course, 95% of respondents agreed that SL has the potential to enhance student learning in education, and 100% of them agreed that it can enhance communication among people. All the respondents (100%) agreed (15%) or strongly agreed (85%) that they enjoyed learning about SL and virtual worlds, and two thirds (68%) agreed

---

1. The numbers in parentheses indicate the frequency of the same or similar responses.

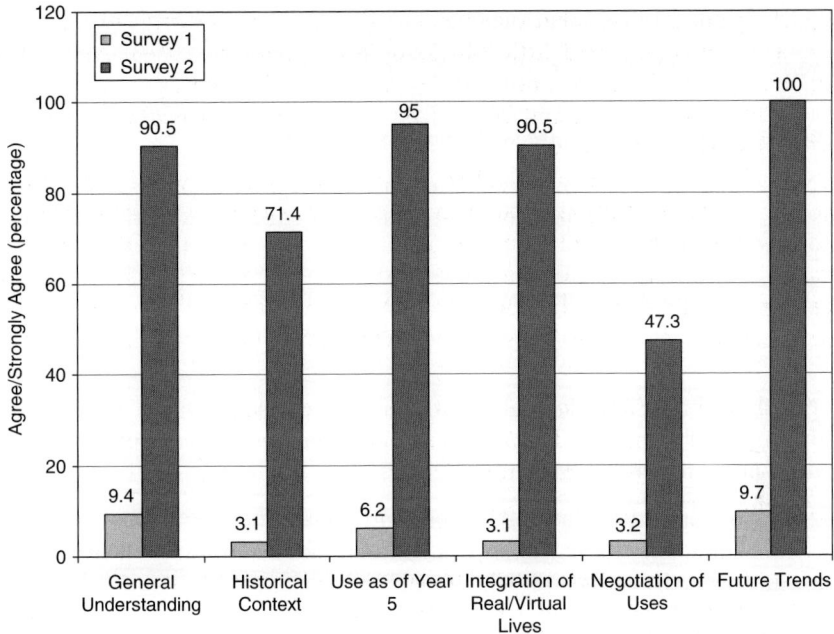

Figure 12.1: Participants' perceptions of virtual worlds

(47%) or strongly agreed (21%) that they felt confident that they now knew enough about virtual worlds and SL to explain them to other people.

In the focus group discussion held after the end of the course, one participant described his intense engagement with the content he learned during the class sessions:

> *I went from being mildly curious to being pretty enthusiastic by the end of the six weeks, because I kept seeing the potential of what this* Second Life *is all about. And, at each opportunity I'd walk away saying I never thought of doing that. I'd go home and tell my wife, "Could you believe today we were in South Africa? And we saw an art exhibit in Tokyo? And we did this today?" And then, I also talked about my experiences in business of constantly videoconferencing and teleconferencing, as well as travel on an international basis. And I'd think, "Hmm, this might have some potential."*

In summary, at the beginning of the course, participants were generally unfamiliar with and psychologically remote from SL or virtual worlds. However, most of them enjoyed and succeeded in learning key concepts of SL in six sessions (Table 12.1), and they reported various societal uses of SL including educational, medical, business, and social applications.

Table 12.1: Second Life course syllabus.

Class No. 1: Introduction to Second Life – Research study part I
Definitions, background, demo. Homework: Discover one new piece of information
  about science and SL to share with the class

Class No. 2: Second Life – Science-related groups, organizations, and activities
Discussion. Homework: Explore media coverage of educational activity in SL and
  bring one story to class

Class No. 3: Second Life: Business- and education-related groups
Organizations and activities. Homework: Explore news stories about health or
  political activities in SL and bring one story to class

Class No. 4: Second Life: Medical, health, and government-related groups
Organizations and activities. Homework: Explore news stories about non-profit
  activities in SL and bring one story to class

Class No. 5: Second Life: Cultural, social, and non-profit groups
Organizations and activities. Homework: Explore news stories about future trends
  for SL and virtual worlds and bring one story to class

Class No. 6: Second Life: Future trends. Research study part II – Volunteers for
  focus group

---

(2) What content and activity aspects of the course were perceived as being most
effective for learning the key course concepts?

According to the results from Survey 2, the older adults responded positively to
most of the instructional strategies that the instructor employed (Figure 12.2). In
particular, all participants (100%) reported that the virtual field trips to actual
working environments in SL and various examples of SL uses projected on the screen
were helpful for them to learn about SL. These results suggest that exposure to actual
people in SL and to their activities facilitated the students' understanding of SL as a
real albeit virtual place. Experiences with expert guest speakers from inside SL (95%)
and the interactive style of the class (91%) were also perceived as helpful by most
participants. It is important to note that the virtual field trips and the guest speakers
were presented using the "voice" capability of SL. That is, the students were able to
hear the actual sounds of the virtual locations (birds, engines, wind chimes) as well as
the voices of the guest speakers. Since in actuality the guests were distributed
geographically throughout the real world, the immediacy of their voices and the
environmental sounds made an observable impression on the students. In addition,
the students were able to ask questions, mediated through the instructor's avatar,
and they were able to receive immediate responses from the guests.

About three quarters of participants reported that the handout of landmarks in
SL and other research and resources (76%) was helpful for learning about SL. One
handout described technical content such as a demonstration of how images,
documents, and web pages can be imported into SL, and 70% of the participants

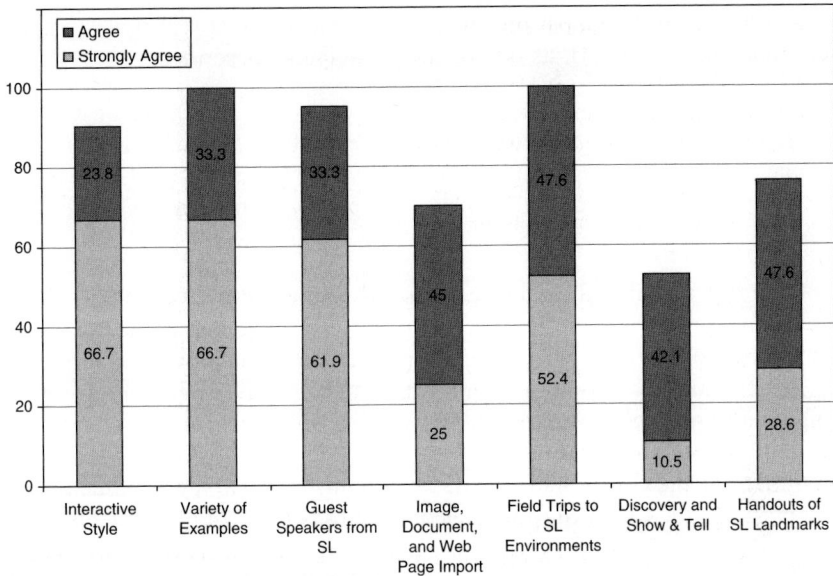

Figure 12.2: Participants' perceptions of the instructional strategies

mentioned it was helpful. This result may indicate that some of the participants were not interested in learning technical details or that some did not intend to actually use SL (discussed later).

Compared to the aforementioned strategies, fewer participants (53%; the rest remained neutral) perceived as helpful for learning the task where students were encouraged to discover something new on their own and to present a show-and-tell. However, this was a voluntary assignment and, as mentioned earlier, there were no grades or credit for the class. The lack of accountability possibly lowered students' involvement in this task.

(3) Will participants use Second Life or other related technologies? If so, why?

Compared to a mere 6% of the participants reporting their own use of virtual worlds at the beginning of the course, many more tried out SL during the course. According to survey 2, close to half of participants (43%) reported using SL on their own, with two thirds of them spending three hours or more in SL. Most of them (6) described their use as casual exploration such as walking, flying, and visiting various locations in SL introduced by the instructor or discovered on their own. Furthermore, by the end of the course, even more participants expressed their intention to use SL or other related technologies on their own in the future, with 81% of them agreeing that they would do so. Among the reasons that the older adults listed for planning to use SL were the desire to travel virtually (4) to meet people worldwide with similar interests, to visit with family, to attend conferences, and to take advantage of SL's vast potential for casual exploration or for various applications (3). Some were motivated by the desire to learn new things (2) and to keep current with new technology (1).

On the other hand, the most prevalent reason participants reported for not using SL were time constraints (4), as one of the participants described:

> *I can imagine when I am at the "wheelchair stage" if I can still remember how to use my laptop, I might find it widens the horizons! I feel I am the wrong demographic at the moment – too old for work – but busy!*

For these older adults, their desire to use SL in the future was mostly driven by specific interests such as language learning (1), learning about health issues (1), finding internationally common values through communication (1), meeting with family and friends (1), staying current with education and psychology topics (1), teaching seniors new technologies (1), and visiting museums (1), rather than general exploration without specific aims (1).

A month after the course had ended, we administered Survey 3 online and found that the participants' use of SL diminished: only 14% (2 of 14 respondents) reported some use of SL, such as revisiting the places that their instructor's avatar visited during the course or pursuing their own interest (e.g., language learning). Three respondents noted that they tried to use SL themselves, but their computers' capacity prohibited them from doing so. The participants' reported intention to try using SL or other related technologies on their own in the future also decreased, with only 31% (4 of 13) expressing their interests to do so. Those who intended to use it on their own were driven by their interests in staying current with cutting edge technologies (2) as well as to satisfy specific existing needs such as foreign language learning (1) and research (1). One the contrary, some reported that they did not intend to use SL because of the significant time investment required from their busy schedule in their first lives (4), because there was no specific use that would bring practical benefit to their lives (2), or because of the high computer capacity requirements (2).

Focus group participants also mentioned similar reasons for using or not using SL. One pattern that emerged in the process was the older adults' strong inclination for using SL for practical purposes related to their professional and personal interests. For one participant, it was psychology:

> *I think it is very good for – my background is psychology and social work – role-playing. You know, for a Ph.D. student to experience different scenarios and interacting with people, and things like that. So, I think that is a very good use of it.*

Another participant mentioned his idea for creating a museum to exhibit historical and creative products of the company that he used to work for. Still another proposed various ways to use SL for distance education. However, when there was no perceived clear match between SL use and their interests, participants had a hard time imagining using SL. One participant expressed:

> *I'm still searching for where I go from here. And how do I use SL to make*
> *it worthwhile for me personally? I keep trying to think of business*
> *applications and all that, and I haven't come up with anything.*

Additionally, even when a match was identified, for some participants the implementation may be difficult because they may feel that they are not in the position to take an action:

> *You know it has to affect us because we've all recognized a great deal of*
> *power and potential there…[in] just about any realm you can think of,*
> *and we saw examples of all of those that already have effects. We're*
> *probably the wrong age group that we'll take action on it, we've taken*
> *action for the most part, most of us are retired. I think SL will probably*
> *be pushed ahead by people who want to be productive in that productive*
> *age. We're in the third age; we don't have to be productive anymore.*

Others in this group of older adults disagreed, and one participant said, "I don't want to be on a shelf even though I'm retired. So, I guess there is potential for this age group." Additional reasons that the focus group participants raised for not using SL include the perceived "cartoonish" nature of the avatars and the technical challenges such as slow bandwidth. They discussed other social networking tools such as WebCT, Eons, Webcam, and teleconferencing, observing that they perform some similar functions as SL but may be easier to use.

Three survey respondents added that they may use SL as a social interaction vehicle. For example, one respondent wrote

> *I do think that it will be a great way to interact when the time comes that*
> *I am not mobile or when the course offerings are more attractive than*
> *what I can find locally.*

One focus group participant, who never entered SL herself, expressed a similar thought, saying:

> *I could see if I was a shut- in, and had no social life, and I lived very far*
> *from my friends, if SL could design, let's say the room that I am living in*
> *with a friend, and then we could sort of visit and play games, or do*
> *anything and it would be virtual kind of situation. But I think it would*
> *have a positive change for people who are infirm or can't get out or want*
> *to reconnect with friends and have more of a social scene.*

In summary, although the participants' use of and intention to use SL increased substantially during the course, their intentions diminished somewhat after the course. Their main reasons for not using SL included the perception that there were significant demands for time and/or computer capacity and not having found a practical use for SL in their current lives. However, this class of older adults also listed a variety of desired future uses of SL that catered to their intellectual and social interests.

(4) What impacts do participants perceive these technologies might have on their lives?

At the end of the course (Survey 2), most of the participants (81%) reported the belief that virtual worlds would have some impact on their future lives. The kinds of impact that they described include sustained or wider social interactions (5), continuing education (2), and staying current with new information (2). Similarly, 71% of the respondents reported their belief that society's use of virtual worlds would have some impact on their own futures such as increased social or business collaboration (3) and communication (3). One participant predicted that SL's use may expand with aging: "as aging occurs some uses for virtual life may evolve." These older adults also saw various possibilities of how SL or other virtual worlds might affect society at large, in particular in education and training. For example, one participant suggested possibilities for:

- Education (especially in learning/ teaching process as in paramedic training, or emergency room or ICU care)
- Learning by doing
- Entertaining ways of introducing new ideas
- Library access
- Visiting sites (like Rome) for learning history

12.7.   Results Related to Social Interaction and Persona

This group of older adults indicated that their new knowledge of or use of SL contributed new topics for communication in their social relationships. At the end of the course (Survey 2), all participants (100%) agreed (57%) or strongly agreed (43%) that they had discussed SL with their family or friends since the beginning of the course. Many of them (10) reported discussing the general concept of SL and the general course content, and some (2) mentioned discussing applications in certain fields such as education and medicine. Also, two reported use of the topic of SL to create a communication channel with the younger generation. For example, one respondent explicitly described asking "my grandchildren to help me choose an avatar, and our experience helped overcome the generation barrier." Furthermore, two others reported extending the discussion to social and psychological issues related to SL, and one mentioned the possibility of the "dangers of 'hiding' behind a persona and opting out of real social contacts."

One month after the course (Survey 3), many continued to discuss SL in conversations, and more than three quarters of participants (79%) reported that they had discussed SL with their family or friends since the end of the course. Similar to the results indicated by Survey 2, in Survey 3 many participants (7) reported explaining what SL was or what the course was about, and several (5) went further and discussed possible practical applications of SL in their interactions with other people. For example, one respondent wrote that she had

> explained in detail what SL was all about and gave them examples of the academic potential that SL represents. We moved beyond the "game" aspect of SL and discussed ways that it could improve one's life, e.g., shut-ins.

Although some participants reported that their knowledge of or use of SL might not affect their relationship with others at all (3), still others suspected that it might allow them to participate in conversations on related topics (4). One wrote, "At least I know what it is and don't have that blank look on my face regarding avatars, etc.", whereas another wrote, "I understand my grandchildren's conversations about their game boxes, Wii, etc."

Beyond using their new knowledge of SL in real-life conversations with others, some participants recognized the value of SL in expanding their social network virtually. In Survey 2, at the end of the course, participants were asked about SL's usefulness in helping to create or expand their social network, and 10% of the participants responded with "very useful," 24% "useful," and 33% "somewhat useful," whereas one third of them (33%) responded with "not too useful" (no one selected "Not at all useful"). Most of the participants (85%) reported that, if they were to use SL, they would be likely to build social connections with a mix of older and younger people, rather than with people around their own age (10%), somewhat (5%) or much (0%) younger than themselves or older than themselves (0%).

Knowledge of or use of SL also appeared to have had some impact on the participants' perceptions of self and other. Although five reported that their knowledge of or use of SL had not affected their self-image at all, four described positive changes, mainly saying that they felt good about themselves after they succeeded in learning about SL, a new technology that they had originally perceived as foreign. One respondent, for example, wrote, "When I decide to invest six weeks of my time in a class, I try to learn all that I can ... I think I succeeded. I would say as a result, my self-image grew." Similarly, a majority of the respondents (6) reported that their knowledge of or use of SL had not changed their perceptions of others; however, three reported different changes. One wrote, "now that you mention it, some of them seem a bit behind or resistant to new ideas and how it may be useful."

In summary, these older adults imagined impacts of SL on various facets of their current and future lives, as well as for society at large. They reported that their new knowledge of SL contributed conversational topics for social interactions, helped to create or expand social networks, and cast a different light on their self-image.

12.8.   Discussion

Several themes emerged from the survey and focus group data in this study with older adults learning about SL in a classroom setting. First, throughout the focus group responses it was clear that, despite some initial trepidation and anxiety in learning about a new technology, participants in the class identified the value of SL in terms of its educational benefit, especially for distance learning and language learning. They also identified its potential in relation to business activities and the concomitant economic possibilities that lie therein. Some very practical applications of SL were noted by focus group participants. For example, one speaker argued that using SL could be highly cost effective:

> *using this in place of videoconferencing. And it would be more real life because we'd all be sitting around a conference table in Cape Town having the same conversation, and when you get bored you teleport to Malaysia and attend the meeting there. And I'd think, well, this could be a big time saver, a carbon footprint saver, and all that, so I got really enthusiastic about it.*

Second, most of the participants in the class found that SL held the potential for increasing their social networks in the future, should their capacity to engage with others decline as they enter the later stages of old age. It is important to recognize that the older adults in this seminar were still actively engaged in both learning and social activities, a fact underscored by their very participation in the class. Thus, this group was not immediately faced with a need to involve themselves with SL. The apparent decline in usage following the course would suggest that SL is not necessarily a context of first choice for creating social networks among this group of individuals.

On the contrary, the possibility for retired individuals to contribute their expertise and ideas to the world was a theme expressed by many. As one participant observed, "that's what I mean about being productive. I think if you find what it is that you want to produce, this is just wide open to you." The theme of productivity came up repeatedly among participants, whether related to being retired or to physical health conditions. One man expressed the ability to contribute virtually through SL in this way:

> *People from banks, from hospitals, from museums, you know they were there to be docents, as doctors, or they were there to be productive. I thought that was maybe to me the most amazing thing: that you could be productive no matter what condition physically you were in. There was something that you could actually contribute to some section of society.*

It is also clear that several participants in the class perceived SL as having future potential for generating social networks should they become disabled. This is an important observation, because it suggests, first, that the young-old (older retired adults who are still active; cf. Neugarten, 1974) are in fact interested in becoming involved in learning environments that allow them to explore and develop knowledge using technologies that can expand or enhance social networks. Second, this study suggests that the aging population is also very interested in acquiring – even through virtual world technology-the capacity to plan for possible disability and to manage the process of declining social networks that can occur among older adults as they lose the capacity to regularly engage with others (McFadden & Atchley, 2006).

Third, there is an interesting subtext found in the comments of some of the participants related to the potential of learning SL, not only for maintaining or creating social networks among age-peers but also for encouraging intergenerational contact. One participant observed that the opportunity to get help from her grandchildren in creating an avatar opened the door for closer understanding and conversation across the generations. This insight suggests that engagement with new technologies such as SL can enhance intergenerational contact and understanding. Another participant commented that he had reconsidered the expense of the games his grandchildren purchase because he now has a more empathetic understanding of their gaming activities. This observation suggests that SL can re-educate elders about the activities of their children and grandchildren by exposing them to opportunities that allow people to rethink their preconceptions about the nature of "gaming" itself.

Along these lines, exposure to SL through the classroom setting, in short, provides two related vectors for creating social networks, one virtual and the other concrete. Being technology and Internet-centred, the course provided a wealth of information and knowledge for older adults to draw upon as they attempted to connect with younger family members. At the same time, experience and learning related to SL provided participants with new information that allowed them to think about ways in which they might manage and maintain social networks, should their capacity to physically do so decline later in their lives.

Some participants reported feeling a sense of connection with the embodied representations of people and of themselves in the form of their avatars. One focus group participant contrasted SL with an online discussion board community, and she noted that, "You are more of a whole person in SL." The focus group participants agreed that their personality would not change between real life and SL, and one woman reported that:

> *I'm not any different in SL than I am in first life. I have a tendency for shyness and reserve in first life and it's the same in SL. Maybe through experience there may be something more there that will elicit from me more gregariousness, but I don't think so.*

This observation suggests how a visual representation of oneself and others through the form of an avatar was seen as a powerful means for generating both an enriched sense of oneself and of connection with others. Another participant discussed the experience of emotion and emotional involvement in SL:

> *I could see, you know, people actually meeting others, falling in love, and all that kind of thing, virtually. I don't know how much it would translate*

to reality, but I could certainly see that emotion being developed with avatars.

Several of the informants also agreed when one focus group member commented on the experts from SL who interacted virtually with the class: "Yeah I thought of them as real people, even the one with tails." The focus group participants were very clear about this sense of embodiment, and one asserted:

I think when you create your avatar and you start to get to know your avatar … You identify with that avatar. It's you. And, I think some of the same feelings you have in first life, you're gonna have in SL. So, if you can do it easy in first life, you can probably do it easy in SL. If you have difficulty in first life, you may have difficulty in SL.

Finally, a male participant made explicit the continuity of his own experience in SL in this way: "When I go in there I feel that's me. I don't feel the least bit different."

12.9. Conclusions

If we return to where we began this chapter with the case of Fred, the paraplegic who had found a new means of creating social networks through SL after 10 years living in a largely housebound situation, it would seem that there is considerable potential for SL as a means for improving the well-being of those who experience impairment in their abilities to maintain social networks, such as some older adults and those who experience certain types of disabilities. Thus, SL may provide a means by which to enhance feelings of self-worth among older adults. The wealth of knowledge, ideas, and experiences that individuals such as Fred are willing to share and the desire to connect with others, both family and strangers, were pervasive among the group of older people who participated in this study. Furthermore, through exposure to SL during the course, these older adults were able to recognize and assess that potential for themselves should the need to make use of SL in this way arise.

However, there are some important cautions that should be noted. First, our informants may represent only a small proportion of older adults. Although recent research suggests that there is a sustainable trend for users to continue investing their time and capital in SL, user acceptance of 3D virtual world environments may still be one of the most critical challenges to overcome (Fetscherin & Lattemann, 2007, p. 20). Courses such as the OLLI seminar provide potential contexts for older adults to experience SL in a safe learning environment alongside their age-peers. Nonetheless, it should be noted that the participants in this class were people already motivated to seek out new forms of information and to explore the potential of the Internet. Furthermore, as several participants noted, overcoming initial preconceptions about the appearance of people's avatars and addressing on-going challenges in the early stages of a new technology will continue to be critical for early adopters.

Cases like that of Fred, our homebound NASA guide, when combined with the very similar social, professional, and business possibilities that our informants offered during the study, suggest that SL can have significant potential to enhance the well-being for older adults. In that light, we suggest that efforts to expose older adults to virtual worlds like SL should be continued and expanded, and at the same time more research should be conducted to develop concrete ways for facilitating older adults' use of virtual worlds.

References

Adler, R. (2002). The age wave meets the technology wave: Broadband and older Americans. *Technical Report for SeniorNet.* Accessed July 3, 2009, from http://www.seniornet.org/downloads/broadband.pdf.

Atkinson, R. K., Mayer, R. E., & Merrill, M. M. (2005). Fostering social agency in multimedia learning: Examining the impact of an animated agent's voice. *Contemporary Educational Psychology, 30*(1), 117–139.

Bollier, D. (1989). *1989 Review conference on new electronic technologies for the elderly: Issues and projects.* Report of an Aspen Institute Conference, Queenstown, MD. (ERIC Document Reproduction Service No. ED315678).

Chadwick-Dias, A., McNulty, M., & Tullis, T. (2003). *Proceedings of the 2003 ACM conference on universal usability,* 30–37. ACM, Vancouver, Canada.

Charness, N., & Schaie, K. W. (Eds). (2003). *Impact of technology on successful aging.* New York: Springer Publishing Company.

Czaja, S., & Sharit, J. (1998). Age differences in attitudes toward computers. *Journals of Gerontology Series B: Psychological Sciences and Social Sciences, 53*(5), 329–340.

Dresang, E., & McClelland, K. (1999). Radical change: Digital age literature and learning. *Theory into Practice, 38*(3), 160–167.

Fetscherin, M., & Lattemann, C. (2007). *User acceptance of virtual worlds: An explorative study about Second Life.* Rollins College: University of Potsdam.

FitzGerald, S. (2007, June). Virtual worlds: What are they and why do educators need to pay attention to them? Paper presented at E-learning Networks June Online Event. Accessed July 3, 2009, from http://seanfitz.wikispaces.com/virtualworldsenetworks07

Fox, S. (2004). Pew Internet & American life project report: Older Americans and the Internet. Accessed July 3, 2009, from http://www.pewinternet.org/PPF/r/117/report_display.asp

Freedberg, D., & Gallese, V. (2007). Motion, emotion and empathy in esthetic experience. *Trends in Cognitive Sciences, 11*(5), 197–202.

Gallese, V., Eagle, M., & Migone, P. (2007). Intentional attunement: Mirror neurons and the neural underpinnings of interpersonal relations. *Journal of the American Psychoanalytic Association, 55*(1), 131–176.

Gallese, V., & Lakoff, G. (2005). The brain's concepts: The role of the sendory-motor system in conceptual knowledge. *Cognitive Neuropsychology, 22*(3/4), 455–479.

Gorini, A., Gaggioli, A., Vigna, C., & Riva, G. (2008). A Second Life for eHealth: Prospects for the use of 3D virtual worlds in clinical psychology. *Journal of Medical Internet Research, 10*(3), e21. Accessed July 3, 2009, from http://www.jmir.org/2008/3/e21.

Iacoboni, M. (2008). *Mirroring people: The new science of how we connect with others.* New York: Farrar, Straus & Giroux.

Jarmon, L. (2009). Learning in virtual world environments: Social-presence, engagement, & pedagogy. In: P. Rogers, G. Berg, J. Boettcher, C. Howard, L. Justice & K. Schenk (Eds), *Encyclopedia of distance and online learning* (pp. 1610–1619). Hershey, PA: IGI Global.

Jarmon, L., Traphagan, T., Mayrath, M., & Trivedi, A. (2009). Virtual world teaching, experiential learning, and assessment: An interdisciplinary communication course in Second Life. *Computers & Education, 53*, 169–182. Elsevier. doi:10.1016/j.compedu.2009.01.010.

Kanayama, T. (2000, April). The pilot study of the uses of electronic mail by the elderly. Paper presented at the 2000 Mid-Year Conference of AEJMC Graduate Education Interest Group, Boulder, CO.

Latimer, C. P. (2001). *Government information focus: The digital divide: Understanding and addressing the challenge.* New York: York State Forum for Information Resource Management.

Lave, J., & Wenger, E. (1991). *Situated learning: Legitimate peripheral participation.* New York, NY: Cambridge University Press.

Lawhon, T., Ennis, D., & Lawhon, D. (1996). Senior adults and computers in the 1990s. *Educational Gerontology, 22*(2), 193–201.

McFadden, S., & Atchley, R. (2006). *Aging and the meaning of time: A multidisciplinary approach.* New York: Springer Publishing Company.

Minardi, H., & Blanchard, M. (2004). Older people with depression: Pilot Study. *Journal of Advanced Nursing, 46*, 23–32.

Moreno, R., Mayer, R. E., Spires, H. A., & Lester, J. C. (2001). The case for social agency in computer based teaching: Do students learn more deeply when they interact with animated pedagogical agents? *Cognition and Instruction, 19*(2), 177–213.

Morgan, R. E. (2005). Technology greets the age wave. *The Gerontologist, 45*, 704–710.

Nardi, B. (2005). Beyond bandwidth: Dimensions of connection in interpersonal communication. *Computer Supported Cooperative Work, 14*(2), 91–130.

Neugarten, B. (1974). Age groups in American society and the rise of the young-old. *Annals of the American Academy of Political and Social Science, 415*, 87–198.

Nycyk, M., & Redsell, M. (2006). The role of computer tuition in community health: A grounded theory approach. *Aging International, 31*, 296–308.

Ondrejka, C. (2005). Changing realities: User creation, communication, and innovation in digital worlds. *Social Science Research Network.* Accessed July 3, 2009, from http://papers.ssrn.com/sol3/papers.cfm?abstract_id = 799468

Petigrew, S., & Roberts, M. (2008). Addressing loneliness in later life. *Aging and Mental Health, 12*(3), 302–309.

Rosenthal, R. (2008). Older computer-literate women: Their motivations, obstacles, and paths to success. *Educational Gerontology, 34*(7), 610–626.

Rowe, J., & Kahn, R. (1998). *Successful aging.* New York: Pantheon/Random House.

Russell, H. (2008). Later life: A time to learn. *Educational Gerontology, 34*(3), 206–224.

Seals, C., Clanton, K., Agarwal, R., Doswell, F., & Thomas, C. (2008). Lifelong learning: Becoming computer savvy at a later age. *Educational Gerontology, 34*, 1055–1069.

Shapira, N., Barak, A., & Gal, I. (2007). Promoting older adults' well-being through Internet training and use. *Aging & Mental Health, 11*, 477–484.

Stein, R. (2007, October 6). Real hope in a virtual world. *Washingtonpost.com,* p. A01. Accessed July 3, 2009, from http://www.washingtonpost.com/wp-dyn/content/article/2007/10/05/AR2007100502391.html

Traphagan, J. (2000). *Taming oblivion: Aging bodies and the fear of senility in Japan*. Albany: State University of New York Press.

White, H., McConnell, E., Clipp, E., Branch, L. G., Sloane, R., Pieper, C., & Box, T. (2002). A randomized controlled trial of the psychosocial impact of providing Internet training and access to older adults. *Aging & Mental Health, 6*, 213–221.

White, H., McConnell, E., Clipp, E., Bynum, L., Teague, C., & Navas, L. (1999). Surfing the Net in later life: A review of the literature and pilot study of computer use and quality of life. *Journal of Applied Gerontology, 18*, 358–378.

Xie, Bo. (2007). Older Chinese, the Internet, and well-being. *Care Management Journals, 8*(1), 33–38.

Author Biographies

Leslie Jarmon, PhD (Second Life: *Bluewave Ogee*) is a Faculty Development Specialist at the University of Texas at Austin with the Division for Instructional Innovation and Assessment. She has designed and taught graduate level courses since 1998 with the Office of Graduate Studies. She is a leader in the university's entry into virtual world environments, specifically Second Life (SL), and she is co-founder of the Educators Coop, a virtual residential community of interdisciplinary educators, researchers, and librarians from around the world (http://www.educatorscoop.org). She has published research papers and presented at numerous conferences on Second Life, including Best Practices in Education in SL, the American Sociological Association, and the New Media Consortium Symposium on Creativity.

Tomoko Watanabe Traphagan, PhD is a research associate in the Division of Instructional Innovation and Assessment at the University of Texas at Austin. She has been involved in the research and evaluation of various instructional technology programs at the university, including webcasting, Second Life, digital media service, course management system, web-based inquiry-based learning, and usability of instructional websites. Her research interests lies in the impact of technology on students' learning behaviors and performance.

John W. Traphagan, PhD is associate professor of Religious Studies and Anthropology at the University of Texas at Austin. He is the author of *Taming Oblivion: Aging Bodies and the Fear of Senility in Japan*, *The Practice of Concern: Ritual, Well-Being, and Aging in Rural Japan*, and co-editor of *Imagined Families, Lived Families: Culture and Kinship in Contemporary Japan*, *Demographic Change and the Family in Japan's Aging*, and *Wearing Cultural Styles: Concepts of Tradition and Modernity in Practice*. His work has appeared in many scholarly journals, including *Alzheimer Disease and Associated Disorders*, *Research on Aging*, *Ethnology*, the *Journal of Cross-Cultural Gerontology*, the *Journal of Anthropological Research*, and the *Journal of Adult Development*.

Lynn Jones Eaton, PhD is the Associate Director of Faculty and Graduate Student Instructional Development in the Division of Instructional Innovation and Assessment at the University of Texas at Austin. She has been involved in teaching and learning at the K-12, college, and post-college levels. Her academic interests focus on teaching and learning within a broad spectrum of rich learning environments.

Author Index

Abbott, J. 161
Abrahams, P. 48, 53
Acutt, B. 185
Adams-Spink, G. 48
Addison, A. 216
Adler, R. 224
Agarwal, R. 224
Alissa, A. 48
Allen, M. 101–102, 110
Allen, T.H. 29\
Andersen, J.F. 102, 106
Andersen, P.A. 102
Anderson, J.F. 102, 162
Anderson, J.R. 119
Anderson, T. 101
Aperia, T. 117
Armstrong, M. 181
Atchley, R. 237
Atkins, C. 147
Atkinson, R.K. 225
Au, W. J. 197
Avtgis, T.A. 111

Bailenson, J.N. 52
Bailey, C. 183
Baker, C. 54
Baker, J. 104
Bakx, A.W.E.A. 208
Baldridge, D.C. 32
Balkun, M.M. 141
Ball, S. 47
Barak, A. 224
Baron, A. 181
Barraclough, R.A. 106
Barrows, H.S. 160
Bartlett, C. 181

Baxter, A. 89
Bayne, S. 182, 187
Beamish, P. 181
Beck, J. 184
Becker, K. 185
Beckwith, R.T. 47
Belei, N. 115
Bell, M. 183
Bennett, B. 205
Benoit, P.J. 30
Benoit, W.L. 30
Biehler, R. 161
Biever, C. 50
Biggs, J. 118
Bignell, S. 51
Biocca, F. 48
Blackall, L 147
Blanc, A. 50
Blanchard, M. 224
Blascovich, J. 181
Blatner, A. 183, 186, 193
Blomeyer 59
Bollier, D. 222
Bolt, M.A. 118
Boos, M. 30, 32–33, 43
Bouloth, M.N.K. 56
Box, T. 224
Branch, L.G. 224
Braswell, R. 49
Bratton, J. 181
Braunger, J. 52
Broadribb, S. 203, 208
Bruner, J. 161
Bunz, U. 32
Burgstahler, S. 58
Burrage, K. 58

Buss, A. 208
Bynum, L. 225
Byron, K. 32

Cagiltay, K. 159
Calongne, C. M. 142
Campbell, S.W. 32
Carey, L. 161
Carlton, I. 181, 183
Carr, D. 48, 53
Carr, M.S. 52
Carter, B. 48
Carter, C. 203, 208
Carter, W.S. 48
Cascio, W.F. 181
Cassell, J. 50
Castronova, E. 216
Chadwick-Dias, A. 222
Challagalla, G.N. 118–119
Chang, T.-W. 163
Chaput, H. 47
Cheng, N. Y.-W. 159, 163
Cheng, Y. 51
Childress, M.D. 49
Childs, M. 48
Christie, B. 30, 103
Christophel, D.M. 103, 106
Clanton, K. 224
Clark, S. 163
Clipp, E. 224–225
Cobb, P. 214
Coleride, S. 15
Corbin, J. 36
Cornelius, C. 30, 33, 43
Corona, G.D. 48
Cowdroy, R. 163–164
Craig, D.L. 159
Crandall, B. 191
Crichton, P. 52
Croucher, R. 182
Czaja, S. 224

Daft, R.L. 30
Davis, B.L. 181
Davis, F.D. 119, 124

De Castell, S. 147
Decker, P.J. 124
Dede, C. 159, 163
Deeley, L. 50
Dev, P. 56
Di Meglio, F. 86, 92
Dick, W. 161
Dickey, M.D.
        162–163
Doesinger, S. 92
Donath, D. 163
Doswell, F. 224
Dresang, E. 225
Dudeney, G. 11
Duffy, T.M. 160
Dunham, P.J. 30–31

Eagle, M. 226
Eaton, L.J. 221
Elliott, J. 57
Ellis, K. 107
Ellis, W. 55
Ennis, D. 224
Ewins, R. 181

Fassett, D.L. 29, 33, 43
Fayer, J.M. 106
Feldman, J.M. 182–183
Felix, U. 207
Feningstein, A. 208
Fenn, J. 13
Fetscherin, M. 238
FitzGerald, S. 225
Fitzpatrick, G. 22
Fleming, M.L. 162
Fletcher, C. 181, 183
Folmer, E. 48
Ford, K. 124
Fox, S. 222, 224
Frederiksen, N. 118
Freedberg, D. 226
Freitas, F.A. 111
French, J.R.P. 182
Friend, R. 208
Furnham, A. 208

Gaggioli, A. 225–226
Gaimster, J. 29, 33, 43
Gal, I. 224
Gallese, V. 226
Gartner 97
Gee, J.P. 153, 184, 190
Georgson, M. 117
Gerhard, M. 103
Ghoshal, S. 181
Glaser, B.G. 36
Glasersfeld, E. V. 162
Goffman, E. 208
Gojdycz, T.K. 29, 31
Gold, J. 181
Good, J. 23
Gorham, J.S. 102–103
Gorini, A. 225–226
Granka, L. 30–31
Gredler, M.E. 214
Grover, G. 124
Gu, N. 159, 162
Guerrero, L.K. 104
Guess, A. 57
Gül, L. F. 159, 162, 172
Gunawardena, C.N. 104

Hackman, M.Z. 104
Haenlein, M. 84, 93–95, 97
Hall, L. 181
Hancock, J.T. 30–31
Hansen, G.J. 30
Hanson, S. 48
Hanson, T.L. 103, 109
Harris, M. 11, 13
Hassall, L. 66
Heinrichs, W. 56
Hemmi, A. 182
Hemp, P. 83, 96
Hine, C.M. 184
Ho, S.S. 32
Hoadley, C.M. 185
Hobbs, D. 103
Hoffman, R. 191
Hollingshead, A.B. 30
Hollins, P. 17, 216

Holzwarth, M. 83
Horspool, A. 49, 52, 58, 60
Horton, L. A. 101
Howland, K. 23
Hubble, K. 57
Hudson, K. 57
Huffcutt, A.I. 182
Hyland, P. 185

Iacoboni, M. 227
Ip, A. 184, 197

Jackson, C.J. 208
Jaime, S. 48
Janiszewski, C. 83
Jarmon, L. 119, 221, 226
Jeffery, C. 216
Jensen, A.D. 102
Jensen, H. 88
Jenson, J. 147
Johnson, D. 159
Johnson, R. 159
Johnson, S.D. 103, 109
Jonassen, D.H. 162

Kahn, R. 224
Kahneman, D. 163
Kanayama, T. 222
Kaplan, A.M. 83–84, 93–95, 97
Kay, E. 182
Kearney, P. 102, 105–106
Keller, K.L. 117
Kelley, D.H. 102
Kelly, B. 48
Kelsey, R.M. 181
Kessels, J.W.M. 118
Killough, L.N. 118
Kirriemuir, J. 47–48, 205
Kitade, K. 104
Klein, G. 191
Koh, H.C. 118
Kraiger, K.J. 124
Kruijff, E. 163
Kuksa, I. 48
Kusumoto, L. 56
Kvan, T. 159, 163

Lakoff, G. 226
Lam, S.S.K. 181
Land, R. 182
Landa, L. 161
Latimer, C.P. 224
Lattemann, C. 238
Lave, J. 226
Lawhon, D. 224
Lawhon, T. 224
Lawty-Jones, M. 208
Lea, M. 30
Lee, E. 31–32
Lee, J.J. 185
Leigh, S. 182
Leitten, C.L. 181
Lengel, R.H. 30
Leonard, L. G. 29, 34
Lester, J.C. 225
Levie, W.H. 162
Lewin, K. 185
Linser, R. 184
Littleton, F. 181, 187
Loftin, R.B. 163
Loh, T. 30–31
Love, E. 65
Love, G. 104
Lowendahl, J.-M. 13
Lucas, R. 181
Lupton, B. 181

Macleod, H. 47, 181
Maher, M. L. 159, 162–163
Margulies, J. 182
Mark, E. 159
Martens, B. 159
Mathieson, H. 181
Mayer, R.E. 225
Mayrath, M. 119, 226
McAllister, G. 22, 104
McClelland, K. 225
McConnell, E. 224–225
McCroskey, J.C. 102–103, 105–107
McFadden, S. 237
McGrath, J.E. 30
McGrath, P. 51

McKinney, S. 49, 52, 58, 60
McLeod, D.M. 32
McNulty, M. 222
Mehrabian, A. 102
Meijers, F. 118
Mennecke, B. 66
Merrill, M.M. 225
Mesko, B. 57
Meyer, H.H. 182
Migone, P. 226
Milena, D. 48
Miller, A.N. 103, 109
Miller, T. 104
Millette, D. 103
Milligan, F. 118
Milyo, J. 30
Minardi, H. 224
Minty, I. 17
Moore, D. 51, 103
Moreno, R. 225
Morgan, R.E. 222
Morse, S. 181–182
Mottet, T.P. 107
Mount, M.K. 181
Muller-Camen, M. 182
Mullins, L. 181, 185
Murphy, T. H. 182
Murray, S. 92
Murthy, N.N. 118–119
Myers, S.A. 106, 111

Naidu, S. 184, 197
Nakamura, L. 182
Nakapan, W. 159
Narayan, M. 169
Nardi, B. 225
Nass, C. 32
Nathan, B.R. 124
Navas, L. 225
Neer, M.R. 32
Nesson, C. 34
Nesson, R. 34
Neugarten, B. 236
Neumann, M.M. 83
Nicol, D.J. 17

Nicosia, L. 148
Norton, R.W. 102
Noteborn, G. 115
Nussbaum, J.F. 102
Nycyk, M. 224

O'Hare, L. 216
Oldenburg, R. 206
Oliver, M. 55
Ondrejka, C. 225
Ostrander, M. 75
Oxman, E. 159

Padden, C. 54
Pallof, R. 159
Pasteur, E. 54, 148
Patterson, B.R. 29, 31
Peachey, A. 203, 205–206
Pearce, R. 47
Peterson, M. 103
Petigrew, S. 224
Pieper, C. 224
Piovezan, S. 94
Plax, T.G. 102, 105
Postmes, T. 30
Powell, N.J. 51
Prasolova-Forland, E. 163
Pratt, K. 159
Prensky, M. 184–185
Punyanunt-Carter, N.M. 30

Ramsay, H. 11
Raskino, M. 13
Redsell, M. 224
Reigeluth, C.M. 161
Rice, R.E. 104
Richlin, L. 49, 52, 58, 60
Richmond, V.P. 102, 105–107
Rieber, L. P. 142
Riegler, A. 161
Ritter-Guth, B. 148
Riva, G. 225–226
Rizzo, A. 58
Robbins, S. 216
Roberts, M. 224

Robertson, I.T. 124
Rocca, K.A. 106
Ron, W. 48
Rose, R.M. 59
Rosenthal, R. 224–225
Ross, S.C. 65
Rowe, J. 224
Russell, H. 223
Ruyter, K.d. 115
Ryan, T. 161

Safie, O. 49, 52, 58, 60
Saidi, N. 50
Salas, E. 124
Sallinen, A. 106
Salt, B. 147
Salzman, M. 163
Sapre, M. 48
Sarvary, M. 94–95
Sassenberg, K. 32
Savery, J.R. 160
Schaubroeck, J. 181
Scheier, M.F. 208
Schlosser, A.E. 83
Schmitt, G. N. 159, 163
Schön, D.A. 160
Schnabel, M. A. 163
Schrire, S. 29, 33, 43
Schrodt, P. 104, 109–110
Schroeder, R. 103
Scott, C.R. 30, 32
Seals, C. 224
Shapira, N. 224
Sharit, J. 224
Sherblom, J.C. 29–30, 34
Shervani, T.A. 118–119
Short, J. 30, 103
Simon, S.J. 124
Sinclair, C. 17
Slator, B.M. 47
Sloane, R. 224
Sloman, M. 181, 183
Smith, V.R. 102
Snowman, J. 161
So, H.J. 43

Sorensen, G. 102
Spady, W.G. 161
Spears, R. 30
Spires, H.A. 225
Stager, G. 152
Stanne, M. 159
Stanton, J.M. 183
Stein, R. 227
Stephenson, N. 142
Stevens, S. 53
Strauss, A.L. 36
Swink, D.F. 208

Tartaro, A. 50
Taylor, L. 184
Taylor, S. 181
Taylor, T.L. 48
Teague, C. 225
Teng, J.T. 124
Teven, J.J. 103, 106–107, 109
Thackray, L. 23
Thelander, N. 13
Thomas, C.E. 102, 224
Tidwell, L.C. 31
Tillema, H.H. 118
Timmerman, C.E. 30, 32
Tomaka, J. 181
Torrington, D. 181
Toth-Cohen, S. 56
Tournish, D. 181–183
Traphagan, J.W. 221, 224
Traphagan, T.W. 119, 221, 226
Trevino, L.K. 30
Triplett, J. 66
Trivedi, A. 226
Trotta, H. 141
Truelove, I. 52
Tullis, T. 222
Turkle, S. 184
Turman, P.D. 110
Tversky, A. 163

van der Sanden, J.M.M. 208
Van Ments, M. 183
Vermetten, Y.J.M. 208
Vess, D. 29, 33, 43
Vgotsky, L.S. 206, 213

Vigna, C. 225–226
Vincent, L.H. 118–119

Wade, M. 184
Walker, K.B. 104
Walther, J.B. 30–31
Wandt-Wesco, N.J. 102
Warburton, S. 47
Watson, D. 208
Weineke, C. 102
Wenger, E. 226
Westrap, F. 203
Wheeless, L.R. 101–102, 110
Whitcomb, K. 124
White, D. 52
White, G.R. 22, 48
White, H. 224–225
Whitton, N. 17
Wilhelm, W. 65
Willers, R. 49, 52, 58, 60
Williams, A.P. 159, 163, 164
Williams, E. 30, 103
Winn, W. 161–163, 169
Withers, L. A. 29, 34
Witmer, D.F. 29
Witt, P.L. 102, 104, 109, 110
Woehr, D.J. 182
Wood, A.F. 29, 33, 43
Woods, D. 160
Wrench, J.S. 30
Wyeld, T. G. 163

Xie, Bo. 225

Yee, N. 52
Yellowlees, P. 58
Yi, M.Y. 119, 124
Yildiz, S. 43
Youngblood, P. 56
Yuan, B. 48
Yukselturk, E. 159

Zastrocky, M. 13
Zedeck, M. 141
Zedeck, S. 181
Zimring, C. 159
Zittle, F.J. 104

Subject Index

3D design, 175
3D patient model, 56

access, 5, 15, 18–20, 22–24, 36–38,
    42–43, 48, 55, 58–59, 72, 74,
    79, 88, 98, 118, 123, 143, 145,
    148, 150, 152–154, 163, 211,
    222, 224–225, 234
access-controlled rooms, 55
accessibility, 5, 12, 48, 51, 54, 56
accessory, 16
accounting, 65, 72, 108–109
Active Worlds, 98, 103
Adidas, 83
Adobe connect, 15, 95
advertising, network, 84
advertising, space, 84
affective learning, 102–103, 105,
    107–108, 110
aging, 197, 221–225, 227, 229, 231,
    233–235, 237
aliases, 16
alumni, 85, 87, 89, 92, 94
anonymity, 30, 32–34, 37, 40,
    42, 53, 186, 188, 192,
    195–196
anxiety, 30–31, 42, 181, 236
ATI Radeon, 18
autism, 49–51
Avatars, 1–3, 6, 14, 16, 20, 26, 38–39, 48,
    51–52, 54–55, 70–71, 74–75, 77,
    85, 87–94, 96, 98, 103, 110, 123,
    129, 145, 150, 152, 169, 172, 182,
    184, 187–188, 190–191, 194–195,
    197, 209, 225–226, 228, 233, 235,
    237–238

Babson College, 84
Barbie Girls, 2
barriers, 5, 8, 11–15, 17, 19–21,
    23–25, 47, 49, 51, 53, 55–58, 65,
    74, 175
Barriers, end-user, 12, 17–18, 20, 24
Barriers, institutional, 12–14
Barriers, pedagogical. 12, 14
Barriers, technical. 12, 74
behavior, consumer, 86, 117, 119
Behaviors, 34, 101–104, 106–110, 118,
    172, 224
Behaviors, immediacy, 6, 101–106,
    108–110
Behaviors, nonverbal, 101
Behaviors, verbal, 102
Blackboard, 145, 152
brand(s), 3, 5–7, 12–13, 15–19,
    22–26, 30–42, 47–56, 68, 70–71,
    73, 76, 79, 83–98, 101–103,
    106–107, 109–110, 115, 117–125,
    127–129, 131, 133–135, 141–146,
    148, 151–152, 154, 160–162,
    166, 169, 172, 181–185, 188,
    190–197, 203–204, 207–208, 211,
    213–215, 217, 221–223, 226, 228,
    230–238
brand, label, 117
brand, management, 6, 81, 115, 117–119,
    121–122, 125
brand,value, 117
branding activities, 121–122
branding strategy, 117, 119–122,
    127–128, 132
Business School Toulouse, 84

business, 1, 3, 5, 16, 41, 65–80, 83–89,
    91–99, 105, 115, 117–118, 122,
    150–151, 182, 184–185, 192, 194,
    216, 223, 228–230, 233–234, 236,
    239
business, school, 83–99

campus, 36, 74, 78, 85–89, 91–94, 98,
    116, 123, 149, 153
Canada, 16, 18, 57
Centre for Open Learning in Maths,
    Science, Computing, and
    Technology (COLMSCT), 205
Cetlment Island, 205
Chaotic Sandpit, 13
chat, 5, 21, 23, 35–39, 42, 54, 67, 70, 105,
    108–109, 111, 142, 172, 174,
    187–188, 192–195, 226
chatterbots, 87, 93
choice of perception, 15
Cisco, 65, 95
Club Penguin, 2
codes, 14, 26, 55
codes of conduct, 14, 26
codetermination, 4
cognitive theory, 162
Colgate-Palmolive, 65
collaborate, 36, 41, 68, 89, 159,
    165
collaboration, 5, 15, 29, 36–37, 41–43,
    49, 52, 68, 141, 144, 149–150, 153,
    156, 160–161, 163–165, 168–170,
    172–176, 187, 207, 214, 225–226,
    234
collaboration, design, 16, 168, 170,
    174–176
collaborative virtual environments
    (CVEs), 225
collaborative, group project, 35, 43
collaborative, learning, 33, 43
collaborative, problem solving, 33
collaborative, processes, 32, 168
communication technologies, 30, 161,
    174

communication, 5, 7–8, 11, 13, 17,
    20–21, 29–39, 41–43, 48–49, 51,
    57, 70, 79, 84, 87–88, 101,
    103–104, 111, 115, 117, 119–120,
    132, 145, 159, 161, 164–165,
    168–169, 172–176, 183, 193, 196,
    212, 224–226, 228, 232, 234
communication, apprehension, 31–33,
    42
communication, challenges, 29–45
communication, group, 30, 32–37,
    41–43, 169
communication, interpersonal, 29,
    31–32, 36–37, 39, 42, 46
communication, social-emotional,
    30, 42
communication, synchronous, 8, 36,
    169, 173–174
competition, 34, 92, 117–118, 121, 125,
    127, 129, 165, 195
composite names, 16
computer ethics, 75
Computer Mediated Communication
    (CMC), 5, 29–35, 37, 42–43, 104
confidence, self, 51, 208
confidence, social, 49, 52
confidentiality, 70
connection, social, 195, 205, 224, 226,
    228, 235
consequential communication, 172
constructivism, 161, 163, 206
constructivist, 17, 159–163, 176, 214
co-presence, 221–223, 225–226
Cornell University Johnson Graduate
    School of Management, 86
creativity, 6–7, 27, 67, 76, 96, 121–122,
    129, 133–134, 150, 152, 154, 160,
    163, 168, 185
credibility, 3, 103, 105–109
credibility, instructor, 103, 105,
    107–108
Cult of Domesticity and True
    Womanhood, 146, 148
culture, teaching, 11
currency, 65, 72–73, 90, 97

Dallas School of Management, 85
deindividuation, 32
Dell, 83
Department for Strategic Management, Marketing and Tourism of the University of Innsbruck, 86
design learning, 7, 159, 161–163, 165, 167, 169, 171, 173, 175
design protocols, 160
design schools, 159, 163
design, collaborative, 159–160, 164–165, 168–169, 172–173, 176
digital native, 4, 21
disability, 52–53, 192, 237
Disciplined Engine Room, 13
distance learning, 54, 67–69, 76, 104, 111, 236
distribution channel, 120

E-Doctoring, 56–57
educational approaches, 160
educational tool, 115, 123, 132–133
educators, 1–6, 11, 14, 16, 19, 23–26, 29–31, 33, 35, 37, 39, 41, 43, 59, 65–66, 68–70, 73, 75, 79–80, 101, 111, 134–135, 160–161, 205, 216
educators, business, 5, 65–66, 69–70
educators, design, 160–161
Eduserv, 57, 205
Eduverse, 123
eHealth, 225
eject permissions, 15
e-learning, 7, 15, 85, 182, 185
Elluminate, 15
embodiment, 47–48, 148, 225–226, 238
empathic understanding, 226
engagement, 17, 21, 33, 49, 54, 67, 147, 153, 156, 175, 190–195, 212–214, 216, 221–222, 225, 229, 237
entertainment, 54, 222, 224
entrepreneur, 69, 81
entrepreneurship, 65
environments, learning, 6, 24, 27, 66–68, 197, 217, 225–226, 237–238,

103–104, 109, 118, 135, 142, 162–163, 172, 176
environments, rich, 156
environments, student-generated, 155
environments, synchronous collaboration, 225
environments, virtual, 23, 49, 51, 58, 74, 86, 98, 103, 106, 110–111, 145, 157, 159, 163, 169, 172, 184, 190, 203–204, 207–209, 212, 214–216
executive education, 7, 89, 95, 98
experiential learning, 49, 79, 119, 128, 159–160, 163, 192
experiments, 1, 50–51, 68, 160, 181

Facebook, 18, 80, 207
face-to-face, 8, 31–33, 37–43, 49–50, 56, 67–68, 89, 103–104, 108–111, 146, 155, 174, 182, 190–192, 195, 197
Faculty Innovation Grant (FIG), 143
faculty, 16, 66–69, 73, 76, 83, 85, 88, 92, 94–95, 98, 105, 123, 129, 143, 206, 223
faculty, business, 66–68, 73, 76
First-hour, 4, 24, 26
First-hour, orientation, 24, 26
First-hour, syndrome, 4
Flickr, 18
Freeview TV, 71
future trends, 223, 228–230

Gaia, 2
Gartner Inc., 97
griefers, 23, 55
griefing, 15, 23–24, 26
group meetings, 41–42, 69

Habbo, 2
Harvard, 83
Heads-Up display (HUD), 21
Healthy Hothouse, 13
High Speed Packet Access, 19
Holyrood Park, 187–189, 195
homebound, 221, 226, 239

House of 7, 6, 143, 145, 149–152,
    154–155
human resource management, 72
human resources, 72, 207, 209, 215
Hype Cycle, 13–14

IBM, 65, 84, 96
identity play, 182
identity, 30–32, 34, 42, 50–51, 53, 55,
    169, 182–186, 190–191, 194–197,
    208, 214
identity, exploration, 184
identity, social, 31
IE Business School, 85
immediacy, 6, 101–111, 226, 230
immediacy, nonverbal, 6, 101–111
immediacy, teacher, 101
immersion, 36, 68, 77, 169, 189–190,
    197
immersive environment, 1, 76, 83, 91,
    148
immersive Simulations, 68
impairments, 51, 53, 56
innovation, 4, 12, 85–86, 91, 96,
    143, 164
INSEAD island, 92
INSEAD, 5, 83–95, 97
Instructional Designer, 143, 146,
    149–150
Instructor Immediacy, 6, 101–103,
    105–107, 109
integrated marketing communication
    (IMC), 117, 119–120, 124,
    127–128
Intel 945 chipset cards, 18
interdisciplinarity, 141
interdisciplinary learning, 58
Internet Protocol, 15, 19
interpersonal expression, 32–33, 42
Interpersonal uncertainty reduction, 31,
    33–34, 42
interpersonal uncertainty, 30–31, 33–34,
    42
in-world, 2–3, 6, 11, 13–14, 17, 20–21,
    23–24, 26, 57–58, 66–71, 73–76,

78–80, 83–84, 97, 104, 109–110,
    123, 142, 144–146, 150–151,
    153–155, 182, 190–191, 193,
    204–206, 209, 213–214
in-world, navigation, 95

Jenkins Graduate School of
    Management (North Carolina
    State University: Raleigh, North
    Carolina), 85
Just Roleplayers, 184

K. Haub School of Business, 85
Kelley School of Business (Indiana
    University, Bloomington,
    Indiana), 84–85
Kingston University, 57
knowledge exchange, 49, 85
Kraft, 65

lag, 37–38, 42–43, 93–94, 110
learning curve, 72, 74, 79, 104, 110
learning platform, 164, 172, 176
learning, modes of, 78, 183
Library, 88–89, 131, 234
lifelong learning, 7, 87, 98, 221–223, 225,
    227, 229, 231, 233, 235, 237
Likert scales, 212
Linden Dollars, 3, 65, 71, 121–122, 124,
    128, 195
Linden Labs, 3, 16, 19, 21
listservs, 66, 141
literary analysis, 141, 143, 145, 147, 149,
    151, 153, 155
Literature Alive!, 54, 142, 148
literature, 6, 15, 29, 33, 42, 54, 86, 122,
    141–144, 147–151, 153, 155, 183,
    224

Maastricht University, 116, 121, 123
Macmillan publishers, 142
Management information systems, 73
managers, 13–14, 16, 69, 118, 134, 181

marketing, 6, 13, 65, 69, 73, 79, 83,
    86–88, 91, 115, 117–120, 122, 125,
    128–129, 133
Massive multiplayer online games
    (MMOG), 2
MBA, 86, 89, 91, 93
medical students, 56–58
membership, 31, 71, 154
Metaverse(s), 3, 5–7, 12–13, 15–19,
    22–26, 30–42, 47–56, 68, 70–71,
    73, 76, 79, 83–89, 91–98, 101–103,
    106–107, 109–110, 117, 122–124,
    129, 131, 133–135, 141–146, 148,
    151–152, 154, 160–162, 166, 169,
    172, 181–185, 188, 190–197,
    203–204, 207–208, 211, 213–215,
    217, 221–223, 226, 228, 230–238
micro-commerce, 65
Microsoft Virtual Earth, 96
mixed reality events, 69
MSc in E-Learning, 7, 182
Multi-user Virtual Environments
    (MUVE), 12, 15, 17, 49

NASA, 221, 226, 239
National Collegiate Inventors and
    Innovators Alliance (NCIIA), 84
Networking, 2, 8, 68, 75, 80, 215, 226,
    233
New Media Consortium (NMC), 143,
    154
notecard, 144, 146, 154
NU-Genesis Island, 165
nVidia GeForce, 18

Olive, 3
once-removed, participation, 47–63
once-removed, persona, 54
OnRez Viewer
Open Life, 205–207, 209
Open Sim, 96
open source, 96
Opera software, 53
organizational behavior, 72
orientation spaces, 21

orientation, 17, 21, 24, 26, 37,
    41–43, 117, 143, 147, 172,
    216
Osher Lifelong Learning Institute
    (OLLI), 222–223, 228, 238

pedagogical advantages, 49, 66–67
Penguin publishers, 2, 142
performance appraisal training, 7, 182,
    185–186, 197
performance appraisal, 7, 181–187, 189,
    191, 193, 195–197
permanence, 6
permission, 48
Pixelbreeze, 92
poetic faith, 15
policy, 72
Positive Monthly Linden Flow
    (PMLF), 1
post-traumatic stress, 58
PowerPoint, 71, 74, 76, 78, 141
practical applications, 235–236
Princeton, 83
problem solving, 33, 67
problem-based learning, 49, 160
project(s), 3–7, 12–13, 15–19, 22–27,
    29–43, 47–57, 68–71, 73, 75–76,
    79, 83–89, 91–98, 101–103,
    106–107, 109–110, 115, 117,
    120, 122–124, 128–129, 131–135,
    141–146, 148–155, 159–162,
    164–166, 169, 171–176, 181–188,
    190–197, 203–208, 211, 213–215,
    217, 221–223, 226, 228, 230–238
project, group, 35, 43
project, Second Life, 4, 6, 13, 16, 26, 27,
    115, 123–124, 129, 132–134,
    137–139, 150–153
project, whole-class, 141
Proteus effect, 52
protocols, 14, 49, 75, 96, 160
proximity, 6, 75
proxy servers, 19
psychological distance, 102–104
psychological harm, 54

Rangsit University, Thailand, 159, 164
Real life (RL), 5–7, 15–16, 23, 34, 37–41,
    49, 51–53, 55–59, 71, 77, 83–85,
    89–93, 96–99, 127, 129, 132, 181,
    183–184, 194–195, 212, 223, 226,
    228, 236–237
rehearsing, 183–184
ReLIVE08, 23, 203
representation, 12, 34, 48, 51, 54, 120,
    144, 168, 172–173, 175, 184–185,
    193, 209, 237
Research and Learning in Virtual
    Environments conference
    (ReLIVE), 203
research, 2, 6, 11–14, 25–27, 29, 31–35,
    50–51, 66, 69, 75, 83–87, 90–94,
    98, 101–111, 134, 141, 144,
    148–153, 155, 159–160, 162–163,
    187, 194, 203–206, 208, 214–215,
    222–227, 230, 232, 238–239
research, cross-cultural, 224
research, lab, 90–94
research, market, 75
research, virtual lab, 93
rez, 72
Role(-)play, 1–8, 11–26, 29–43, 47–59,
    65–76, 78–80, 83–99, 101–111,
    115, 117–129, 131–135, 141–155,
    159–166, 168–169, 171–174, 176,
    181–198, 203–209, 211–216,
    221–228, 230–233, 235–239

Salem, Massachusetts, 144
schizophrenia, 58
SchomeBase, 205–206
scripting language, 25, 73
SDA Bocconi, 85
Second Life Best Practices in Education
    conference, 11, 13
Second Life Business Review, 88
Second Life Educators List (SLED), 3,
    11, 19, 22, 24
Second Life, 1–8, 11–27, 29–30, 32–43,
    47–56, 58, 65–80, 83–86, 88, 91,
    94, 101, 103–111, 115–116,
        119–125, 128–129, 131–135,
        141–155, 159–161, 163–167, 169,
        171–175, 181–182, 185–189,
        192–198, 203–209, 211–217, 221,
        223, 225, 227, 229–231, 233, 235,
        237
Seton Hall University, Pirate Island,
    143–144
shared virtual environments (SVEs), 225
silver generation, 7
SimTeach wiki, 20
simulations, 57, 65, 68–69, 79, 118–119,
    185, 197, 226
simulations, business, 69, 75
simulations, group, 79
Skype, 15, 20, 154
SL Dreams, 227
Sloodle, 214
slope of enlightenment, 25
social connectedness, 221–222, 224
social factors, 75
social media, 85, 95, 97
social networking, 2, 80, 215, 226, 233
social Presence, 30–32, 34, 42, 68,
    103–104
Source credibility measure, 106
standardization, 95–96, 98
Stanford, 83
Star Doll, 2
State Motivation Scale, 106
strategies, appraisal, 181
strategy, 7, 17, 72, 75, 95, 117, 119–122,
    127–129, 131–132, 134, 203
strategy, branding, 117–125, 127–128,
    132, 139
strategy, business, 9
strategy, investment, 72
Strathclyde, Business School Newsletter,
    16
streaming media, 20
student recruitment, 84–85
student, recruitment, 84–85
Student-instructor relationship, 101–111
students, 2–3, 5–7, 12, 14, 16–19, 22–24,
    26–27, 29–30, 32–37, 40–43,

47–50, 52, 54–59, 65, 67–72, 74–80, 83, 85, 87, 89, 91–92, 95–98, 101–111, 115, 117–125, 127–129, 131–135, 141–155, 159–166, 168–169, 172–177, 182, 184–187, 193, 197, 203–208, 223, 226, 230–231
students, business, 67, 74, 78, 80
students, graduate, 105, 119, 146–151
students, undergraduate, 105, 159
support, institutional, 14, 18, 25, 204
surnames, 16
suspension of disbelief, 12, 15–16, 184
synchronous communication, 8, 36, 169, 172–174
Synthetic Environments for Emergency Response Simulation (SEER), 57
Synthetic Worlds Initiative, 86

teaching effectiveness, 76, 101
team projects, 85
teamwork, 85, 165, 173–176
technical constraints, 131–132
technological infrastructure, 2, 5, 8
teleport, 16, 22, 111, 187, 236
telepresence, 103
texture, 71
Thailand, 7, 159, 164
The Open University, 7, 203, 205, 207, 209, 211, 213, 215
There.com, 2, 98
Thincbook, 146, 154

UK Higher Education, 13
Ulm University, 86
Universal Design for Learning principles, 58
universities, 2, 35, 41, 48, 56, 66–67, 73–74, 78, 83, 98, 154, 165
University Dalhousie, 16
University of Alberta, , 18
University of California Davis, 56, 58
University of California Los Angeles, 56
University of Chicago Booth School of Business, 98

University of Derby, 51, 57
University of Edinburgh, 85, 182, 187, 198
University of Liverpool, , 19
University of Newcastle, Australia, 159, 164
University of Plymouth's Sexual Health SIM, 56
University of Strathclyde, 16, 19
University of Sussex, , 22
url(s), 3, 5–7, 12–13, 15–19, 22–26, 30–42, 47–56, 68, 70–71, 73, 76, 79, 83–89, 91–98, 101–103, 106–107, 109–110, 117, 122–124, 129, 131, 133–135, 141–146, 148, 151–152, 154, 160–162, 166, 169, 172, 181–185, 188, 190–197, 203–204, 207–208, 211, 213–215, 217, 221–223, 226, 228, 230–238
user training, 12
user-created content, 225

videoconferencing, 92, 229, 236
virtual business classrooms, 34, 68
virtual campus, 78, 86–87, 89, 91–94, 97–98
virtual classes, 85, 92–93, 98, 105
virtual commerce, 95
virtual community, 120, 206, 221
virtual design studios, 159, 163
virtual economies, 86
virtual environments, 12, 48–49, 58, 98, 110–111, 159, 163, 169, 172, 203–204, 207–209, 214–216, 225
virtual field trips, 230
virtual goods, 3, 65
virtual home, 7, 159, 165–169
virtual homes, 7, 166
virtual lifestyle, 65
virtual meetings, 69
virtual products, 75
virtual teams, 65, 85
Virtual University of Edinburgh (VUE), 187

virtual worlds, 1–2, 6, 11, 25, 29, 47–52, 54–59, 65, 78, 83–87, 89, 91–98, 101, 115, 135, 141–142, 147, 149, 151, 159–160, 162–166, 168–169, 172–176, 181, 185, 187, 203, 205, 215, 217, 221–222, 225–231, 234, 239
Voice over Internet Protocol (VOIP), 2, 5, 15, 18–20, 23

Web 2.0, 18, 75, 79–80, 204
web 3D, 11
web host server charge, 13
Webex, 95, 97

webinars, 92
webquest, 150
Wells Fargo, 83
Wheelies Club, 53
white listed, 19
Whiteboard, 71, 77–78
Whiteboard, message, 71, 81
Whiteboard, presentation, 71, 81
Whyville, 2
wikis, 2, 66, 141, 174
workshops, 12, 153, 211–216
World of Warcraft, 216

YouTube, 18, 52, 125, 145